Right Belief and True Belief

Right Belief and True Belief

DANIEL J. SINGER

Oxford University Press is a department of the University of Oxford. It furthers the University's objective of excellence in research, scholarship, and education by publishing worldwide. Oxford is a registered trade mark of Oxford University Press in the UK and in certain other countries.

Published in the United States of America by Oxford University Press
198 Madison Avenue, New York, NY 10016, United States of America.

Library of Congress Control Number: 2023938146

ISBN 978–0–19–766038–6

DOI: 10.1093/oso/9780197660386.001.0001

Printed by Integrated Books International, United States of America

Contents

Introduction 1

1 Normative Epistemology 10
- 1.1 What Should We Believe? 10
  - 1.1.1 Traditional Epistemology and What We Should Believe 11
  - 1.1.2 Getting Clearer About the Question 16
- 1.2 Normative Ethics 18
- 1.3 Normative Epistemology 23
  - 1.3.1 Right Belief and Why It's Not Correct Belief 25
  - 1.3.2 What Is Normative Epistemology? 29
  - 1.3.3 What Is Right Belief? (Take 2) 31
  - 1.3.4 The Methodology of Normative Epistemology 34
- 1.4 Toward a Theory of Right Belief 37

2 Truth-Loving Epistemic Consequentialism and Trade-Offs 39
- 2.1 Believe Truth! Shun Error! 39
- 2.2 Intuitions in Favor of Epistemic Consequentialism 41
- 2.3 On Trade-Offs: Part 0 52
  - 2.3.1 The Shape of Permissible Epistemic Trade-Offs 55
  - 2.3.2 Trade-Offs in Pedagogy 56
  - 2.3.3 Trade-Offs in Changes of Worldview 58
  - 2.3.4 Indirect First-Personal Trade-Offs 61
- 2.4 Permissible Trade-Offs Are Rare 65
- 2.5 Some Benefits of Accepting Some Trade-Offs 67
- 2.6 Moving Toward More Discussion of Trade-Offs 69

3 On Specific Trade-Off Objections 71
- 3.1 More Trade-Off Objections 71
- 3.2 The Target of Epistemic and Ethical Consequentialisms 72
- 3.3 The Specific Trade-Off Objections 75
- 3.4 Responding to Specific Trade-Off Objections, Round 1 77
  - 3.4.1 The Analogy 77
  - 3.4.2 Epistemic Consequentialism as a Theory of Deontic Notions 83
  - 3.4.3 An Explanation of the Directionality of Epistemic Notions 86
- 3.5 Deontic Trade-Offs 87

3.6 Responding to the Deontic Trade-Offs 89
3.7 Accounts of Justification and Rationality 94
3.8 How Plausible Is the Sophisticated View? 97

4 On Veritism and Promoting the Epistemic Good 101
4.1 The Truth-Loving Theory of Value 101
4.2 On the Promotion of Phone Book Beliefs 106
4.3 Littlejohn's Promotion-Based Objection 113
4.3.1 Is True Belief Good qua Belief? 114
4.3.2 Is True Belief Good for the Believer? 115
4.3.3 Is True Belief Just Plain Good? 117
4.3.4 Expanding the Roadmap to Understanding Goodness 119
4.4 Promoting Epistemic Consequentialism 121

5 Consequentialism and Epistemic Utility Theory 123
5.1 Aiming at Truth in Our Beliefs and Credences 125
5.1.1 Gibbard's Argument Part 1: Epistemic Rationality and the Value of Truth 125
5.1.2 Gibbard's Argument Part 2: Epistemic Rationality as Maximizing Guidance Value 128
5.2 Immodesty and Truth-Based Approaches to Epistemic Normativity 131
5.2.1 Explaining Immodesty Without the Practical 131
5.2.2 Why It's OK to Be Epistemically Modest 136
5.3 Objections to Dominance and Expected Value Arguments 142
5.4 Dominance Avoidance and Truth-Loving Epistemic Consequentialism 146
5.5 Epistemic Value for Consequentialists and Epistemic Utility Theorists 149
5.6 Are Epistemic Utility Theory and Truth-Loving Consequentialism Opposed? 152

6 On Racist Beliefs and Moral Encroachment 155
6.1 The (Apparent?) Conflict Between Epistemic and Moral Norms 155
6.2 Irrational or Racist: The Puzzle 158
6.3 Dilemmism, Moral Encroachment, and Purism 163
6.4 Why Moral Encroachment Doesn't Solve the Puzzle 168
6.5 How to Be a Dilemmist 179

7 Consequentialist Epistemology 189
7.1 On Epistemic Deontic and Responsibility Terms 191
7.1.1 On Constraining Views of Epistemic Responsibility 192
7.1.2 On Instrumentalist Views of Epistemic Responsibility 197

7.2 Going Global 205
7.2.1 What Global Epistemic Consequentialism Is 206
7.2.2 Why Global Rather Than Local Consequentialism 207
7.2.3 The Broader Global Truth-Loving Epistemic Consequentialist Picture 214
7.3 The Global Truth-Loving Framework for Inquiry 219
7.4 Global Truth-Loving Consequentialism and Naturalized Epistemology 224
7.5 Conclusion 228

References 231
Index 243

Introduction

This book follows a long line of philosophy books and articles that are titled with a conjunction of noun phrases (the most clever, of course, being Larry Sklar's *Space, Time, and Spacetime*). And the title of the book makes sense, since the book will have a lot to say about right belief and true belief. That said, for many reasons (avoidance of a trademark lawsuit not among them), it might have made more sense to title the book *Epistemic Consequentialism for Dummies*. This introduction will give several reasons why that title would have made more sense, and in doing so, it will provide a broad overview of the aims and limitations of the project undertaken here.

Epistemic Consequentialism for Dummies

For those unfamiliar with the reference, the *For Dummies* series is a media franchise of instructional, self-help manuals. The most well-known instances of the series are guides to computer operating systems, including the best-selling *DOS for Dummies* and *Windows for Dummies*. Most *For Dummies* books start with a high-level overview of their subject and follow that with detailed explanations of particularly central or important aspects of the subject. *Windows 95 for Dummies* (Rathbone 1997), for example, begins with a short overview of what Windows 95 is and how to get it installed on your computer, and the rest covers topics like how to move files in the Windows interface, how to use particularly important applications, and how to troubleshoot common problems. Unlike an owner's manual, *For Dummies* books don't aim to give a comprehensive deep dive into every aspect of their subject. Instead, *For Dummies* books provide readers with a broad overview of the topic, and by working through central aspects of the topic and representative everyday use-cases, *For Dummies* books empower readers to better understand the topic on their own.

Right Belief and True Belief. Daniel J. Singer, Oxford University Press. © Oxford University Press 2023.
DOI: 10.1093/oso/9780197660386.003.0001

This book isn't about computer operating systems. It's a philosophy book aimed primarily at academic philosophers (although much of it should be accessible to non-academic readers). But the book will take a tack similar to the *For Dummies* books in fleshing out and defending a theory of what we should believe, a theory I call 'truth-loving epistemic consequentialism':

> TRUTH-LOVING EPISTEMIC CONSEQUENTIALISM A belief that *P* is right for an agent to have if and only if among the available options for belief, believing *P* promotes the greatest overall balance of having true beliefs and not having false beliefs.

The book fleshes out the motivation and contours of this view (including how it can be extended to credences) while defending it from several different kinds of objections. In doing so, it adopts a methodological approach to theorizing about what we should believe that I call 'normative epistemology.' Normative epistemology looks a lot like normative ethics, except that where normative ethics is about what we should *do*, normative epistemology is about what we should *believe*. Chapter 1 is dedicated to spelling out that methodology. The rest of the book uses the methodology to flesh out and defend truth-loving epistemic consequentialism.

It would be impossible to do a deep dive into all aspects of normative epistemology and truth-loving epistemic consequentialism in a single readable book. Normative epistemology is a methodological approach to epistemic questions that's as vast and complex as the methodology of normative ethics (a topic there are already thousands of books on). And truth-loving epistemic consequentialism aims to be a complete theory of what we should believe in any situation and one that can serve as a framework for thinking about epistemology more generally. So instead of trying to spell out every detail of both and defend both from every possible objection, this book starts with a broad overview of the methodology and the view to be defended. It then describes the most central and novel aspects of the view and defends them from objections. Like a *For Dummies* book, this book aims to help the reader to understand its core ideas and empower the reader to see for themselves how those ideas can be fleshed out further and defended from future objections. This is one reason the book might have been better titled *Epistemic Consequentialism for Dummies.*

Anti-Consequentialists as the Dummies

The main claim of truth-loving epistemic consequentialism is that the question of what we should believe in any situation is a question of what gets us at the truth. As I'll argue throughout the book, this claim is simple, intuitive, and compelling, and it's an idea that philosophers have flirted with for hundreds of years. Despite that, very few (if any) philosophers have really gone to bat for the view, mainly because the view is subject to a number of powerful objections. Most of this book (the second half of Chapter 2 and all of Chapters 3 to 6) is structured around showing how truth-loving consequentialism can escape those objections.

Chapters 2 and 3 consider trade-off objections to epistemic consequentialism, like those put forward by Firth (1998, written in 1978), Fumerton (1995), Jenkins (2007), Greaves (2013), and Berker (2013a, 2013b). These trade-off objections accuse epistemic consequentialists of wrongly sanctioning trade-offs of the goodness of some of our beliefs for the overall goodness of our doxastic state. The second half of Chapter 2 argues that, contra what some of these authors claim, there are some epistemically permissible trade-offs. Chapter 3 asks whether we should be worried about any of the particular trade-offs that truth-loving epistemic consequentialists sanction. It argues that epistemic consequentialists should borrow three lessons from ethical consequentialists to respond to what might appear to be objectionable trade-offs. First, the view should be construed as an account of right belief, which we should distinguish from other epistemic notions like rational and justified belief. Second, the view should be 'sophisticated' in the same way that Railton (1984) argues that ethical consequentialism should be sophisticated. And third, the view should be 'global' in that it extends the consequentialist criterion of evaluation beyond belief to also include agents' dispositions, decision-making procedures, and the like. An important upshot of this chapter, one we see repeated several times throughout the book, is that epistemic consequentialists can avoid many objections to their view by mirroring the best consequentialist views in ethics.

Chapter 4 looks at objections to truth-loving epistemic consequentialism that focus on its claim that we should promote having true beliefs. It starts by asking whether truth-loving epistemic consequentialism falls prey to the generalized swamping problem discussed by Sylvan (2018) and argues that it does not. It then turns to an objection from Grimm (2009), which says that views that call for the promotion of having true beliefs erroneously entail that we should spend our time learning trivial truths by, for example, memorizing entries in a phone book or counting blades of grass. This chapter shows that there are a few peculiar and misleading elements of these purported counterexamples, which means that they don't really undermine truth-loving consequentialist views. Chapter 4 also considers an objection from Littlejohn (2018), which claims that there is no sense of 'goodness' in which epistemic goodness is to be promoted. While the chapter doesn't commit the consequentialist to a particular way of responding to Littlejohn's charge, it does show that there are several possible paths forward, each of which leads to a different metanormative way of thinking about the view.

Epistemic utility theorists and truth-loving epistemic consequentialists share a starting place in thinking that epistemic norms are about maximizing accuracy in our doxastic states. Chapter 5 focuses on two objections to epistemic utility theory that look like they might translate to truth-loving epistemic consequentialism. It starts by considering an objection from Gibbard (2007), which says that aiming at the truth is insufficient to explain all of the requirements of epistemic rationality. It then considers objections from Caie (2013), Greaves (2013), and Carr (2017), which say that despite what the theorists claim, epistemic utility theorists can't use the standard tools of decision theory (i.e., dominance and expected utility theory arguments) to justify their conclusions. Chapter 5 argues that the objections to epistemic utility theory don't transfer to truth-loving epistemic consequentialism. The upshot is that, even though the two views share an intuitive starting place in thinking that epistemic norms are about getting at the truth, the two views are importantly different. The key differences are about the targets of the view and how the epistemic consequences are measured.

Chapter 6 looks at a puzzle first discussed by Gendler (2011) that motivates some theorists to give up on the thought that beliefs should be evaluated solely with respect to traditional epistemic factors, like what one's evidence is. According to moral encroachment theorists (e.g., Basu 2019b; Bolinger 2020a; Moss 2018), moral factors can also be relevant to how we should evaluate beliefs. As Chapter 6 shows, moral encroachment views don't hang together well with truth-loving epistemic consequentialism, even if they are, strictly speaking, compatible. The chapter goes on to argue against moral encroachment views by undercutting their motivation. The chapter shows that moral encroachment views can't satisfactorily reply to Gendler's puzzle, and it argues that the best reply is actually the one that truth-loving epistemic consequentialists would most naturally give.

Chapter 7 breaks the mold of the previous chapters by not being primarily structured around objections to epistemic consequentialism. Chapter 7 starts by fleshing out and further defending two of the most novel (and likely most controversial) aspects of the view: (1) the aspect of the view that treats right belief as importantly distinct from justified and rational belief, and (2) the aspect of the view that says that epistemic evaluations apply to things other than belief. Chapter 7 then goes on to show how we can think of truth-loving epistemic consequentialism not just as a theory of what we should believe but also as the foundation of a broader truth-centric conception of epistemology. In doing that, the chapter discusses and responds to several smaller objections to truth-loving epistemic consequentialism, including an objection that says that the view is self-undermining and an objection that says that the view is too radical in extending epistemic evaluation to things other than belief.

Most of the book is structured around responding to objections to truth-loving epistemic consequentialism. As I'll argue, truth-loving epistemic consequentialism can withstand these challenges, and the objections fail. So, if I'm right (and I think I am), a second sense in which this book might be better titled *Epistemic Consequentialism for Dummies* is that it shows the ways in which objectors to epistemic consequentialism miss the mark.[1]

Epistemic Agents Are the Dummies

A third sense in which this book might be better titled *Epistemic Consequentialism for Dummies* is that the conception of epistemology offered here takes seriously the fact that real human agents are deeply and persistently limited in their ability to get at the truth. As Hume famously pointed out, in any given moment, we only have access to what's going on at that moment and what we remember about the past. And even in a moment, we only have access to a tiny, tiny fraction of all the facts, at most those concerning what's

[1] I hope it's clear that my insinuation that the objectors to epistemic consequentialism are dummies is completely in jest. Even though I believe that the objections fail, I find each of the objections to be compelling and insightful, otherwise I wouldn't have seen them as worth engaging with here. In fact, it has been quite an honor to be able to engage with each of these objectors' writings.

going on around us at that moment and whatever small portion of the other facts we can infer from those. On top of that, we're subject to a huge number of memory, attention, and information-processing limitations that thwart our ability to work with and store the facts that we do get access to.

In Chapter 1, I argue that our limited nature gives us an easy way to see why there even is a substantive question of what we should believe. In Chapter 2, I argue that our limited nature means that there will be some cases where it's permissible for us to trade off the accuracy of some of our beliefs for the accuracy of others. In Chapter 3, I argue that consequentialists can explain the apparent backward-lookingness of epistemic rationality and justification by appeal to our limited nature, I argue that we can gain some traction on seeing what beliefs are right by thinking about less limited creatures, and I argue that our limitations help explain why the best versions of epistemic consequentialism deny that we ought to think in consequentialist terms. In Chapter 4, I argue that real human limitations help explain why epistemic consequentialists are not committed to thinking we should spend time counting blades of grass or memorizing the phone book. In Chapter 5, I appeal to cases of limited agents to argue that Gibbard's objection to epistemic utility theory fails, and I argue that our limitations give rise to an epistemic paradox of truth-seeking that's analogous to the ethical paradox of hedonism. And in Chapter 7, I argue that any plausible theory of justification and rationality should incorporate facts about the ways we're limited, and I spell out a broader truth-loving framework for epistemology that centrally locates the strengths and limitations of real epistemic agents.

So, the exposition and defense of the consequentialist view given here crucially relies on the fact that real epistemic agents face severe limitations and are, in that sense, dummies. That's the third reason titling the book *Epistemic Consequentialism for Dummies* might have made more sense.

The Unguided Reader Is a Dummy

A fourth way in which this book might have been better titled *Epistemic Consequentialism for Dummies* is that, like *For Dummies* books, readers need not read this book straight through to understand many of the central points. While I do recommend that readers who have the time read all of it (and in the order I've given it), there are some alternative paths for readers with more limited time or interest.

Chapter 1 is dedicated to laying out the methodology used in the rest of the book, a program I term 'normative epistemology.' Readers with some background in philosophy will likely be familiar with the basic methodology of normative ethics. Normative epistemology is meant to mirror normative ethics in being a search for a complete and correct theory of what we should believe (rather than a theory of what we should do). So while Chapter 1 does lay out some important methodological points and caveats that would help a reader better understand arguments in later chapters, readers who just want to learn about the truth-loving consequentialist theory can skip Chapter 1.

Chapters 2 and 3 are both quite central to the project. Chapter 2 lays out a lot of the motivation for going in for truth-loving epistemic consequentialism, and it begins to respond to trade-off objections, one of the most prominent types of objection to the view. Chapter 3 continues the response to trade-off objections, and in doing so, it introduces three of the most important aspects of the view, the bipartite, global, and sophisticated aspects. So I'd advise readers not to skip either Chapter 2 or Chapter 3, but Chapter 3 is probably the most central to the book (both in pagination and in content).

Chapters 4, 5, and 6 are primarily focused on responding to different kinds of objections to truth-loving epistemic consequentialism. These chapters develop central aspects of the view in response to the objections, but none of these aspects of the view is so crucial that a reader would be fundamentally confused if they skipped one of these chapters. Chapter 5 would probably be the most interesting of these chapters to readers with a background in formal epistemology, since this chapter compares truth-loving epistemic consequentialism to the most common formal approach to understanding epistemic normativity. And although Chapter 5 engages with quite formal work on Bayesianism, I've written it in a way that I hope is accessible to readers without a strong formal background.

Chapter 7 begins with a quick summary of five defining aspects of the view developed in the preceding chapters. That summary might be a useful reference for readers at any point. As mentioned above, Chapter 7 then delves deeper into further fleshing out two of the most important aspects of the view and showing how truth-loving epistemic consequentialism can give rise to a general truth-centric approach to epistemology that extends beyond questions of what we should believe. This chapter has a distinctly 'metanormative' feel in contrast to the more 'first-order normative' feel of the preceding chapters. Instead of thinking about example cases and finding ways to structure the view so that it gets the right verdicts, Chapter 7 discusses the nature of epistemic normativity and how different kinds of epistemic normative notions hang together. So readers who are interested in the higher-level metanormative aspects of the view will likely find this chapter to be the most interesting, but those just looking to get the bare bones of the theory need not make it their top priority.

I Am the Dummy (Acknowledgments)

Like all real epistemic agents, I too am a dummy, and despite there being only a single name on the cover of this book, many others are due credit for their role in helping support this project. I'm profoundly grateful to everyone who helped me work through the ideas themselves, everyone who helped me think about the broader picture, everyone who helped by reading and giving comments on drafts, and everyone who supported me being in a position to do this work.

The main consequentialist idea is one I've been working through since graduate school and is deeply inspired by Jim Joyce. I'm very grateful for my graduate program at the University of Michigan and particularly my committee, Jim Joyce, Allan Gibbard, and Sarah Moss, for helping me get started in philosophy. I'm also extremely grateful to J. Dmitri Gallow and Alex Silk for the hundreds (thousands?) of hours of conversations in graduate school that laid the foundations for these ideas. Starting in graduate school but continuing for a decade since then, I've worked closely with Patrick Grim in using the consequentialist framework to do more applied work in social epistemology using agent-based computer models, and I'm extremely grateful to Patrick for all of the support and guidance he has provided. I'm also extremely grateful for the long-term, big-picture support provided by my former undergraduate mentor and current department chair, Michael Weisberg. And of course, I couldn't have done any of this without the practically endless emotional support of my partner, Meredith Tamminga.

The general framing and presentation of this project were inspired by conversations with Ram Neta, and I'm extremely grateful to Ram for his help on that. Too many people to name provided helpful feedback about the ideas presented here over the last decade, but I'm particularly thankful for the careful and supportive feedback from Errol Lord, Daniel Wodak, Nate

Sheridan, Sukaina Hirji, Sandy Goldberg, Sara Aronowitz, Carlos Pereira Di Salvo, William "Zev" Berger, Oxford University Press editor Peter Ohlin, several anonymous reviewers of the proposal for this book, and the students in my epistemology graduate seminar in spring 2021, Afton Greco, Sara Purinton, Vanessa Schipani, and Shira Silver.

The vast majority of what is written here is new, but some portions of it do borrow from work I've previously published. Chapter 3 is a highly revised and improved version of my 2018 "How to Be an Epistemic Consequentialist," published in *The Philosophical Quarterly* (Volume 68, Issue 272, pp. 580–602). I'm extremely grateful to Justin Bernstein, Julia Driver, Amy Floweree, James Joyce, Jason Konek, Ram Neta, Kate Nolfi, David Plunkett, Keshav Singh, and Kurt Sylvan; students in my seminar on epistemic normativity at Penn; audiences at the Institut Jean Nicod in Paris, the University of British Columbia, Dartmouth College, and the Penn Ethics Breakfast; and anonymous referees for their helpful feedback on that work. The second part of Chapter 2, which begins the response to trade-off objections, is based on my 2019 "Permissible Epistemic Trade-Offs," published in the *Australasian Journal of Philosophy* (Volume 97, Issue 2, pp. 281–293). The main ideas for that were formulated over dinner at a PeRFECt conference, and I'm very grateful to Selim Berker, Julia Driver, Kate Elgin, James Joyce, Jason Konek, Ram Neta, David Plunkett, Keshav Singh, Meredith Tamminga, Charles Côté-Bouchard, and the audience at the Chapel Hill Normativity Workshop for their feedback on them. The responses to Grimm and Littlejohn given in Chapter 4 are based on my 2019 "Demoting Promoting Objections to Epistemic Consequentialism," published in *Philosophical Issues* (Volume 29, Issue 1, pp. 268–80). I'd like to thank Lisa Miracchi for organizing that issue, and I'd like to thank Clayton Littlejohn, Eliot Michaelson, Lisa Miracchi, Kate Nolfi, and Meredith Tamminga for their feedback on the ideas. Finally, while Chapter 6 hasn't been previously published, it did benefit significantly from feedback on earlier drafts by Sukaina Hirji, Ian Peebles, Errol Lord, Daniel Wodak, and everyone at the Penn Normative Philosophy Group.

In formulating these acknowledgments, I'm sure I've accidentally overlooked the names of many folks who have supported me, and I sincerely apologize for that. As anyone who has done academic work knows, we all stand on the shoulders of those who come before us and those who support us in myriad ways during the process. I am eternally thankful for everyone's support.

1

Normative Epistemology

1.1 What Should We Believe?

Some of the most important questions in life are questions about what we should do. “I could go to college, get a barista job, or try my hand at being a street artist. What should I do?” “I could have a chicken sandwich or falafel for lunch. What should I do?” “If I tell the CEO about my supervisor’s fraudulent behavior, I risk losing my job, but if I don’t, I might get caught up in his underhandedness. What should I do?” “I could spend my savings on new binoculars for my bird-watching hobby or donate it to charity. What should I do?” “Human activity has given rise to climate change that’s on track to kill millions and make Earth uninhabitable. I feel like I can at most make a small impact on this. What should I do?”

I think we should see questions about what to *believe* as at least as important as questions about what to *do*. One reason is that what we believe affects what we do. Whether I’ll tell the CEO about my supervisor’s underhandedness depends on what I believe about how accepting the CEO is of tattletales and how easily expendable I am to the company. Whether I’ll choose chicken or falafel for lunch depends on what I believe about the prices of the options and whether one is likely to be more filling than the other. Whether I’ll try to make a difference on global warming issues depends on what I believe about the efficacy of the various proposed solutions and what the potential costs are. What we believe is also as fundamental to our identity and life experience as what we do. In the same way that our actions define us, our beliefs do too. Buying into Nazi beliefs makes someone a Nazi in the same way that devoting one’s life to helping the poor makes someone a good person. So more generally, if we care about who we are and what we should do, we should equally care about what we should believe. This book is about what we should believe.

Right Belief and True Belief. Daniel J. Singer, Oxford University Press. © Oxford University Press 2023.
DOI: 10.1093/oso/9780197660386.003.0002

1.1.1 Traditional Epistemology and What We Should Believe

Most professional philosophers will say that the question of what we should believe is a question in epistemology. But if you pick up almost any epistemology textbook, you'll be told that epistemology is the 'theory of knowledge,' not the theory of what we should believe (see, for example, Audi 2010, Dancy 1985, Feldman 2003, Lemos 2007, Nagel 2014, Pritchard 2018). And in the table of contents, you'll likely see that the theory of knowledge is conceived of as involving a few related themes and questions like the following:

1. What is knowledge, and can it be broken down into component parts, such as justification and true belief?
2. How do perception, memory, and testimony create and maintain knowledge and justified belief (if they do)?
3. How do reasoning and introspection create knowledge and justified belief?
4. How do different forms of inference (such as deduction, induction, and abduction) create knowledge and justified belief?
5. What is required for justified belief? In particular, how must one's reasons be arranged for one's beliefs based on those reasons to be justified? And does anything other than how one's reasons are organized matter for justified belief?
6. What are the limits of what we can know? In the face of skeptical worries, can we even have knowledge at all? How can we know, for example, that we're not dreaming or in a realistic computer simulation?
7. How do the knowledge and justified beliefs of individuals depend on and influence the knowledge and justified belief of others?

Importantly, you won't see the question of what we should believe, at least not in those terms. The focus of traditional epistemology is knowledge, and what motivates the epistemologist to pursue questions like these is the idea that by getting at different aspects of knowledge with these questions, we'll get a better account of knowledge. The main goal of this book is to give and defend a theory of what we should believe, regardless of whether those beliefs also constitute knowledge.

To better understand the question, let's consider a few mundane examples:

> MICROWAVE Today, just as he has done at lunch for years, Justin put a Hot Pocket in the microwave and set it for 2 minutes. While he waited, he could see that the microwave looked and sounded like it was working normally. Just before Justin reached in to grab the Hot Pocket, he could see the steam coming off the Hot Pocket, and he believed it was hot. In fact, the Hot Pocket was hot.

> DRIVING TIME Daisy needs to drive to the zoo. According to Google Maps it will take 22 minutes, but according to Apple Maps it will only take 18 minutes. Daisy doesn't have any reason to think one mapping service is more or less likely to be right than the other. So Daisy believes it will take between 18 and 22 minutes to drive there.

> YOUTUBE VIDEO Earl is reading a thread on Facebook about whether hydroxychloroquine has clinical benefits for COVID-19 patients. The thread starts with a compelling Youtube video claiming that hydroxychloroquine helps, but the comments link to many sources debunking the claim. Earl is well educated, but he isn't a scientist. So Earl emails his niece, who is a medical researcher. Earl's niece replies with links to several recent studies and survey articles in top medical journals that show that hydroxychloroquine does not help COVID-19 patients, and one survey even mentions this particular YouTube video as a misleading and politically motivated source of the idea that it does. Earl thinks his niece is qualified to evaluate these articles, and on her advice, he comes to believe that hydroxychloroquine does not help with COVID-19.

There are several questions we can ask about the people in these examples. The traditional epistemological question is whether their beliefs constitute knowledge. Traditional epistemologists might try to answer that question by consulting a theory of knowledge that might tell them what factors to think about. They might, alternatively, consult their intuitions about the situations. Either way, what they'd be doing is trying to figure out whether the belief state has the epistemic status of knowledge.

A distinct question we could ask about these beliefs is whether they are the beliefs the agents should have. Should Justin believe the Hot Pocket is hot? Should Daisy think it will take between 18 and 22 minutes to drive to the zoo? Should Earl trust his niece and believe that hydroxychloroquine does not help with COVID-19? Or should these agents have some other attitude (or no attitude at all) about these propositions? Notice that if we decide that each agent should believe what they do, that doesn't answer the question of whether their beliefs are knowledge. For one, if the beliefs were false (perhaps because the microwave was broken, there will be a traffic jam, or hydroxychloroquine does in fact help with COVID-19), the beliefs certainly wouldn't be knowledge, even if they are what the agents should believe. So, the question of what we should believe isn't the same as the traditional epistemological question about what constitutes knowledge.

That said, I think that a lot of what epistemologists have had to say really is, in part, about what we should believe. There is some work directly on this question in the literature that goes under the heading 'ethics of belief.' That heading subsumes many different questions, including questions about general theories of epistemic normativity, ethical implications of our beliefs, whether we can control our beliefs, whether there are connections between epistemic norms and other kinds of norms, the nature and aim of belief, and so on. See Chignell (2018) for a general overview. Some parts of that literature do aim to directly address the question of what we should believe. Feldman's "Ethics of Belief" (2000) is probably the clearest example. There, Feldman aims to defend an evidentialist conception of what we should believe, according to which, if we have a belief about a topic, we should have the belief supported by our evidence. (For Feldman, this lines up perfectly with what it takes for a belief to be justified, but let's put aside whether those are the same for now.)

Dating further back, in his own "Ethics of Belief," Clifford (1877) defends a norm similar to Feldman's, but Clifford takes the norm to have an ethical foundation. Clifford gives the example of a shipowner who, without evidence, convinces himself to ignore his own doubts about the seaworthiness of his vessel and believes it will be fine. When the ship goes down, Clifford argues, the owner is morally responsible both for the deaths and for failing to satisfy a norm of belief. James (1979) famously dissents from Clifford's view and argues that in some cases (like about a Christian God) it's permissible to believe without sufficient evidence.

There is relatively little other discussion that is *explicitly* about what we should believe in epistemology, but many other things that epistemologists study probably are, at least in part, about what we should believe. Consider a simple example: The peer disagreement literature (e.g., Feldman 2006; Elga 2007; Kelly 2010; Christensen 2010) asks what we should believe in very particular situations. This work usually assumes that an agent has a belief about some topic. Let's suppose, for example, that the agent believes that their restaurant bill sums to $67. They then learn that an epistemic peer disagrees with them, like if they learn that their equally well-informed and mathematically skilled dining partner believes the sum is $65. The question is then what the subject should believe in light of the disagreement. Notice the question here is about what belief they should have, not whether that belief would count as knowledge.

Bayesian formal epistemology (see Talbott 2016) is another place where it's clear that the extant work is largely about what we should believe. Bayesian epistemologists think of our belief states as probabilistic, rather than on or off. They assume that we view certain things as probabilistically likely in a certain way before we get new evidence. Bayesians then ask the question of what we should believe when we gain new evidence. Bayesians argue that we should use the particular formal rule of conditionalization to update our beliefs. So Bayesians also make claims about what we should believe (in a probabilistic sense and given that we have certain prior beliefs).

I think that much of the extant work on theories of justification can also be seen as being about what we should believe. Evidentialists about justification, for example, hold roughly that an individual's belief that *P* is justified if and only if their evidence overall supports *P* (e.g., Feldman and Conee 1985). That is a claim about justification, but I take it that evidentialists also typically think this tells us something about what we should believe. An extreme view here might be Feldman's (2000) view mentioned above—i.e., that we should believe that *P* if and only if that belief would be justified in this way. There are weaker options available, though, like holding that a belief not being justified is a mark against holding it. In that way, much of the work on justified belief can be seen as in part about what we should believe.

Much of the work on skepticism about knowledge also relates to what we should believe.[1] The standard approach to responding to skeptical arguments is about showing how we can have knowledge in the face of those arguments. It's natural to think of those responses as also being about

[1] For an overview of the relevant discussion, see Comesaña and Klein (2019).

what we should believe in light of the skeptical arguments. The question, so posed, is "In the face of skeptical scenarios being phenomenologically indistinguishable from non-skeptical ones, should we believe we're in the non-skeptical ones, as we usually do?" We can see Moore's fallibilist approach (1939), for example, as claiming that we should believe we have hands, even if that belief could be mistaken.

Work on theories of knowledge is often motivated by and has implications for what we should believe too.[2] Consider tracking views of knowledge, which say that knowledgeable belief tracks the truth about its subject matter (e.g., Nozick 1981, pp. 172–96). Proponents of these views will naturally hold that our beliefs ought to track the truth, since it's those beliefs that are knowledge when true. On other views of knowledge like virtue-theoretic ones, knowledge is an especially good kind of belief or mere belief, is a deficient kind of knowledge (see, e.g., Sosa 2007 and Williamson 2000). Proponents of these views will naturally hold we should have the beliefs that are knowledge, since those are the best (or at least the non-deficient) beliefs.

Finally, we can also see work in epistemology about particular ways we gain and maintain justified beliefs, like work on visual perception, memory, testimony, etc., as being in part about what we should believe. Questions about whether we should rely on visual perception, for example, just are questions about whether we should believe the deliverances of visual perception. Narrower questions about what is produced by visual perception can also be seen as questions that are in part about whether visual perception should (or even can) directly influence what we believe. With work on memory and testimony the story is similar: much of the work can be seen as either directly asking whether to believe what memory and testimony support or as asking about how memory and testimony influence what we should believe.

What these examples show is that, even though it isn't typically formulated as such, much of the extant work in epistemology is already about what we should believe, at least in part. But each of the approaches mentioned above is either limited or not directly about the question (or both). Discussions of what we should believe in the context of peer disagreement are limited to peer disagreement contexts. Discussions of what we should believe on the basis of perception, memory, and testimony are equally limited

[2] For an overview of this literature, see Ichikawa and Steup (2018).

to those contexts. Conditionalization in Bayesian epistemology is limited to cases where we learn something with certainty, and even then, the Bayesian needs a story about what the right starting probabilities are. And as I'll argue in Chapter 3, we should be careful to distinguish what we should believe from what beliefs are justified or knowledge. This will mean that theories of justification and knowledge won't fully answer the question of what we should believe.

1.1.2 Getting Clearer About the Question

The aim of this book is to focus squarely on the question of what we should believe and try to defend a complete answer to that question, one that tells us what we should believe in any particular situation. As I hope the examples have made clear, when I talk about belief, I don't mean to exclude attitudes that might also constitute knowledge or mere opinions. Belief, the way I'm conceiving of it, is the attitude we have toward a content when we take that content to be true. This is the attitude I have toward there being a computer in front of me right now, the attitude you have about these words being on this page, the attitude devout Jews have about Moses crossing the Red Sea, and the attitude doctors have about the high efficacy of COVID-19 vaccines. This attitude is meant to include all the things agents believe, know, or have opinions about, in the ordinary ways those words are used. So this attitude isn't limited to what agents believe about particularly controversial topics (like political topics) or about how agents settle their stance on issues for which they lack sufficient evidence (like many folks' beliefs about God). What this attitude does not include are what agents might be imagining or what they wish to be true.[3] I also won't assume that we must explicitly or consciously believe something in order for it to count as a belief. In the relevant sense of the term, even before reading this sentence, you had the belief there are more people on Earth than there are on moons of Earth, but that belief probably wasn't explicit or conscious until now. So the question of what we should believe, the way I'll understand it here, is the question of how we should think about the world (including anything in the world and ourselves) in the broadest sense.

[3] Much ink has been spilled on exactly how to characterize belief in contrast to other attitudes. I don't intend to take a stand on those issues here. See Schwitzgebel (2019) for an overview.

On the traditional picture, belief is thought of as coming in three categorical varieties: belief, disbelief, and suspension (also known as 'withholding') of belief. On this way of thinking about how we represent the world to ourselves, for any given proposition, we might believe it, disbelieve it, or suspend belief about it. As mentioned above, Bayesian theorists (along with many others) think that the three-modes model is too limited. On the Bayesian picture (e.g., Joyce 2013), how we represent the world to ourselves is modeled by probability functions. These functions assign a real-valued credence to each proposition, and that value represents the 'degree of belief' we assign to the proposition. As I'm thinking of it, the question of what we should believe is about how we should represent the world to ourselves, be it with the traditional modes of belief or with degreed beliefs (or whatever other doxastic attitudes we might have). Most of what I say will straightforwardly apply to either way of thinking about belief, but I'll mostly write in traditional ('full belief') terms for ease of exposition. The exception will be Chapter 5, where I'll focus on degreed ways of thinking about belief.

Importantly, the question of what we should believe is normative—it's about what we *should* believe. It's not about what people typically do believe or what others think they should believe. I'll say more later in this chapter about exactly what kind of 'should' this is, but first a few quick remarks: I'll assume there are facts about what different people should believe in different situations, at least in a weak sense of 'fact' that allows us to think that answers to that question can be right or wrong. And while I'll focus on the question conceived of in terms of what we 'should' believe, I'll sometimes talk about what we 'ought' to believe (which I'll take to be synonymous with 'should'). I'll also assume that the 'should' in play expresses a relation between agents and 'havings' of belief states—e.g., that the agent Bobby should have the belief state with content *P* (following how Schroeder 2011 thinks of the deliberative 'ought'), although I'll relax this assumption in the last chapter.

Part of what I hope to show in this book is that we can fruitfully approach the question of what we should believe using the same kind of methodology used by ethicists to approach the question of what we should do. So, it will help to get clear on what I take that methodology in ethics to be. The next section will give a brief (and opinionated) overview of the relevant methodology. I'll then turn to how it can be applied in epistemology.

1.2 Normative Ethics

Whereas epistemology is typically construed as the theory of knowledge, ethics is typically construed as the theory of morally right action. The goal of ethics, so understood, is to investigate what we should do morally speaking. Ethics is distinct from fields like sociology and anthropology, which might answer the question of what different people or cultures do and think we should do. Ethics aims to answer the normative question of what we should do, which, in theory at least, could be independent of what people think we should do.

Ethics is typically thought of as consisting of three distinct branches: metaethics, normative ethics, and applied ethics (e.g., Fieser 2020). Applied ethics is the part of ethics that looks at particular ethical issues and aims to determine what the right actions are on those issues. Examples of applied ethical questions are ones like whether abortion is permissible, whether we should have kidney markets, whether the wealthy should donate large portions of their wealth, and whether it's OK to eat animals. Work in applied ethics focuses on particular questions, and often that work appeals to particular facts about the issues in play that might not generalize to other questions.

Metaethics is on the opposite end of ethics, conceptually speaking. Metaethics asks general and abstract questions *about* ethics, as opposed to asking ethical questions. Questions commonly considered to be metaethical ones include questions like the following: Are there truths of ethics? If there are truths, are they relative to cultures, speakers, or anything else? If there are truths of ethics, what makes them true? I.e., are there special moral truth-makers or can normal physical stuff make moral claims true? How can we know ethical truths and what does that knowledge consist in? When we make moral judgments, what are we making judgments about and what is going on in our mental and neural states when that happens? What is the connection between God or other supernatural beings and moral truths? What do our moral claims mean? All of these metaethical questions ask about the nature of moral facts, knowledge, meaning, and related issues. They're not about any particular ethical claim. Rather, they're questions about the very idea of ethics and what morality is.

Normative ethics is about figuring out what is ethically right in a general way. Unlike research in applied ethics, which aims to figure out the morally right answer to particular moral questions, normative ethics aims for a theory of what actions are right and wrong in any case. So normative ethics is more general than applied ethics. But unlike metaethics, normative ethics aims to directly answer the question of what we should do in different situations, not to answer questions about the nature of morality.

The goal of normative ethics is often put in terms of determining which set of 'moral principles' or 'general rules' correctly tells us which actions are right or wrong (see, for example, the preliminary chapter of Kagan 1998). This formulation of normative ethics rules out possible views of moral rightness that deny that it can be productively understood in terms of principles or general rules, like many forms of moral particularism (see Dancy 2009). Instead, I propose that we take the goal of normative ethics to be producing a function from possible situations agents might find themselves in to what actions the agents should do morally speaking in those situations. I'll call a theory that does this for every possible situation 'complete.' So a complete ethical theory of rightness is one that tells us for every possible situation which actions are morally right and wrong in that situation.

On this conception of normative ethics, a theory will be *correct* if for every scenario an agent might find themselves in, it gives the right verdict about exactly which actions are morally right for that agent in that scenario.[4] Two theories will disagree if they are different functions—i.e., if there is a scenario that a subject might find themselves in and the two theories don't share the same output of what action is morally right in that scenario. Notice that this conception of normative ethics still allows for moral principles to play a role; they can be seen as either determining or summarizing parts of the function. For that reason, I see this conception of normative ethics as more general than the principle-based one.

The two most widely discussed general classes of theories of normative ethics are consequentialism and deontology. There are many different versions of both kinds of view. Broadly speaking, ethical consequentialists

[4] Here I am assuming that the *correctness* of an ethical theory only depends on its extension—i.e., what it says to do or not to do in every situation. This is a common assumption, and it motivates many who go in for 'consequentializing' (e.g., Brown 2011, Dreier 2011; for an overview, see Portmore 2009). That said, some push back on this idea by holding that theories can importantly differ not only in what they say is right or wrong but also in how they explain what makes those things right or wrong. One might then think that the goal of normative ethics is not only to find a theory that gets the right answers about rightness and wrongness but also to find a theory that properly explains why those things are right or wrong (e.g., Hurley 2020). Here I'll use the term 'correct' to pick out theories that give the right verdicts independently of how they explain those verdicts. In doing that, I don't take myself to be disagreeing with opponents of consequentializing; we can simply see those folks as demanding more from normative ethics than that it just give a correct theory, in my sense of the term.

think that we can understand the ethical rightness of an action solely in terms of the consequences of the action. The simplest kind of this view, known as 'hedonistic utilitarianism,' says that an action is the right one when, among the available actions, it produces the most amount of happiness for everyone. More sophisticated versions of consequentialism might include a more complex conception of the relevant consequences and a more complex determination function of rightness in terms of the consequences. I'll introduce more elements of ethical consequentialist theories in later chapters to develop my epistemic consequentialist view by analogy, but for more focused information on ethical consequentialism, see Sinnott-Armstrong (2015). Ethical deontology is typically understood as the view that the ethical rightness of an action doesn't *only* depend on the consequences of the action. As such, deontology is typically understood as the denial of consequentialism. That said, paradigmatic deontological views take that to an extreme by claiming that the consequences don't matter at all. For example, one way of understanding Kant's deontological ethical view is that it takes the ethical rightness of an action to depend exclusively on what principles the agent used in performing the act (Johnson and Cureton 2019). These two standard approaches to normative ethics have in common that they aim to give a complete theory of when an action is right—i.e., one that will tell us for each possible action in any possible scenario whether the action is right or wrong.

How are such theories defended? One part of defending normative ethical theories involves appealing to intuitions about example cases. Kagan (1998) offers the example of setting a child on fire for the pleasure of watching the child burn. By reflection on this idea, we can see that this is clearly morally wrong. What we're doing when we determine that is we're consulting our intuitions, and in some cases like this one, our intuitions are strong enough and clear enough that we see that any correct normative ethical theory should make that prediction. It's standard methodology in normative ethics to treat intuitions like these as a kind of non-empirical evidence about the correct ethical theory (see, for examples, Driver 2006, Kagan 1998, Timmons 2012). So one way ethicists get insight into the correct ethical theory is by appeal to intuitions about particular cases.

Intuitions about particular cases typically aren't going to be enough to fully defend a theory, since ethical theories will make claims about infinitely many scenarios, most of which we'll never consider and many of which are too complex to clearly think about. Another source of evidence for ethical theories comes from our intuitions about general moral principles, not just cases. It might strike you as plausible, for example, that human life should be preserved at every cost. Or it might strike you as plausible that it's impermissible to determine what punishment someone deserves for a crime by appeal to their race. Like intuitions about particular cases, these intuitions about moral principles can be used as evidence for or against a moral theory by checking whether the theory agrees with them.

Intuitions about moral principles come in different levels of generality. Some principles apply only to a few cases. For example, you might think that there's just a brute moral principle that abortion is impermissible. Alternatively, you might think that one principle is right because it's entailed by a more general principle about the value of human life. As Kagan (1998) highlights, our intuitions sometimes extend beyond general moral principles to features of moral theories themselves. For example, we might have the intuition that any correct moral theory should be able to explain all purportedly right actions in terms of the value of human happiness. Such an intuition is not about any particular moral principle, but rather, it's about the general structure of the theory itself.

Altogether, there are three kinds of intuitions used to defend theories of normative ethics: intuitions about particular cases, intuitions about moral principles, and intuitions about features of moral theories. Unfortunately, these intuitions don't always seem to support the same theories and sometimes they straight forwardly conflict. For example, an intuition about a principle about killing others might conflict with an intuition about a case of self-defense. When conflicts occur, moral theorists try to find the theory that has the best fit with the intuitions.[5] In some cases, some intuitions are stronger than others, and ethicists take that as evidence about which ones we should give up. My intuition that it's wrong to light someone on fire for artistic purposes is much stronger than my intuition that producing works of art is always good. So when the two conflict, the former should override the latter. In other cases, we might be willing to let go of our intuitions about particular cases to save moral principles. In some cases, it's not clear what we should give up. In those cases, theorists might argue that some of our intuitions are faulty and should be abandoned, perhaps because they are confused or the product of unreliable processes or

[5] This is an instance of a more general process of reflective equilibrium discussed by Goodman (1983), Rawls (2005), and Daniels (1979).

ills like racism, sexism, etc. In other cases, moral theorists might prefer one theory over another because of one theory's theoretical virtues, including things like the theory's simplicity, explanatory fecundity, or internal consistency.[6]

Of course, there is also substantial disagreement among moral theorists about how to decide which theories are best, how best to deal with conflicts of intuitions, whether there are other sources of evidence for moral theories, and, among some moral theorists, whether intuitions count as evidence at all. We'll put those issues aside here. What I'll argue below is that we can approach epistemology with a methodology that's analogous to this standard methodology for normative ethics. So for the sake of this project, if we should engage in these controversial issues, it will make more sense to do it when they're about theories in epistemology rather than theories in ethics (and I will engage with some of these in later chapters).

For now, let's operate with a simple conception of normative ethics as being exclusively about morally right action. Admittedly, this leaves out important work done by normative ethicists on moral value, moral responsibility (including praise and blame), moral virtue, moral worth, and many related topics. I've given you no reason to think that complete theories of right action will answer questions about these other things as well. It's commonly thought, for example, that someone can act wrongly without being blameworthy for it, like if I take your coat because I mistakenly think it is mine. This should make us think that the right-action-only conception of normative ethics is too anemic. It's probably more accurate to view normative ethics as having understanding right action as one of its primary aims, not its only aim. Doing so matches many standard conceptions of the field (see, for example, Driver 2006, Fieser 2020, Kagan 1998, Rachels and Rachels 2015, Timmons 2012), and it matches how Socrates describes the main task of ethics in Plato's *Republic* (352d) .

For now, let's stick with the simple conception of normative ethics as being only about right action. Doing this will help us more easily grasp the approach to the question of what we should believe that I think we should use in epistemology. Ultimately, nothing I say in this book will depend on accepting a right-action-only picture of normative ethics, and in fact, I'll

[6] The similarities between using intuitions to support moral theories and using empirical evidence to support scientific theories should be obvious here. I'm inclined to think the two are instances of a common type of inquiry, but that claim is highly controversial and one I won't pursue here.

argue later that the analogy is stronger when we bring topics like moral responsibility back into our conception of normative ethics. But for now, it will make explicating the project easier if you join me (at least temporarily) in adopting the simple picture of normative ethics. In the next section, I'll flesh out the methodology of my approach to what we should believe as analogous to the methodology of the right-action-only conception of normative ethics. The rest of the book will be dedicated to employing that methodology to defend a particular theory of what we should believe and filling in more details of the analogy.

1.3 Normative Epistemology

Most philosophers think that questions about what we should believe are outside of the domain of ethics. Ethical norms, on the standard view, only tell us about what we should do, not what we should believe. Similarly, epistemic norms, on the standard view, only apply to beliefs, not what we should do. This distinction is often motivated by looking at cases where the two kinds of norms seem to come apart. A standard example is Pascal's Wager.[7] Simplified, we can think of Pascal's Wager as involving an agent who forms a belief in God because of the practical upshots of doing so (like getting into heaven, avoiding hell, making friends at church, etc.) without having any evidence to think that God exists. Most people think there is something amiss with Pascal believing in God for these reasons. One common diagnosis of the problem is that Pascal is trying to use practical reasons (including ethical reasons) to form his belief even though only epistemic reasons bear on belief. Proponents of this kind of view hold that practical reasons (including ethical reasons) are the wrong kind of reason to use in supporting a belief; only epistemic reasons can do that.

I agree with the standard view that we should distinguish epistemic and practical reasons. In Chapter 7, I'll argue against the standard way of distinguishing these, but I do think we can use cases like Pascal's Wager to tease them apart. Practical normativity, we can say for now, is the kind of normativity that paradigmatically applies to action, and ethical normativity is a subset of that kind of normativity, the subset that contains all and only our moral obligations. Epistemic normativity is the kind of normativity that paradigmatically applies to belief. Exactly how to

[7] For more information on Pascal's Wager, see Hájek (2018).

distinguish these two is something I take to be up for debate, and part of what I hope to argue for in this book is a particular conception of epistemic normativity that I will flesh out more explicitly in Chapter 7. The reader will have to wait (or jump ahead) to find out what I think that is.

For now, let's assume that there are at least two kinds of normativity including epistemic and practical normativity (of which ethics is a particular subset). I'm inclined to think there are many other kinds of normativity as well, including aesthetic normativity, legal normativity, and social normativity, but whether that's right is beside the main point here. The point of distinguishing ethical and epistemic normativity here is so that we can clarify the aim of ethical and epistemic theorizing. Normative ethics, as I described it above, has the aim of creating a complete and correct account of right action. Importantly, though, for this conception to be correct, we must limit the 'right' in 'right action' to ethical or moral rightness. Normative ethics doesn't attempt to capture which actions are right in the sense that it is right for someone to visit the beach over the mountains when they prefer beach settings, since this is a kind of practical normativity that falls outside of moral normativity. So normative ethics, properly conceived, has the aim of creating a complete and correct account of *morally* right action.

Earlier I introduced the question of what we should believe. We should restrict that too. The question is really about what we *epistemically* should believe. Like in Pascal's Wager, notice that we can be completely convinced that the practical and ethical considerations count in favor of or against believing something (like, for example, if believing would make everyone very happy) but still be unsure whether an agent should believe it, in the relevant sense. So the question, more clearly stated, is what agents *epistemically* should believe. (Of course, if you think that only epistemic norms apply to belief, then whether one epistemically should believe something reduces to the bare question of whether one should believe it.)

In normative ethics, the term 'morally right action' is used to refer to what an agent should do morally speaking. Analogously, I propose that we use the term 'epistemically right belief' to refer to the belief the agent epistemically should have. In most cases, the context will make it obvious whether I mean ethical or epistemic rightness when I say 'right action' or 'right belief,' so I'll drop the modifiers 'ethically' and 'epistemically' unless they're needed for clarity. The focus of most of the rest of the book will be about how to understand what right belief is. Let's start with some clarifications.

1.3.1 Right Belief and Why It's Not Correct Belief

To start getting a grip on what I mean by 'right belief,' first notice that using the term to refer to what we should believe doesn't perfectly mesh with how English-speakers sometimes use it: When we're getting soaked in the rain, we might say, "I thought it wasn't going to rain because the forecaster said it would be sunny. But I guess that wasn't right." In that use of the term, 'right' seems to be a synonym for 'true.' For clarity in this part of the discussion, I'll use 'right$_t$ belief' to talk about the natural language version of 'right belief' that picks out true belief, and I'll use unmodified 'right belief' to refer to the belief we should have. As we'll see, the theory I argue for will have a natural explanation for why it's so easy for us to conflate these different uses of the term.

We should also distinguish 'right belief' from 'correct belief.' Shah (2003) and Wedgwood (2002) argue that it's a conceptual or normatively fundamental truth about BELIEF that a belief is correct if and only if it's true. On Wedgwood's picture, we can explain the rest of epistemic normativity in terms of this more basic epistemic norm. When we ask what belief someone should have, in the sense I aim to explore, we're not asking if the belief is true. We're instead asking whether it's the belief the agent should have. If these two were the same, it would follow that agents should only have true beliefs. As I'll argue below (and separately in the next two chapters), that's not quite right. For now, just notice that right belief sometimes seems to be more sensitive to agents' evidence and circumstances than correct belief is.

We now have three different terms in play. In natural language, we have 'right$_t$ belief,' which is co-extensive with 'true belief' (because they're synonymous). We have the notion of 'correct belief,' which is also co-extensive with 'true belief.'[8] I've also proposed we use 'right belief' in a circumscribed way to pick out the belief we should have. Let's consider how these notions might relate to each other.

'Right$_t$ belief' and 'correct belief' both have true belief as their extension. A natural thought is that the distinction between 'right belief' and the other two terms should map onto the distinction metaethicists often make between subjective and objective versions of 'ought' claims. Subjective 'ought'

[8] I say that these two terms are 'co-extensive' since, on the face of it, the former looks normative whereas the later looks non-normative. I won't take a stand on whether that's true. Shah (2003) convincingly argues otherwise.

claims are the ones that are true in light of the information an agent has, whereas objective 'ought' claims are true in light of all the facts. Here's a case to make the distinction easier:

> JACK'S FRIEND Jack's friend is in the hospital and close to passing away, and no one knows why. In fact, Jack has a rare bacterial infection and would be saved by using a particular over-the-counter antibiotic that Jack could easily get 20 minutes away from the hospital, but no one knows this. What Jack does know is that his friend would be much happier if Jack comforted him in his final moments in the hospital.[9]

In this situation, what Jack objectively ought to do comes apart from what he subjectively ought to do. In the objective sense (i.e., in light of all the facts), Jack ought to go get the antibiotic that will save his friend, but in the subjective sense (i.e., in light of the information he has), he ought to spend his time comforting his friend in the hospital.

When it comes to epistemic 'ought' claims, the standard view is that what we objectively epistemically ought to believe is always the truth (see, for example, Gibbard 2005, p. 340; Boghossian 2003; Shah 2003; Wedgwood 2002; Schroeder 2015; Whiting 2010). Consequently, it's natural to think that both 'correct belief' and 'right$_t$ belief' also pick out what we objectively ought to believe (which is also always the truth). 'Right belief' seems to pick out a notion that's more subjective, so the natural thought is that it must refer to what we subjectively ought to believe.

Why think that what we objectively epistemically ought to believe is always the truth? The standard line of argument goes like this: What one objectively ought to believe is just what one ought to believe in light of all the facts (from the definition). So, for any proposition *P*, the fact of whether *P* is always in the information set that the objective 'ought' applies in light of. And, in light of some fact, one should always believe that fact. Why does this last step supposedly hold? I take it that the idea is that to determine when an 'ought *in light of* some information' claim is true, we should imagine that the agent (or some idealized version of them, some idealized advisor of them, etc.) has the relevant information and then ask what they ought to do under that condition (or what they ought to be advised to do). But surely, if an agent has the information that *P* is true, they ought to believe that *P* (or be so advised).

[9] This is a simplified version of the Sick Mother case from Lord (2015).

I think this argument fails, and I think its failure undermines the idea that what we objectively ought to believe is always the truth. The rest of this book can be construed as a defense of that claim, but there's a different (and shorter) argument we can look at here: One problem with the argument is that it implicitly (and incorrectly) assumes that all agents are able to have true beliefs about all topics. Consider six-year-old Clara, who, let's suppose, has a nascent interest in physics but isn't in a position to believe that spacetime is non-Euclidean (or its negation), perhaps because she lacks the relevant concepts or intellectual ability. Clara can't even comprehend the thought that spacetime might be non-Euclidean, so it seems to me that she can't be objectively required to believe it (despite it being true).

Defenders of the standard view will likely have a quick retort: They'll restrict their view by saying it only applies to topics that agents have beliefs about. So then the view would be better described as saying that for every proposition *P*, *if one has a belief about whether P*, one objectively ought to believe the truth about *P*.

While this move avoids the worry about Clara's belief about spacetime's Euclideanness (something Clara doesn't have a belief about), I think it misses the larger issue. To see that, let's additionally stipulate that Clara believes that it's a conceptual truth that parallel lines never intersect (something that's false but only because of the possibility of non-Euclidean spaces). If Clara were questioned about whether parallel lines could intersect, she would be confused about the question and argue that her belief necessarily follows from the definitions of "parallel" and "lines"—she can't even conceptualize what the truth is like (i.e., that it's possible for parallel lines to intersect) because she hasn't yet developed the ability to think about non-Euclidean spaces. In this extended case, believing the truth about parallel lines just isn't an option for her. The options for what she can believe are limited, and the truth is not among the available options. So if there is something she objectively ought to believe about parallel lines, it must be the case that she objectively ought to believe something false.[10]

[10] Notice that it wouldn't be an attractive option for my opponent here to deny the assumption that there is something she objectively ought to believe in this case. The central motivation for the view said that what we objectively ought to believe is just what we ought to believe in light of all the facts. On the most natural way of understanding that view, what the predicate 'ought to believe in light of all the facts' does is pick out a best option for belief from a given set of options. It would be odd to think that the predicate just doesn't apply to any of the options if the truth isn't among them (and the set is non-empty). Why wouldn't there be a next-best option? Compare the practical case: Suppose we were in a situation where we were deciding what to do and the options only differ in respect of how many lives are saved out of 100 at-risk people. Obviously, we objectively ought to do

The carve-out my opponent made in the previous paragraph doesn't help them here, since Clara does have a belief about the relevant topic. The issue is that even though she has a belief about it, she can't (in the relevant sense) have a true belief about it, and for that reason, it can't be the case that she objectively ought to have a true belief about it.

Because this conclusion runs counter to a strong tradition of thinking that we objectively ought to believe only truths, I imagine some readers still won't be happy with it. So let's look at the argument a little harder. The argument for thinking that we objectively ought to believe only truths had as a premise that in light of *P*, one objectively ought to believe *P*. I've claimed this fails in cases where the agent involved cannot believe *P*, since for a sufficiently strong sense of 'cannot,' it can't be the case that we both objectively ought to believe something and cannot believe it. To see this more clearly, let's compare the epistemic case to the practical one: In JACK'S FRIEND, we said that Jack objectively ought to go get the antibiotic. Why didn't we instead say that Jack objectively ought to go back in time and prevent his friend from getting the infection? Or why didn't we say that Jack objectively ought to focus his mental energy into tiny lasers that go into his friend's infected cells and kill the bacteria? Or why didn't we say that Jack should sing a magical song that destroys all unhealthful bacteria in the world? I take it that we excluded these actions because they are not, in the relevant sense, things Jack can do; they're not actions available to Jack, and we think that what one objectively ought to do is limited to which actions are available. What I'm claiming here is that in the epistemic case, like in the practical case, we should think that we can only be objectively required to believe something if having that belief is available to us. In cases like Clara's, the truth is not an available option, so she can't be objectively required to believe it.[11]

the option that saves all of the people, if that option is available. It would be odd to think that if that ideal option isn't available, it automatically follows that there isn't anything we objectively ought to do. But this is the analogue of what my opponent would be saying in Clara's case: The truth isn't an available option for belief, so there just isn't anything she objectively ought to believe.

[11] Notice that appeals to purported 'definitions' of the objective 'ought' don't really help here. It's hard to understand what it would mean for Clara to 'have' the information that spacetime is Euclidean but also not be able to believe it. It doesn't help to retreat to thinking that what's involved in an 'ought' claim being true in light of some information is that some idealized version of the agent or some idealized advisor of the agent has the information, since the problem is that Clara cannot have the belief, not that we can't understand the proposed translation of 'in light of.'

This argument shows against the claim that what we objectively ought to believe is always the truth. This means that neither 'right$_t$ belief' nor 'correct belief' picks out the objective epistemic 'ought' (assuming both of those have true belief as their extension). It makes more sense to think of 'right$_t$ belief' and 'correct belief' as offering objective standards of evaluation for belief, rather than as a prescription for what beliefs we should have. Describing a belief as 'correct' or 'incorrect' ('right$_t$' or 'wrong$_t$') tells us whether it meets a certain ideal standard, that of being true. But as is widely recognized in the metaethics literature, we must distinguish merely evaluative uses of 'ought' and 'should' from their prescriptive uses (see, e.g., Schroeder 2011). 'Right belief,' in the sense I intend it here, doesn't merely evaluate a belief; it also tells agents what they should believe in a prescriptive sense.

So here I'll think of 'right$_t$ belief' and 'correct belief' as providing a standard of evaluation for belief, neither of which lines up with what we objectively or subjectively ought to believe. This leaves open how we should think of 'right belief.' Should we think of 'right belief' as picking out an objective or subjective kind of rightness? I'll return to this question below. But first, let's turn to how we might theorize about right belief.

1.3.2 What Is Normative Epistemology?

Above I characterized normative ethics as the subfield of ethics that's concerned with giving a complete and correct account of morally right action, of what we morally ought to do. I propose that we carve off a kind of epistemic theorizing that's analogous to normative ethical theorizing. Let's use the term 'normative epistemology' to refer to the kind of epistemic theorizing that aims to give a complete and correct theory of epistemically right belief, of what we epistemically ought to believe.[12] Just as normative *ethics* aims to produce a complete and correct theory that tells us for every possible situation which actions are morally right and wrong in that situation, normative *epistemology* aims to produce a complete and correct theory that tells us for every possible situation which beliefs are epistemically right and wrong in that situation.

[12] I caution my reader not to confuse normative epistemology in this sense with the epistemology of the normative (a.k.a. moral epistemology), the subfield of philosophy that aims to understand how we know about normative issues.

Normative epistemology, so characterized, is focused on producing a theory of right belief. As mentioned above, in ethics, there are many normative and evaluative notions other than right action that ethicists aim to understand, like moral responsibility notions (e.g., praise and blame). Similarly, in epistemology, there are many normative and evaluative notions epistemologists aim to understand other than right belief. Epistemologists also care about justification, rationality, knowledge, etc. Let's leave open for now whether a belief being right is the same as (or even has any connection with) it being justified, rational, knowledge, etc. We'll revisit this issue in Chapter 3, where I'll argue that we shouldn't see right belief as lining up exactly with any of those notions, and in Chapter 7, where I'll explore general approaches for thinking about these other epistemic notions that work well with my preferred view of right belief. As I'll conceive of it here, normative epistemology is primarily focused on giving and defending a theory of right belief, not these other notions.[13]

You might worry that by stipulating that we use '(epistemically) right belief' in a particular way and forcing us to disconnect it from extant theorizing on justified belief, knowledge, etc., I've made the task too easy for myself. The goal is to get a complete and correct theory of right belief, so the worry is that by stipulating what the task is and disconnecting it from justified belief, knowledge, and related notions, (1) I'll end up crafting a theory that just fits the stipulations, rather than something of real interest, and (2) the theory will be immune from objections having to do with justified belief, knowledge, and related notions, since it's a theory of a notion carefully fenced off from those.

I don't see it that way at all, though. Normative ethics starts with the important and interesting question of what we should do. The goal of normative ethics is to create a complete and correct theory of right action to answer that question. The way I see it, when compared to the question of what we should do, the question of what we should believe is at least as interesting and important. This is especially true recently where misinformation is widespread and there's profit in changing how we see the world.

[13] Also, as noted above, some authors, like some opponents of consequentializing, hold that normative ethicists must go beyond giving a complete and correct theory of moral rightness by also giving a kind of explanation of moral rightness. Similarly, one might expect more of normative epistemology, perhaps that normative epistemology similarly explains epistemic normativity. What I'll assume here is that giving a complete and correct account of right belief is at least one of the central goals of normative epistemology.

And as I mentioned above, just as much is at stake in deciding what we should believe as there is in deciding what we should do, in part because the former is often an element of the latter. The idea of normative epistemology is to start with the question of what we should believe. It uses the term '(epistemically) right belief' to refer to that. By carving off right belief from extant theorizing on justification, knowledge, etc., normative epistemologists are freeing themselves to focus on the main question of what we should believe by putting aside questions of whether right beliefs must be justified, knowledge, etc. If it turns out that a theory of right belief looks like a theory of justified belief, rational belief, or knowledge, that would be evidence that right belief overlaps with those notions, and that might help further research on both topics. But as I see it, if that happens, that would be a fringe benefit of normative epistemology. Normative epistemology is, in the first instance, motivated by trying to answer the question of what we should believe.[14]

1.3.3 What Is Right Belief? (Take 2)

With this conception of normative epistemology in mind, let's return to the question of what 'right belief' is. Above, I argued against the standard view that says what we objectively ought to believe is always the truth. That argument made space for thinking that 'right belief' might involve either an objective or subjective kind of rightness. Since we've crafted normative epistemology in the mold of normative ethics, I propose we understand this aspect of 'right belief' on analogy to 'right action.' I take it that normative ethicists, in giving theories of right action, aim to give theories of what we objectively morally ought to do.[15] Hedonistic utilitarianism, for example, is a paradigmatic normative ethical theory, and it doesn't give agents' perspectives any special place in issuing verdicts about what's morally right. For that reason, it seems implausible to construe it as giving a theory of what agents subjectively ought to do. Smart (1973, p. 13) agrees. Despite offering a consequentialist moral theory that's heavily tied to agents' perspectives, Smart distinguishes 'right action' from 'rational action,' where 'right action'

[14] If you're the sort of person who reads footnotes, it's worth reminding you that this project isn't entirely new. As I discussed above, many projects in epistemology contribute partial answers to this question. What separates this project from others is it being primarily aimed at generating a complete and correct theory of right belief.

[15] For a dissenting view, see Gibbard (2005).

is what the normative ethical theory is about and picks out what the agent ought to do in light of all the facts. Following normative ethicists, I propose that we see 'right belief' as involving an objective kind of rightness, one that applies in light of all the facts.

I imagine many readers will be hesitant to get on board with this proposal because they'll still be stuck in thinking that we objectively ought to believe only truths. As we saw above, the natural reason to think that is because you think that *in light of the information that P*, agents always objectively ought to believe that *P*. I argued above that this claim is false. Despite that, I imagine it will help some readers if we returned to this. So let's reconsider the question of how we can think of right belief as involving an objective kind of epistemic normativity without thinking 'right belief' is co-extensive with 'true belief.' Here I'll attempt to convince you that it's possible for there to be cases where, in light of some information *P*, it's not true that an agent objectively ought to believe that *P*. This should again help to undermine the thought that the objective epistemic 'ought' always picks out the truth, which will again make space for thinking that the right belief, in my sense, is the one we objectively ought to have.

It's not hard to see how this could work if we construe normative ethical and epistemic theories as I did above. Above I suggested we think of normative ethical theories as functions from situations agents might find themselves in to what the right actions are in those situations, and I proposed that we understand normative epistemic theories as similar functions to what the right beliefs are. Conceived of as such, different theories of right belief (and action) might take into account different amounts and kinds of information in determining what the right belief is in a situation. For example, a simple evidentialist theory of right belief might say that the relevant pieces of information to take into account are only those about what evidence the agent has. An evidentialist theory so construed will ignore all facts that aren't about the agent's evidence. In determining whether an agent's belief that grass is green is right, the theory will take into account only facts about *the agent's evidence about* whether grass is green, not facts about whether grass is in fact green.[16] So for an agent whose evidence supports thinking grass is purple, the theory will say the belief that grass is purple is right, even in light of the fact that grass is green (because, again,

[16] More formally, we could think of this evidentialist theory as giving the same output for all inputs that share the same evidence-facts. So two inputs that differ only in the color of grass will share the same output.

the theory doesn't care about non-evidence facts). On this way of thinking about theories, there is no problem in thinking that a theory of normative epistemology might hold that an agent ought to have a false belief, even in light of all the facts. This shows there is no tension in thinking that the paradigmatic theories of right belief are theories about what we objectively ought to believe and that they sometimes say the right belief is a false belief.

This way of thinking about how theories take facts into account in determining what we ought to believe also undermines a natural argument for thinking that the only interesting epistemic 'ought' claims are ones that are true in light of the information available to the agent (i.e., it undermines the idea that all interesting epistemic 'ought' claims are subjective 'ought' claims). As we saw above, by including all of the facts in the information set that the 'ought' applies in light of, theories of the objective epistemic 'ought' can use both facts about the agent's perspective and facts not about the agent's perspective in determining what the agent objectively ought to believe. That is strictly more information than theories of the subjective 'ought' can use, since they are limited to applying in light of only the perspective-internal facts. For example, suppose there is an agent Brian to whom the cup in front of him appears green and who believes that the cup is green. Let's also suppose that, unbeknownst to Brian, he only believes that the cup is green because of a complicated set of mirrors that would make the cup appear green even if it weren't. Now consider theories of what Brian ought to believe. Subjective theories of what Brian ought to believe can only take into account the information available to Brian, so the only information the theories can apply in light of is information about how the cup appears to Brian and his belief that the cup is green. Objective theories of belief rightness can apply in light of strictly more information: they can apply in light of facts about how the cup appears to Brian, the fact that Brian believes that the cup is green, the fact that the cup is in fact green, and the fact that Brian is in this odd mirror-involving situation (since these are all facts of the situation). What this means is that any prediction a subjective theory of rightness can make about a situation, an objective theory of rightness can also make. Objective theories have strictly more flexibility. They can appeal to information in the agent's ken (or not), and they can appeal to information not in the agent's ken (or not). This undermines the idea that when it comes to epistemic 'ought's, we should only be interested in subjective theories. Objective theories of epistemic rightness can do anything subjective theories can do and more.

These considerations show that the objective epistemic 'ought,' the one that tells us what we objectively ought to believe (rather than merely evaluating our beliefs as true or false), need not be a simple kind of 'ought' that only prescribes true belief. The objective epistemic 'ought' is as ripe for interesting theorizing as its subjective counterpart. This opens up space for thinking that, following normative ethicists, the natural starting place for normative epistemic theorizing is theorizing about right belief conceived of as picking out what we objectively epistemically ought to believe. That's the conception of right belief that I'll employ here.

That said, even if the reader disagrees with me about how to understand these metanormative aspects of the concept of right belief, I doubt it will matter much for how we should actually do normative epistemology (i.e., how we should develop and defend a theory of what we should believe in practice). We can do normative epistemology, I propose, by using the term 'right belief' in a way analogous to how normative ethicists use the term 'right action.' And just as normative ethicists routinely defend theories of right action without a fully worked-out metaethical theory of the kind of moral obligation involved, in the rest of this book I hope to show that we can develop and defend a theory of right belief without a fully worked-out metanormative theory of what kind of epistemic obligation is involved. So, even though I think it's natural to think of 'right belief' as being about objective epistemic normativity, when it comes to doing the kind of normative epistemology I'll do in most of the rest of this book, I'll only need the reader to follow me in thinking of right belief as involving the kind of normativity that's central to normative epistemology—the kind of normativity that tells us what we should believe in the real situations we find ourselves in. With that in mind, I'll put aside for now questions about whether the notion is objective or subjective, whether it's evaluative or prescriptive, and how it relates to other epistemic notions like justified belief and knowledge. I'll turn instead to looking at the methodology normative epistemologists might use to develop and defend theories in actual practice.

1.3.4 The Methodology of Normative Epistemology

How can we develop and defend a theory of right belief in practice? Perhaps unsurprisingly, I'll propose we take cues from normative ethicists to answer this question. Like in normative ethics, research in normative epistemology primarily works by appeal to intuitions about right belief. Mirroring standard accounts of the methodology of normative ethics, we can class those intuitions into three kinds: intuitions about particular cases, intuitions about epistemic principles or general rules, and intuitions about features of epistemic theories. We saw above the case of Earl and what he should believe about whether hydroxychloroquine helps with COVID-19. I imagine most readers will have the intuition that Earl should not believe hydroxychloroquine helps. If that's right, then a theory of normative epistemology predicting that will have a mark in its favor, and a theory not predicting that will have a mark against it. Luckily, we have tons of clear and straightforward intuitions about mundane cases that we can use to evaluate possible theories of right belief.

We also have intuitions about general epistemic rules and principles. We might think, for example, that if we don't have any evidence at all about a certain proposition, we shouldn't believe it. Again here, a theory agreeing with that (by making the correct relevant predictions in each particular case) will have a mark in favor of it, and vice versa. The same point applies to intuitions about features of epistemic theories. You might have the intuition that whether a belief is right for an agent to have should depend only on the agent's evidence and maybe the agent's history. This is the idea that Berker (2013a) describes as the 'backward-lookingness' of epistemic notions. If that's right, then again, a theory having that feature will have a mark in favor of it.

Like in normative ethical theorizing, in normative epistemological theorizing, there will sometimes be clashes of intuitions. We might discover, for example, that our intuition that we shouldn't believe things we don't have evidence for clashes with an intuition that it's permissible to believe in God. If so, then we must give up on one of the intuitions or find a way to square them. This is what much of the work in normative epistemology will consist in. And again like in normative ethics, many things might bear on which intuitions it makes sense to preserve and which we should abandon.

Sometimes in cases of conflict of intuitions, we can come to see that one of the intuitions is misleading and abandon it for that reason. Sometimes, for example, we might have the intuition that a general rule is true because we generalized from some apparently representative cases. We might then come upon a new case we hadn't considered and that clearly shows against the generalization. It would then make sense to reject the generalization.

Not all cases of conflicts are so straightforward, though, and in practice, we'll see that no theory can perfectly account for all the intuitions. So what we should expect from a successful defense of a theory of normative epistemology is that it shows why the theory fits *best* (even if not perfectly) with the intuitions.

There is no fixed formula for deciding when a theory fits best with our intuitions, and arguing that certain theories do or do not fit well will be a lot of what normative epistemology is about. That said, there are some things we should expect of a theory that fits well with our intuitions. The theory should be well motivated by our intuitions about general principles and features of theories. Part of that is showing why the theory would be worth exploring in light of the intuitions we have. A theory that fits well with our intuitions should also be able to fend off objections based on apparent counterexamples and explain away any apparent tensions with our intuitions about epistemic principles and features of epistemic theories. We might also think that theories that are simpler and more elegant will naturally fit better with our intuitions, either because we have the intuition that such theories are more likely to be right or because we expect that simpler and more elegant theories would be easier to grasp, which would explain how we're able to know about them. Of course, what the criteria for fit should be and how well any theory meets these criteria will be up for debate, and successfully defending a theory of normative epistemology will involve grappling with those issues.

Realistically, we shouldn't expect even the best theories to have a fully satisfying answer for every concern. We might find a theory that fits very well with almost all of our intuitions and doesn't fit at all with a small proportion of them. In that case, its defenders might try to get us to just give up on those intuitions and treat them as spoils to the victor. But even if a theory cannot make sense of some intuitions, we might think a theory is better if it can help us understand why we were misleadingly attached to those problematic intuitions. In other words, we might see a theory as better if it can explain why we might have been concerned about the things we were concerned about. Of course, how we treat all of these factors in evaluating theories of normative epistemology is up for debate, so again, grappling with them will be something we have to do to find a complete and correct theory of what we should believe.

1.4 Toward a Theory of Right Belief

The rest of this book aims to develop and defend a particular theory of right belief. The theory that will be developed is consequentialist in structure and is centrally motivated by the idea that epistemic norms are about getting the most accurate representation of the world possible. In Chapters 2 through 6, I outline and defend the theory using the methodology just described. The first half of Chapter 2 lays out the many intuitions that support the theory. Because the intuitions are so pervasive and widespread and because the theory is so simple and intuitive, I propose that we treat the consequentialist theory as the default view. The second half of Chapter 2 and Chapters 3 through 6 serve as defense of that default: they consider what intuitions might show against the theory and attempt to incorporate them or explain them away. In the last chapter of the book, I work out implications of the view for our conception of epistemic normativity more generally and ask how the view of right belief I defend might sit with theories of justification and rationality. That final chapter gives the reader a better conception of how the theory both fits into and grounds a broader conception of epistemology, one that can be used to further projects both inside and outside of philosophy.

A complete defense of the view would need to show that the view fits the intuitions better than any possible alternative theory. Showing that isn't a task I will complete here. Here I'll focus on how showing how good the fit of my view is with our central intuitions about right belief by bringing out the kinds of intuitions that support the view and showing how the view can be developed in response to objections. In several places along the way, I'll sketch some ways proponents of my view might respond to things my opponents might say in favor of their views, but I'll leave it to the future of normative epistemology to decide whether my view really does offer the best overall conception of right belief.

Before moving on to defending the view, I want to mention (and quickly put aside) a common objection to all views of what we should believe. Alston (1988) worried that all talk of what we should believe in a prescriptive sense is confused, since it falsely presupposes that our beliefs are things we have control over. I, for example, distinctly remember having oatmeal for breakfast this morning, and it seems as clearly true to me as anything else.

I couldn't decide to change that belief no matter how hard I put my mind to it. So what sense does it make to say that I either 'should' or 'shouldn't' have that belief? Alston's worry was that because we lack the right kind of control over our beliefs, no prescriptive 'ought' or 'should' claims apply to them. If that's right, it seems to show against the whole project of normative epistemology, the way I've described it.[17]

There are many responses to Alston's worry already in the literature. Feldman (2000), for example, denies that epistemic obligations, permissions, and responsibilities require control. Feldman thinks that epistemic obligations are what he calls "role oughts"—'ought's that apply to us in virtue of a role we occupy. Teachers, for example, might have an obligation to explain things so that their students can understand them even if teachers can't control whether the students understand them. Similarly, Feldman thinks that all agents occupy the role of being a believer, and epistemic norms apply to us in virtue of us occupying that role, regardless of whether we can control our beliefs. Another popular kind of response to Alston in the literature claims that we do have the relevant kind of control. Ginet (2001), Hieronymi (2006), Steup (2008, 2011), and Weatherson (2008) all give some version of this line. Steup (2011), for example, argues that we can conceive of the required control in terms of our beliefs being reasons-responsive, mirroring popular compatibilist responses to the problem of free will (like the one given by Fischer and Ravizza 1998). Because there are already well-worked-out responses to Alston's worry in the literature and because the worry applies to all theories of what we should believe (not only theories like the one I hope to defend but also any theory that has prescriptive implications for what we should believe, even including theories of peer disagreement, Bayesian updating, and many theories of justification), I will ignore Alston's objection here (although I will return to Alston's central idea in the last chapter to ask whether it motivates a particular way of thinking about justification). With that out of the way, let's turn to looking at the truth-loving epistemic consequentialist theory.

[17] Of course, though, if the objection were right, we could likely modify the aims of normative epistemology accordingly. We could, for example, think of 'right belief' as picking out an evaluative standard rather than a prescriptive kind of normativity.

2

Truth-Loving Epistemic Consequentialism and Trade-Offs

2.1 Believe Truth! Shun Error!

According to Exodus, God (through Moses) used a strong wind to part the Red Sea so that the Israelites could cross and escape the Egyptian army. Should we believe that really happened? A common thought is that we should believe what our evidence supports. So to determine whether we should believe it, we might ask what evidence we have about it. We have evidence that strong winds cannot usually part large bodies of water (and certainly not long enough to allow people to walk through). On the other hand, we also have evidence that the Israelites did somehow escape the Egyptians, so that is some (weak) evidence in favor. Suppose we collected all of our evidence on this question. Would that determine what's right to believe?

Evidentialists, like Feldman (2000), say that what you should believe is completely determined by what your evidence supports. I'm not sure that's right. Here's why: When we ask ourselves what we should believe, we ask ourselves what's true.[1] We all know that evidence can be misleading, and when it is misleading, that means that if someone relies on it, it would lead them astray from the truth. So when we're asking ourselves what to believe, we should think that if our evidence is misleading, relying on it would lead us astray too. Of course, it's impossible for us to tell from the inside if our evidence is misleading. But, even if we can't tell, we do think that *if our evidence is, in fact, misleading, we shouldn't rely on it*. What this means is that we don't think we should always believe what our evidence supports. Instead, we think we should treat our evidence not as a determiner but as a *guide* to what we should believe. Our evidence, we think, generally guides us to believing truths, but it's a fallible guide. When it comes to what's right to

[1] See Shah 2003 on this phenomenon, which he calls 'transparency.'

Right Belief and True Belief. Daniel J. Singer, Oxford University Press. © Oxford University Press 2023.
DOI: 10.1093/oso/9780197660386.003.0003

believe about the parting of the Red Sea, it seems more like the truth is what determines what you should believe. If it did happen as described in Exodus, then that's the right thing to believe, and if it didn't, then it isn't. On this picture, we use our evidence as a tool for determining what's true, because the truth (not our evidence) is what determines what's right to believe.

In this chapter I'll argue that reflection on cases like these and others motivates the view I call 'truth-loving epistemic consequentialism.' In a nutshell, that view says that a belief that *P* is the right one for an agent to have if and only if among the available options for belief, believing *P* promotes the greatest overall balance of having true beliefs and not having false beliefs. In the next section, I'll canvass many different kinds of examples that all purport to show that true belief and the lack of false belief are all that matter for whether a belief is right, and I'll argue that these cases should make us think that truth-loving epistemic consequentialism is the best starting hypothesis for epistemic theorizing. In that section, I'll also clarify why I think evidentialists cannot as easily make sense of these cases.

In Section 2.3, I'll begin to respond to an objection to the general structure of truth-loving epistemic consequentialism that accuses the view of incorrectly sanctioning epistemic trade-offs. I'll argue that sanctioning trade-offs isn't always wrong. In fact, there are cases where it intuitively seems right to think that the rightness of one belief is a function of the truth of others. Section 2.4 will show that even though there are some intuitively acceptable trade-offs, acceptable trade-offs will still be rare according to the truth-loving epistemic consequentialist. The rarity of those trade-offs will help alleviate some concerns about the view. In Section 2.5, I'll argue that views that sanction trade-offs, like truth-loving epistemic consequentialism, have some explanatory virtues over those that don't, and in Section 2.6, I'll wrap up and set the stage for further discussions of trade-offs in the next chapter.

As I mentioned in the last chapter, it is not the goal of this chapter (or even this book) to give a conclusive defense of truth-loving epistemic consequentialism, nor is it to give knock-down arguments against competitor views like evidentialism, other kinds of consequentialism, or other nearby views. Rather, the approach I take in this book is one motivated by the analogy to normative ethics discussed in the previous chapter. This chapter will bring out many different kinds of intuitions that favor the view. The view, I'll argue, is the most natural one and we often seem to accept it as the obvious default view. As we'll explore more in depth in later chapters, the view has been subject to many objections, and those objections have motivated most theorists to give up on the initially appealing view. Later chapters will aim to undermine those objections. Altogether, this chapter along with the coming ones aim to defend the view by showing how it is supported by many strong intuitions (this chapter) and how it can overcome many apparently contrary intuitions (later parts of this chapter and later chapters). No particular intuition or argument against the hostile intuitions is essential to the defense of truth-loving epistemic consequentialism that this book aims to give. Rather, the book aims to be a kind of guide for how to best get on board with the consequentialist picture.

2.2 Intuitions in Favor of Epistemic Consequentialism

In the example about the parting of the Red Sea, it seemed like what was right to believe was determined by the truth. Examples about biblical events are controversial, though. So let's consider a more mundane case. Consider MICROWAVE (from the last chapter, repeated here):

> MICROWAVE Today, just as he has done at lunch for years, Justin put a Hot Pocket in the microwave and set it for 2 minutes to heat it up. While he waited the 2 minutes, he could see that the microwave looked and sounded like it was working normally. Just before Justin reached in to grab the Hot Pocket, he could see the steam coming off the Hot Pocket, and he believed it was hot. In fact, the Hot Pocket was hot.

I hope the reader joins me in thinking that Justin's belief is right in this case, and it's right because of its connection to the truth. This example hopefully also makes it clear how typical it is that we judge our own and others' beliefs to be right because of their connections to the truth. Abe is driving on the highway and believes the car in front of him is slowing down because he sees the brake lights illuminate. In fact, the car is slowing down because the driver is pressing the brake, so Abe's belief is right. We look up in a grocery store and notice a sign saying that the avocados are on sale. We believe the avocados are on sale, and because what the sign says is true, our belief is right. It should be easy for the reader to generate more cases.

According to the view I'll begin to flesh out in this section, true belief and the lack of false belief uniquely determine what we epistemically ought to believe. As the examples make clear, this idea is intuitive, but it's also quite established in the epistemology literature. Lots of writing in epistemology (including this chapter) starts with William James's injunction to "Believe truth! Shun error!" (1979, p. 24) or a discussion of how belief "aims at the truth." In *The Meditations*, Descartes took his goal to be "to arrive at the truth" and "avoid ever going wrong" (1985, p. 41). Three hundred years later, Alston (1985, p. 83) took 'the epistemic point of view' to be "defined by the aim of maximizing truth and minimizing falsity in a large body of beliefs." Even more recently, Goldman (2001, p. 32) has claimed that "true belief is the ultimate value in the epistemic sphere."

This idea also seems to underpin a lot of how we try to regulate our own beliefs in our day-to-day lives. Consider what it's like when you ask yourself whether to believe you'll get up early enough tomorrow to make it out for a run before sunrise. To decide whether to believe this, you might ask yourself whether you've been able to do this in the past, whether your alarm clock is reliable, whether you'll actually get out of bed when it goes off, etc. The reason we ask ourselves these questions is that we're trying to discern whether *it's true* that we'll get up early enough for a run, and the answers to each of these questions give us some hint at whether it's true. So in first-personal reasoning, we seem to assume that whether we should believe something is determined by whether it's true.[2]

For another example, suppose you're a scientist who has just collected a bunch of data about a question you're investigating. The exact nature of the question doesn't matter; we could suppose it's about bird migratory patterns, how vowel sounds have shifted in the Northeast, or whether the political party in control of Congress affects stock prices. Not being sure which statistical test to use to analyze the data, you ask a statistician. She tells you that Welch's t-test is designed to be used in cases like yours and that it's very likely (and more likely than any other test) to give you the true answer. You're convinced that Welch's t-test is the most conducive to you forming a true belief about the question you're investigating. Given that, should you use that test?

If you didn't want to use Welch's t-test, there are lots of possible excuses you could give, even if you grant everything the statistician told you. You could say that the test is too computationally or logistically difficult to use. Or you could say that you don't have enough time to compute the result

[2] For further discussion of this phenomenon, see Shah (2003) and Shah and Velleman (2005).

before you have to pick up the kids from football practice. Or maybe computing Welch's *t*-test would use resources that would otherwise be used for more important tasks, like curing someone of cancer. Those would all be practical and moral justifications for not using the test. By adding some cute details to the story, I bet we could also come up with potential aesthetic or legal justifications for not using the test. But could there be an epistemic case for not using the test? It seems like the answer is no. Once it's established that Welch's *t*-test is the test that's most likely to give the true answer, there's no further question about whether you *epistemically* ought to use it rather than other tests. So here again, it looks like it's the truth that's the unique determiner of what's epistemically right.

In interacting with others, we also usually assume that our interlocutors will think that truth-promotion uniquely determines what we should believe. Consider what it's like to teach introductory logic or critical reasoning. (I'm betting several readers will have had this experience, but it's not too hard to imagine, if not.) When explaining the fallacy of affirming the consequent, we might say something like "We cannot infer 'not-*Q*' from 'if *P* then *Q*' and 'not-*P*' because the premises can be true without the conclusion being true." We might follow up with an example: "It doesn't follow from 'If the battery is dead, then the car won't start' and 'The car won't start' that 'The battery is dead.' " If we're trying to be really, really explicit, we might additionally add something like "So inferences like that don't preserve truth from the premises to the conclusion." Notice that it would be odd to take it a step further and add "... and you shouldn't infer in ways that aren't conducive to the truth." We don't need to be that explicit with our students. Why can we leave that last step implicit? The reason is that we can assume our students already know that the promotion of true beliefs and the lack of false beliefs are what determine what we should believe, so if a method doesn't promote truth in our beliefs, it's not helpful (and maybe even detrimental) in helping us form the right beliefs.

This example brings out an important reason to think truth-loving epistemic consequentialism is right: Our interactions with others about what we should believe are typically structured by a joint assumption that we should believe truth and avoid error. This is easy to see in teaching contexts. There, faculty are trying to influence students' beliefs, and we have the aim of doing that in a truth-directed way. But this is true even in less formal contexts. On the bus on the way home, if the stranger next to you starts telling you about the police encounter he had earlier, you'll both know that you're forming beliefs about his experience and take for granted that you're forming beliefs that what he said is true. If, for example, you discover halfway through questioning him about part of the experience that he was, in fact, just making stuff up the whole time, you can reasonably be frustrated that he's violated your trust. What this shows is that it's a deeply ingrained assumption of how we interact with others that the truth determines when our and others' beliefs are right. The assumption is so deeply ingrained that we don't even think we need to teach it, let alone argue for it, even in contexts where we're being very explicit about what constitutes good reasoning, like critical thinking classes.

As I mentioned above, evidentialists like Feldman (2000) argue for a view that says that what our evidence supports, not what's true, determines what we should believe. I don't intend to give a full argument against evidentialism, but I will try to sketch where the truth-loving epistemic consequentialist should think the evidentialist goes wrong. The main issue is that evidentialists can't account for cases where the evidence is misleading. When we're deciding for ourselves what to believe, we ask ourselves what's true, not what our evidence supports. Sure, we use our evidence to determine what we think is true, but that doesn't mean we're aiming for our beliefs to line up with what our evidence supports, any more than a runner with a four-hour marathon goal wants their running time to line up with when their watch says four hours has passed. If the watch is running slow or the evidence is misleading, our running times and beliefs will fall short. It's probably true that our evidence is the only guide we have to the truth, so in cases where our evidence leads us astray, we're doing the best we can by following our evidence. But when our evidence leads us astray, there's a kind of evaluative remainder that sticks around. If we follow our evidence and get a false belief, we're in an epistemically unfortunate situation, where the belief that seemed right isn't really the right one.

So, the truth-loving epistemic consequentialist should think that evidentialists miss the mark in these cases because they confuse what belief *seems* right with what belief *is* right. Really, we should see our evidence as a *guide* that we use to determine what's true. We use our evidence to determine what we think is true because we care about the truth in deciding what to believe. But evidence is a fallible guide, and when it leads us astray, what seems like the right belief (according to the evidence) and what really is the right belief can come apart. Evidentialism cannot accommodate there being distance between these notions. This is why the truth-loving epistemic consequentialist should think evidentialism doesn't get the right results about right belief.[3]

It's easy to come up with more cases where it seems like the truth, not the evidence, determines whether a belief is right. Consider how we think about right scientific beliefs. The primary statistical method used in most scientific disciplines is null hypothesis significance testing (NHST) (Fisher 1925, Neyman and Pearson 1933). In brief, scientists use NHST to determine whether the data they've collected (their evidence) is strong enough to tell them that some effect was observed, or as it's typically construed, that they can 'reject the null hypothesis.' NHST is primarily structured around balancing two different kinds of errors: rejecting the null hypothesis when it's true ('type I error') and not rejecting it when it's false ('type II error'). In different disciplines, there are different norms for how to weigh avoidance of these two kinds of errors against each other, and this is reflected in the '*p*-value' that the discipline uses for when they count results as significant. So even formalized reasoning in science fits the mold of how I've been claiming we regulate our beliefs. When deciding what to believe (as a scientist, in this case), it's the truth of the hypothesis (measured by avoidance of error about the hypothesis) that's the unique consideration. We use the scientific evidence as a guide to truth, but it's the truth that we really care about.

Even in more subtle cases of statistical reasoning, scientists focus on what's true, rather than what their evidence supports, as the determining factor for what to believe. For example, commonly used parametric statistical tests, like the two-sample *t*-test and ANOVA that many of us are familiar with, make certain assumptions about the distributions that are producing the data they operate on. Some of these assumptions are subtle, and often scientists are confused about what those assumptions are and whether they're satisfied (for more discussion, see Shaver 1993). So whether it's appropriate to perform a two-sample *t*-test on some data, for example, can sometimes be a subtle matter. Suppose then that a scientist performs a two-sample *t*-test on their data and draws some conclusion on that basis. If the assumptions of the *t*-test are not satisfied, it's an appropriate rebuke of the scientist to reject their use of that test. This is true even if the scientist's evidence supported thinking the test's assumptions are satisfied.

[3] As a reminder, I don't take this to be a knock-down argument against evidentialism. The goal here is to provide a broad picture of how to be an epistemic consequentialist. What I've offered here is a way for the consequentialist to conceive of what's gone wrong in evidentialist reasoning.

What matters is whether the test's assumptions were, in fact, satisfied. So here again it looks like a belief can be wrong even if it is supported by the holder's evidence.

Now suppose we have a scientist who is properly using a statistical test. Does that mean if the scientist bases her belief on the test, it must be right? Continuing with the picture offered above, I think we should see the scientist's statistical test as a guide she is using to try to reach the right belief. But the proper use of a technique to produce some outcome shouldn't be confused with a successful reaching of that outcome. Just as properly following a cake recipe to bake a cake doesn't guarantee that you'll have a cake at the end (the oven could break, the cake could fail to rise, etc.), so too does proper following of one's evidence not guarantee that you'll reach the right belief. Later research might uncover, for example, that even though she had excellent evidence for the conclusion at the time, that evidence was misleading. In that case, she might have tried her hardest to have the right belief, and she might not be blameworthy for failing to have it, but nonetheless, the belief wasn't right despite it being supported by the evidence. So yet again, it seems like truth, not evidential support, is what determines whether a belief is right.

Let's consider yet another area where we think truth is what makes a belief right: There's a long line of research in psychology about when human judgment errs or is beaten by simple heuristics. In a classic book, Meehl (1954) discussed a series of twenty experiments in which simple heuristics were on average better than humans at making predictions. There are probably hundreds of other experiments in psychology showing the same thing in different contexts. Simple prediction rules have been shown to be better than experts in predicting academic performance (Dawes 1971, DeVaul et al. 1987, Swets et al. 2000), quality of wine (Ashenfelter et al. 1995), the existence, location, and causes of brain damage (Wedding 1983), and the list goes on (see Bishop and Trout 2004 for a longer list). Meehl (1986, pp. 372–373) summarized this research by saying, "There is no controversy in social science which shows such a large body of qualitatively diverse studies coming out so uniformly in the same direction as this one." Meehl went on to draw a normative conclusion from this: "When you are pushing [scores of] investigations, predicting everything from the outcomes of football games to the diagnosis of liver disease[,] and when you can hardly come up with a half dozen studies showing even a weak tendency in favor of the clinician, it is time to draw a practical conclusion."

The "practical conclusion" that Meehl was referring to is that we ought to use statistical prediction rules to reason, rather than relying on expert or clinician reasoning, and a long line of research in psychology agrees with him. See Bishop and Trout (2004, pp. 14–15) for a longer list of examples, and see the entire book for a well-worked-out way of implementing the upshots of this literature in a general conception of epistemology.

There are several things to notice about this research for our purposes. First and most obviously, the "practical conclusion" that we should reason in truth-conducive ways, which is consistently offered by authors in this literature, is also exactly what the proponent of truth-loving epistemic consequentialism would say. So here we have a long list of experts on reasoning who seem to be explicitly endorsing the central tenant of truth-loving consequentialism. Moreover, it seems like these researchers must be endorsing the truth-based norm over the evidentialist alternative, since it's compatible with the results in this literature that the humans' judgments were supported by their evidence.[4] Finally, notice that a natural conclusion to draw from these studies is that, at least in the contexts these studies described, we're pretty bad at how we reason. If that's right, we must think that the reliability of our reasoning processes is what determines their goodness or badness. If so, then again here, it seems like we're focused on production of true belief, rather than adherence with evidence, as what determines the goodness of our reasoning.

At this point, we've seen many different examples that all purport to show that what's true is what determines whether a belief is the one we should have. We saw this in mundane cases like about whether we should believe a Hot Pocket is hot right after being microwaved, whether we should believe the car in front of us is slowing down when its brake lights are on, and whether we should believe the avocados are on sale when the sign says they are. We saw this when we reflected on choosing a way to form a belief, like choosing which statistical test to do. We also saw the centrality of truth for right belief in first-personally deciding what to believe about a topic. There, we quickly slide from asking ourselves what to believe to asking

[4] The evidentialist might object by holding that, in fact, the humans erred and the evidence generally supported what the heuristics said, not what the humans devised, in these cases. But this move will work against any opponent of evidentialism, since in any case where the opponent says that the right thing to believe is *P*, the evidentialist will just hold that the evidence does, in fact, support *P* in that case. I take it that if this evidentialist move is going to have any theoretical merit, we'll need a substantive story about why we should think the evidence supported *P* in those cases.

ourselves what's true. We saw that in conversations with others, we assume that they're aiming for truth in their beliefs, in both formal and informal reasoning contexts. We saw that the truth is the main factor in scientific and statistical reasoning, and we saw that even those who study how humans actually reason seem to assume in their research that truth centrally determines right belief.

What can these examples teach us about right belief? There are several things. As I've emphasized throughout, the examples motivate a truth-focused view of epistemic rightness over the evidentialist alternative. The examples motivate thinking that the truth, not our evidence (or anything else), is ultimately what matters when it comes to what we should believe. Following Goldman (2001), let's call this claim about what epistemically matters *veritism*:

> VERITISM All and only true beliefs (accurate credences) have final epistemic value, and all and only false beliefs (inaccurate credences) have final epistemic disvalue.

Veritism is a view about what's ultimately epistemically valuable. It says that what ultimately epistemically matters is the accuracy of our doxastic states, not whether those states are supported by our evidence, whether they're justified, whether they constitute knowledge, or whether they constitute any other kind of epistemic success.

Veritism, by itself, doesn't answer the question of what we should believe; there's a further question of how (or whether) right belief connects to epistemic value. The hypothesis defended in this book is that we can understand right belief in terms of *maximizing* veritistic epistemic value. That's what truth-loving epistemic consequentialism says:

> TRUTH-LOVING EPISTEMIC CONSEQUENTIALISM A belief that *P* (a particular credence) is right for an agent to have if and only if among the available options for belief (credence), having a belief that *P* (that credence) promotes the greatest overall balance of having true beliefs (accurate credences) and not having false beliefs (inaccurate credences).

According to this view, epistemic norms are about *maximizing* the accuracy of our beliefs (credences).

It's possible to accept VERITISM without being a truth-loving epistemic consequentialist—that is, one could think that VERITISM is true but what we should believe is not about maximizing the accuracy of our beliefs. Sylvan (2020), for example, defends a veritist non-consequentalist view that says that right belief is about *respecting* the accuracy of our beliefs, where respecting accuracy doesn't always require bringing about more of it.[5] So why should we think that the intuitions favor the maximizing conception of epistemic norms over a non-maximizing alternative?

One reason is that several of the examples seem to more directly intuitively support the maximizing view over the alternatives. In Chapter 4, I'll defend this more directly, but for now, reconsider the last example I mentioned above, the research in psychology about when human reasoning is beaten by heuristics. The central result that motivates that research and what guides its 'practical conclusion' is that *when it comes to maximizing our accuracy across a wide variety of topics*, simple heuristics do better than human reasoning. So it seems like *maximizing* veritistic epistemic value must be the goal that's presupposed in that research. We can see the same thing in thinking about the goal of statistical reasoning/tests: What makes one form of statistical reasoning (or a statistical test) better than another is that, within the given context, it gets a more accurate result in more cases. So here again, it looks like *maximizing* accuracy is the goal. Finally, think about what's wrong with telling people misleading truths. A natural thought is that a misleading truth is one that, though true, will lead our interlocutors to infer many falsehoods. So the natural story about what's wrong with it is that giving someone a misleading truth fails to *maximize* the overall accuracy of their beliefs. Here again, it seems like the intuitive view is that *maximizing* accuracy is the epistemic goal.[6]

Another mark in favor of the maximizing veritist view is the fact that it's already accepted by many theorists. As I mentioned above, Alston (1985, p. 83) puts this explicitly in saying that 'the epistemic point of view' is "defined by the aim of maximizing truth and minimizing falsity in a large body of beliefs." Goldman (1999) uses the maximizing approach to veritistic value as the basic building block for a broad framework for social epistemology. And as we'll discuss further in Chapter 6, the maximizing

[5] Sylvan puts his view in terms of what beliefs are 'justified,' but I take it that what he is talking about is what I would call 'right' belief.

[6] I imagine defenders of non-consequentialist veritist views will be quick to produce ways of explaining what's going on in these cases in their own terms. My point here is not that these cases show decisively in favor of the maximizing approach but rather that these cases more straight forwardly appear to support that view. As I spell out below, I think this helps support thinking we should see the maximizing view as a plausible hypothesis.

approach to veritistic value undergirds the prominent project in Bayesian formal epistemology that goes under the headings 'epistemic utility theory' and 'accuracy-first epistemology' (see, e.g., Joyce 1998, 2009; Greaves and Wallace 2006; Leitgeb and Pettigrew 2010b; and Pettigrew 2016).

But the best reason, in my opinion, to at least *start* theorizing with the maximizing view is that it's the simplest and most intuitive way of understanding the connection between right belief and true belief. The maximizing view says the right belief is simply the one that maximizes veritist value. Non-maximizing veritist views will all have to give a more complicated account of the connection between right belief and epistemic value. The kind of view Sylvan (2020) defends, for example, says that right belief must manifest the appropriate kind of respect for veritistic value, where manifesting the appropriate kind of respect is a complex notion that requires minimizing a certain kind of epistemic disvalue as well as meeting several other Kantian-flavored demands. This level of theoretical complexity could, in theory, be needed to give a plausible account of right belief if the target phenomenon is equally complex, but in doing normative epistemology, I suggest we start with the simplest theory and only move to more complex theories when we're forced to.[7]

All of the above considerations together should make us think that truth-loving epistemic consequentialism is a plausible, well-motivated, and intuitive proposal about how to understand right belief in terms of true belief. For those reasons, I propose that we see truth-loving epistemic consequentialism as a good simple starting hypothesis for normative epistemic theorizing. We should treat it as the default view and ask whether there's any good reason to give it up. If after careful consideration we decide that there's no good reason to abandon the view, its intuitive plausibility along with its ability to fend off objections should count as sufficient reason to accept it.

Luckily for our ability to test this methodology, the epistemology literature is full of objections to truth-loving epistemic consequentialism, and many authors have taken the view to be an obvious non-starter on the basis of one objection or another. So, the bulk of the remainder of this book will make the case for truth-loving epistemic consequentialism by looking at those objections and showing how truth-loving epistemic consequentialism avoids them. In doing so, it will flesh out many aspects of the view further,

[7] Here I take myself to be appealing to a standard aspect of scientific methodology that views simplicity as a theoretical virtue. For an overview, see Fitzpatrick (2022).

and, as I'll argue in the last chapter, what we'll be left with is a sophisticated global truth-loving consequentialist view of epistemic norms that can serve as the basis for a broad and fecund general conception of epistemology.

But before digging into the details, it's worth highlighting a few important basic elements of the view. First, as I'll discuss more in the next chapter, the view is an *objective* consequentialist view in that it says a belief is right when it *in fact* promotes the best outcomes. *Subjective* views, by contrast, hold that what appears to the agent as best is what determines what's right. And although the view defended in this book is veritist, I'll remain agnostic about *why* true belief and the lack of false belief are valuable. Much ink has been spilled on exactly this question (e.g., David 2001, Horwich 2006, Pritchard et al. 2018), but most views about the value of true belief will be compatible with the normative epistemological theory defended here.

It's also important to notice that truth-loving epistemic consequentialism is not the same as the view that says that right belief just is true belief. I considered the latter view in the previous chapter and argued that one reason it fails is that it falsely assumes that a true belief is always available to the agent. Truth-loving epistemic consequentialism says that a belief that *P* is right if and only if, among the available options for belief, believing *P* conduces to the best overall balance of having true beliefs and not having false beliefs. On this view, whether a belief is right will depend not only on whether the belief itself is true but also on whether having it promotes having other true beliefs and not having other false beliefs. As we'll discuss in the next section, this aspect of the view means that it will license epistemic trade-offs, and cases of permissible trade-offs will also be cases where the right-belief-as-true-belief alternative fails.

As a reminder, even though I've been discussing the view in terms of right *belief*, the view is intended to be about how we should represent the world to ourselves more generally, and so it is meant to be a view about whatever doxastic attitudes we have, be they beliefs, credences, or anything else. On the degreed version of the view, a credence function will be right for an agent to have if and only if, among the available options for a credence function, having that credence function best conduces to accuracy.[8] Although most of the discussion in this book will be cast in the

[8] The notion of 'gradational accuracy,' introduced by Joyce (1998), is meant to be a degreed notion of accuracy that measures how closely a credence function matches the truth. Joyce (1998, 2009) fleshes this notion out more completely and uses it as a defense of part of the Bayesian approach. As I'll discuss in Chapter 5, there is an important difference between how Joyce and I conceive of the kind of accuracy that we should associate with a credence function.

traditional categorical terms for ease of exposition, everything I say here translates naturally to formal versions of epistemic consequentialism with degreed notions of belief. The exception will be Chapter 5, where we'll look at some of the issues facing degreed versions of the view more directly.

Finally, I want to highlight that I'll (intentionally) be switching between two conceptions of the theory being defended here. Narrowly construed, truth-loving epistemic consequentialism is a complete theory of right belief (or credence), in the sense discussed in Chapter 1. The theory tells us for every situation what beliefs (credences) are epistemically right for an agent to have in that situation. One goal of this book is to argue for that theory. But I also hope to motivate and encourage the reader to further explore a broader conception of epistemic normativity that has maximizing true belief at its core. On this broader conception of epistemic normativity, it's not only about what to believe; it's also about how to live one's life and set up social institutions in ways that promote the ultimate epistemic end of having true beliefs and not having false beliefs. On this broader conception of epistemic normativity, epistemic normativity tells us not only what beliefs to have but also what thought patterns to have and encourage in ourselves, how to discuss ideas with others, how to research our hypotheses, how to set up our experiments, how to process and store our data, how to structure grant-giving agencies, how to set up the criminal justice system, and, as Chapter 7 will argue, even what to eat. The narrower theory of right belief is separable from the broader framework, so those who find themselves wed to a more traditional conception of epistemic normativity need not abandon it to consider the central arguments of the book.

With those clarifications aside, I'll turn now to one of the most central arguments in the book, a defense of truth-loving epistemic consequentialism from trade-off objections. As we'll see, there are two different worries about trade-offs, so we'll continue the discussion of trade-offs into the next chapter as well.

2.3 On Trade-Offs: Part 0

Consequentialists (in both ethics and epistemology) think that whether some action or belief is right is to be understood exclusively in terms of whether the action or belief conduces to the best consequences. Truth-loving epistemic consequentialism is a particular kind of epistemic consequentialist view. Other epistemic consequentialists might take different views about what epistemic goodness is (popular options include true belief and knowledge, and less popular ones are justified belief and understanding), what epistemic rightness is (e.g., justification, rationality, warrant, or what one epistemically ought to believe/do), and what the conduciveness relation is (e.g., maximizing over the long term, or indirectly promoting). Process reliabilism (Goldman 1979) is probably the most popular form of epistemic consequentialism. That view takes a belief to be justified when it is the product of a process that reliably produces true beliefs (as such, it is a form of *indirect* consequentialism). Truth-loving epistemic consequentialism is the much simpler view that belief rightness is to be understood directly in terms of having true beliefs and not having false beliefs.

In both ethics and epistemology, consequentialists sanction trade-offs that their opponents reject. Recently in epistemology, some opponents of consequentialism have claimed that epistemic normativity doesn't admit of any trade-offs at all, contra consequentialists' commitments. Here, I will argue that there are at least *some* permissible epistemic trade-offs.[9] I'll give three different kinds of examples. What I aim to show in the rest of this chapter is that some epistemic trade-offs are permissible. That leaves room for the opponent of consequentialism to object to particular trade-offs that the consequentialist sanctions, but it doesn't allow them to reject the view simply on the basis that it admits of any trade-offs at all. We'll consider the more particular kind of trade-off objection in the next chapter.

According to trade-off objections to consequentialism, consequentialists incorrectly sanction actions or beliefs that sacrifice the good of some for the overall greater good. In ethics, a prominent example of this is the organ-harvesting case (Foot 1967, Thomson 1976), in which a consequentialist doctor is committed to trading off the life of one patient to save five others. In the epistemic realm, trade-off objections work analogously: Objectors say that consequentialists wrongly sanction trading off the epistemic goodness of some of one's beliefs for the overall goodness of their doxastic state. Examples of trade-off objections to epistemic consequentialism can be found in Firth (1998), Fumerton (1995, p. 12), Jenkins (2007), Greaves (2013), Berker (2013a), and Berker (2013b).

[9] Much of what I say here stems from what I previously published in Singer (2018b), but the arguments are improved here.

The most straightforward trade-off objection to epistemic consequentialism comes from Jenkins (2007). Here is that case as formulated by Andow (2017):

> TRUTH FAIRY Suppose you start with no reason to believe that *P* is true and no reason to believe that it is false. The Truth Fairy is a very powerful being, and she makes you the following credible offer: You accept *P* as true, and she will make your epistemic situation very, very good overall. She will arrange for you to have many, many true, justified, knowledgeable beliefs and very, very few false, unjustified, or unknowledgeable ones. However, she does not guarantee that your trust in *P* itself will have any particular epistemic status as a result of her actions.

In this case, consequentialists are committed to thinking that you should believe *P* (or that it's justified, rational, warranted, etc.), but of course, the natural intuition is that you should suspend belief.

There are many other formulations of trade-off objections to epistemic consequentialism, and there are formal versions of the trade-off objections that apply to Bayesian conceptions of epistemic consequentialism (see Greaves 2013). Some defenders of consequentialism have tried to rework their consequentialist views to avoid particular purported counterexamples (e.g., Ahlstrom-Vij and Dunn 2014 and Goldman 2015), but opponents of consequentialism typically take the worry to generalize past particular examples. Berker, for example, says that his goal is "not to argue by counterexample" (2013a, p. 365) and tries to show that sanctioning trade-offs uncovers more a general problem with consequentialism.

According to Berker (2013a), the more general problem with consequentialism that trade-off objections bring out is that consequentialism ignores the "separateness of propositions," a notion that is meant to be analogous to the "separateness of persons" issue for ethical consequentialism.[10] Berker thinks that epistemic normativity treats what's right for any individual proposition as distinct from the goodness of other beliefs. Berker (2013b) revises his view by arguing that the problem with consequentialism is actually that it tries to understand epistemic rightness in terms of promoting or conducing to some end. Berker thinks that whether an agent is justified or rational is typically viewed as a question of whether she *responded to* or *respected* her evidence (or something like that), and these are essentially backward-looking notions. On the

[10] For background on the structural worry about ethical consequentialism, see Brink (1993).

consequentialist picture, epistemic rightness has the wrong directionality: If consequentialism were right, epistemic rightness would be forward-looking, since it'd be about *bringing about* epistemic consequences. For that reason, the view can't account for the structure of epistemic notions like justification and rationality, Berker claims. Greaves (2013, p. 918) agrees that the trade-off objections show something more general about consequentialist views, but she puts the problem in terms of epistemic consequentialism's propensity to accept 'epistemic bribes.' In the next chapter, I'll take up the more specific task of responding to particular trade-off worries, and I'll respond directly to Berker's claims about directionality. In this chapter, I'll focus on arguing for the positive claim that some trade-offs are epistemically permissible. If that's right, it shows that these authors are wrong to try to generalize the trade-off objections to show against all theories that admit of trade-offs.

2.3.1 The Shape of Permissible Epistemic Trade-Offs

In TRUTH FAIRY, you're asked to consider a situation in which *you* have no reason to believe or not believe *P*, and a fairy offers *you* a bribe for believing *P*. As it's presented, the most natural way to consider the case is from the first-person perspective—i.e., we imagine ourselves as the subject in the case. In thinking about that case, we naturally ask ourselves, "Would it be the case that *I* should have this not-apparently-true belief for the sake of having other epistemically good beliefs, were *I* in that scenario?" Many of the other trade-off objections to epistemic consequentialism also have this first-personal flavor, including those from Firth (1998) and Fumerton (1995, p. 12), and I suspect we often consider cases from the first-person perspective even when they might not be presented that way. Let's call cases like this *first-personal-deliberative cases.*

First-personal-deliberative cases are particularly helpful to the opponent of consequentialism. As Shah (2003) discusses, first-personal doxastic deliberation exhibits the phenomenon of *transparency*, that "when asking oneself *whether to believe that p*, [one must] immediately recognize that this question is settled by, and only by, answering the question *whether p is true*" (2003, p. 447).[11] With transparency, in first-personal-deliberative cases,

[11] Whereas Shah (2003) and Shah and Velleman (2005) take it that transparency holds as a matter of conceptual necessity, Steglich-Petersen (2006) denies that transparency obtains *as a matter of conceptual necessity*, as does Chappell (2005). All of the authors accept that the phenomenon is prevalent among real agents, though, even if it's not conceptually necessary.

the question of whether to believe *p* will be settled by whether *p* appears true, which is a question we try to settle using our evidence (and maybe prior beliefs) about *p*, not the epistemic goodness potentially produced by holding that belief. So transparency means that from the first-person perspective, questions of epistemic rightness appear to be settled only by the truth of (or maybe the evidence about) that particular proposition, which is exactly the result the opponent of consequentialism wants.

Because of that, to find cases that intuitively look like cases of permissible epistemic trade-offs, we'll need to avoid straightforward first-personal-deliberative cases. If there are permissible trade-offs in straightforward first-personal-deliberative cases, they would have to involve an agent who doesn't exhibit transparency, or they would have to be some kind of trade-off where the only epistemic consequences in play are ones that can be understood in terms of the value of the right belief itself (and no other beliefs). It would be hard to find straightforward permissible trade-off cases like that, so let's not start looking there. In the next three subsections, I'll offer three examples of permissible epistemic trade-offs, none of which is a straightforward first-personal-deliberative case. In the first two kinds of cases, we'll be asking about what others should believe. In the third kind of case, we will consider our own beliefs in the first person, but we will do that indirectly. For that reason, it too is not a case where transparency is involved.

2.3.2 Trade-Offs in Pedagogy

The first kind of permissible epistemic trade-off involves pedagogy. For the past few months, your seven-year-old daughter Samantha (the older sister of Clara from the last chapter) has been showing interest in spacecraft design. Today, after school, she was asking you questions about how we know where spacecraft will go and how fast they'll get there. You want to help Samantha learn about this, so you decide to teach her some physics. You could teach her about simple Newtonian mechanics, which would allow her to get many close-to-true (but false) beliefs now, or you could teach her the general theory of relativity (and non-Euclidean geometry), most of which would go over her head.

In this case, I take it that the natural thing to do is to tell Samantha *what she ought to think*, rather than what is true. You might say something like, "You should think about this in terms of Newtonian mechanics," and follow that with instruction about forces, lines that are in flat geometries, etc. The idea is that teaching her about spacecraft movement with the simpler (but false) theory first will enable her to later come to have true beliefs about how spacecraft really move (either by approximation to the truth or by serving as a stepping-stone to learning about relativity).[12]

What you say to Samantha in this case strikes me as true; that is, it's true that she ought to think about it in Newtonian mechanical terms. But were Samantha to think about it that way, she would be coming to have false beliefs now as a way of trading off for epistemically valuable beliefs in the future. Because of that, this is a case of a permissible epistemic trade-off.

My opponent might push back by saying that it's not literally true that Samantha ought to think about it in Newtonian terms. Rather, she ought only to use Newtonian mechanics as a rough guide to the truth or as a heuristic, while keeping in mind that it's, strictly speaking, false. But this strikes me as an unrealistic conception of how humans work. In real humans, beliefs (but not working assumptions, mere guides, or heuristics) play a particularly efficient role in guiding deliberation and inquiry, both of which impact future belief-formation. Because of our limited memories and computational power, in some cases real humans ought to have false beliefs when those beliefs will help us get a better grasp on the rest of the world. For example, in our everyday lives, the attitude that we take toward 24 hours being the amount of time it takes Earth to rotate about its axis (something most of us know is, strictly speaking, false) is no different from the attitude we take toward grass being green. It's only in contexts like this one, where it's made salient that one of them is known to be false, that we're inclined to say that the attitude we have toward the first is not really belief.

We can also stipulate that, in this case, Samantha has no reason to suspect that you might be misleading her, so even though it might make sense for *us* to treat Newtonian mechanics as a heuristic, it wouldn't make sense for Samantha to do that. *We* know that she would be forming false beliefs by following your advice, but we also know that teaching children about Newtonian mechanics is the first step to getting them to understand relativistic physics later on. That's why this case involves a permissible epistemic trade-off: Samantha ought to think about spacecraft movement in Newtonian terms, and in doing so, she should sacrifice the epistemic goodness of

[12] Kate Nolfi (2018) gives a somewhat similar example of a case like this involving a subway map.

the beliefs she has now for the goodness of her future beliefs. It's easy to generalize this case to other cases of pedagogy, so let's turn to another kind of permissible trade-off.

2.3.3 Trade-Offs in Changes of Worldview

It's popular to think that sometimes we should have a belief in part because of its connections to other beliefs. For example, it's often assumed that a belief explaining other things an agent believes can count as a mark in its favor.[13] Coherentists (e.g., BonJour 1985 and Davidson 1986) think that belief justification works exclusively like this, but of course, less extreme versions of this view, where coherence is seen as some kind of epistemic virtue, are extremely common. Let's call the rightness of a belief outward-looking when it depends on the belief's connections to the holder's other beliefs. The second kind of permissible epistemic trade off involves the goodness of beliefs that have outward-looking rightness being traded-off in changes of worldview i.e., big-picture, systematic changes in what we believe.

Before we get to the main example of this section, notice that not just any case of outward-looking rightness involves a trade-off: If Sandy knows some large class of phenomena that needs explaining and learns that *P* explains them, it could be that *P* is the right thing for Sandy to believe. It would be right for Sandy to believe *P* because of how that belief would relate to the other things Sandy believes (so the rightness is outward-looking), but there is no trade-off. For it to be a trade-off, the goodness of the belief in question would have to be sacrificed for the overall epistemic goodness of Sandy's doxastic state. But in this case, Sandy's belief that *P* is supported by abduction on the things he knows. So coming to believe *P* is a win-win situation, not a trade-off.

In contrast, consider Eli's case: When she was young, Eli was a member of an extreme religious sect that holds that Earth is roughly 6,000 years old. A couple of years ago, Eli went away to college and took a course on evolution. At that time, Eli rejected evolutionary theory. Eli would admit that evolutionary theory would be a simple and highly explanatory theory were it true, but she also firmly held that the world wasn't old enough for evolutionary

[13] Of course, this is an instance of a broader kind of view that takes theoretic virtues such as explanatory power, simplicity, and fecundity to be reasons for belief.

theory to be right. Now, a year after finishing the course, Eli is reconsidering her stance on the age of Earth. When Eli thinks about her evidence that bears directly on the question of Earth's age, she takes her evidence to overall support thinking that Earth is young. But she recognizes that were she to believe that Earth is older, she would come to have many new reasons to form beliefs about the evolutionary origin of species, many of which she would then regard as knowledge. In this situation, I take it that it is permissible for Eli to start believing that Earth is older, and this case, unlike Sandy's, is a case of a permissible epistemic trade-off.

To see why, contrast Eli with her twin, Teli. Teli was also brought up being given evidence and arguments that Earth is roughly 6,000 years old. But Teli, unlike Eli, never left the religious community. Because of that, Teli isn't familiar with all of the data evolutionary theory might explain, she doesn't understand the mechanisms evolutionary theory provides, and she hasn't been put into a position to reconsider her belief about the age of Earth. In this case, unlike Eli's, it isn't permissible for Teli to revise her belief about Earth's age. What makes the difference? It's that for Eli (but not Teli), revising her belief enables her to better the state of many of her other beliefs by tying them into a common explanatory theory. Eli can avail herself of the evolutionary explanations of the visible differences, similarities, and changes of living species. Teli is not in a position to reap similar benefits, which is why a change in her belief is impermissible. So what makes it permissible for Eli to revise her belief is the overall increase in epistemic goodness of her doxastic state that it enables.

You might think that Eli's case is just like Sandy's. Just like Sandy, after taking the evolution class, Eli knows a lot of things that stand in need of explanation. So, isn't what makes it permissible for her to revise her belief that the revised belief best explains the new things she knows, not that it leads to greater overall epistemic goodness in her epistemic state? Don't all of Eli's beliefs (including the belief about the age of Earth) end up better off? If so, then there is no sacrifice of the goodness of the one belief for the overall benefit, and hence no trade-off.

To see why this isn't right, first notice that Eli's case is importantly different from Sandy's in that in Eli's case, the changed belief is not the one that does the explaining. Sandy simply adopts the belief that is already abductively supported by the other things he believes. Eli would only be able to adopt the beliefs that are abductively supported by her other beliefs if she could stop believing that Earth is too young for evolution to have happened. But when Eli reflects on the age of Earth, she is faced with evidence that overall supports thinking that Earth is young. Eli is stuck in what we might think of as an epistemic bottleneck:[14] She would be in a much better epistemic state overall if she could just get past this one sticking point about Earth being too young for evolution to have worked. The trade-off happens for Eli because in adopting the new beliefs, she sacrifices the apparent epistemic goodness of this one bottleneck belief for the goodness of the others.

Let's consider one way the details of this case might be further fleshed out. Suppose the case involves a progressive change in Eli's beliefs: She first comes to believe that Earth is old, and then later she comes to believe the evolutionary facts. On this precisification, Eli sacrifices the goodness of her belief about Earth's age for the goodness of her other (future) beliefs. In the time after Eli adopts the belief about Earth's age but before she works through the implications, that belief isn't well supported for her—it conflicts with the things she believes from her upbringing.[15] It is only after she goes through the process of reasoning through the implications of her new belief and connecting it to beliefs about evolutionary explanations that the belief about Earth's age comes to cohere with her other beliefs. So, in this way of precisifying the case, she sacrifices the goodness of her belief at the earlier time for the goodness of her overall epistemic state later.

In changes in worldview that happen progressively like this one, although the vast majority of our beliefs end up better supported than they were previously, some beliefs may end up being less well supported. In cases where what makes a belief permissible to hold in the new worldview is its connections to other aspects of the new view, the agent may have little or no other reason to accept it. In those cases, the amount of support for that particular belief may decrease despite an increase in the overall goodness of

[14] Thanks to an anonymous reviewer for putting it in these terms.

[15] The reader might worry that if we take a belief to be good iff it's true, then we can't make sense of these claims, since how well supported a belief is doesn't determine its goodness. Two responses: First, regardless of what we take epistemic goodness to be, we'll surely take being well supported as a sign of a belief having epistemic goodness. If so, then this case shows that we gladly accept *apparent* epistemic trade-offs, which should be enough to undermine the claim that no epistemic trade-offs are permissible. Second, we could modify the case slightly to be one where Eli comes to believe something false that would then lead her to believe many truths and give up the false belief. We could imagine, for example, that Eli starts by believing that the world is only a little older than 100,000 years, just old enough to explain the appearances of low-level organisms. She then reasons from there that it's more likely that Earth is much older still. It still seems permissible for her to take that first step.

the full picture warranting the change. When that happens, the epistemic status of those less-well-supported beliefs is sacrificed for the greater overall epistemic good. These cases are the second kind of permissible epistemic trade-offs.

If you're worried that a progressive adoption of a new worldview like this is impermissible, consider another way of fleshing out the details of the case. Suppose Eli just adopts the whole swath of new beliefs in a single step. Instead of first changing her belief about the age of Earth, she works through the potential implications of adopting that belief, and then she adopts that new combined doxastic state in a single change. Of course, real belief change rarely works this way; when we change our beliefs in major ways, it takes a while for us to realize the implications of those changes. Notice, though, that if we think of the case this way, Eli doesn't *sacrifice* the apparent goodness of her belief about Earth, since there is no time where that belief becomes less well supported. So this is not a trade-off case in a strict sense. But this precisification of the case would still show against the trade-off-based objections to consequentialism. That's because in this case, revising her belief about Earth's age is permissible *in virtue of* it leading to the betterment of the overall epistemic goodness of her full set of beliefs. The difference between Eli and Teli, who could not avail herself of evolutionary explanations by changing her belief, is that Teli cannot better her overall belief state by revising her belief. What makes it permissible for Eli to change her belief is that changing her belief about the age of Earth enables a new and dramatically better systematic approach to understanding the natural world. So on this precisification, despite the case not being a trade-off in the strict sense, it still demonstrates that the epistemic rightness of one belief can be dependent on the epistemic goodness of many others, which is the feature of theories that licenses trade-offs. Let's turn then to the third kind of permissible epistemic trade-off.

2.3.4 Indirect First-Personal Trade-Offs

The last example of a permissible epistemic trade-off involves an indirect doxastic decision. Here's the case: You've just passed your qualifying exams as a graduate student in chemistry, and you're trying to decide what to do your dissertation work on. You know that project α is ingenious and would give us new foundational insights into molecular bonds and shape the research field for generations. Project α is difficult, though, and you know there would be many skeptics until the project takes root, which may take a half century. So, if you pursue project α you expect to be less professionally successful and less happy than you'd like. The alternative is project β. The lasting impact of project β would be minimal, but it would produce some new knowledge that project α would not produce. In particular, you would come to know whether *Q*. Knowing whether *Q* would advance our understanding of how a certain protein folds, but it would not generate much other knowledge. Project β is in a very hot area of chemistry right now. So, if you pursue project β, you'll be a lot more professionally successful and happier. If you pursue α, you will suspend belief about whether *Q*. If you pursue β, you will suspend belief about the numerous foundational insights project α would have created.

Is it permissible to choose to work on β? Regardless of whether pursuing β is permissible all things considered (something I'll remain agnostic about), if you do pursue it, there is a sense in which you would be criticizable. What we'd criticize you for, were we your future colleagues, for example, is the harm you would have caused to yourself and the field in epistemic opportunity cost: "Think of how far the field would have advanced were you to have pursued that other project!" we might say. The criticism can't be a practical one, since the practical aspects of the case count in favor of β. The criticism is about the loss of knowledge, true belief, understanding, etc. So, what the appropriateness of that criticism shows is that, *epistemically speaking*, what you should do is pursue project α, even if that's not what you should do all things considered (again, a claim I'll remain agnostic about).

Recall that choosing α produces a much better overall epistemic outcome than β, but you'll come to know whether *Q* iff you pursue β. So, given that you should pursue α (epistemically speaking), this is a case where you should trade off your future knowledge of whether *Q* for the epistemic gains of the other project, and hence, it is a case of a permissible epistemic trade-off.

If you're not convinced this is a trade-off case, compare this case to paradigmatic ethical trade-off cases. Take Thomson's (1976) trolley case: There is an out-of-control trolley heading toward five people strapped to the tracks, and you have the opportunity to divert the trolley toward just one person. Taking the trade-off would be to divert the trolley. Doing so is trading the life of the one to save the lives of the five. Here's the analogy: Professionally, you're heading right for project β, but you have the opportunity to 'epistemically divert yourself' toward project α, which is significantly epistemically better. But pursuing α means that you won't come to know whether *Q*. So, diverting your professional trajectory would be sacrificing your potential true belief about whether *Q* for the better epistemic outcome of project α. This is a permissible epistemic trade-off.

A natural worry here is that the trade-off isn't *epistemic*. It's a choice about what research project to work on, and it's common to think that epistemic questions are only questions about what to believe. Since we're focused on a choice of a research project (which is a 'doing' rather than a 'believing'), doesn't that show that the issue is practical and not epistemic?

I don't think it does. Despite the common assumption among epistemologists that we cannot, we do seem to evaluate some 'doings' as either epistemically permissible or impermissible. For example, consider someone who follows Pascal's advice to "act[] as if [one] believed" to "cure [one] of unbelief" in God (1941, sec. III). A common critique of Pascal's suggestion is that, regardless of whether so acting is practically right, there is something epistemically amiss about it. That is an epistemic evaluation of an action. Consider also people who search out more evidence about a hard question or run statistical tests on data to learn more about the data's structure. These actions seem epistemically evaluable too: You could be epistemically criticized for biasedly seeking out evidence or praised for running the right statistical tests.

Sometimes we deliberate about actions that will knowingly have substantial impact on our future doxastic states, like by affecting whether we'll have enough evidence to support our beliefs about the data or whether we'll know whether *Q*. These kinds of decisions are about what to believe just as much as they're decisions about what to do. But unlike the cases of doxastic deliberation that Shah (2003) considers, in these cases your deliberation doesn't directly result in you having a belief. What makes these cases *indirect* doxastic deliberation is that you choose features of your doxastic state by choosing an action that will knowingly give rise to those features. These decisions are epistemically indirect, but they're still decisions about what to believe, so we can evaluate them along the epistemic dimension (in addition to practical, moral, and other dimensions).

Does it matter that in direct doxastic deliberation one is choosing the content of one's beliefs rather than just choosing whether to have a belief on a given topic? I don't think it does. That's because there can be cases of indirect doxastic deliberation where the deliberation is about particular contents. Pascal's case is an example: Pascal's suggestion is that one choose to act in a certain way in order to come to believe a particular content, namely that God exists. We can also modify the case above to make it one where you're choosing the content of your beliefs by choosing a research project. Suppose, for example, that folks who work in the area of project β all accept a particular methodological claim about how to study protein folding. As of yet, you do not accept that claim, but you're sure that you'll come to believe it if (and only if) you choose project β. Then by choosing project β, you would be knowingly (but indirectly) choosing the content of your future belief. So, if you think we can only epistemically evaluate deliberation about specific contents, this modified example still contains a trade-off.

Another natural worry here is that the reasoning overgenerates. Almost every decision we make and action we perform has an impact on what we believe. If I order a chicken burrito rather than a veggie one for lunch today, that will influence whether I believe I am eating meat later. So doesn't that mean that, if we accept the reasoning above, we must think that all of those actions are epistemically evaluable?

My inclination is to bite the bullet and think that all actions are epistemically evaluable, and this will be a major topic of Chapter 7. One need not accept anything nearly that radical in order to accept my argument here, though. For the purposes of this argument, one only need accept that *some* actions are epistemically evaluable (and that among them are cases like the trade-off I described above). I hope to have made that intuitively plausible by pointing to cases where epistemic evaluations of actions seem ordinary, like the cases of collecting new evidence, analyzing data using statistics, and getting oneself to believe by self-indoctrination. It's open to the reader to think that it's only a very small class of actions that are epistemically evaluable. Perhaps it's ones where it is (or should be) obvious or salient to the agent that the decision or action will have significant and particular doxastic impacts. In cases like that, you make an indirect doxastic choice—you choose between options that in part include changes to your doxastic state. And, in some such cases, there are permissible epistemic trade-offs.

2.4 Permissible Trade-Offs Are Rare

So far I've tried to convince you that, in some cases, accepting an epistemic trade-off is the epistemically right thing to do, which is exactly what the truth-loving epistemic consequentialist would predict. I imagine that some readers might still be skeptical. But the truth-loving epistemic consequentialist has a good explanation of why skepticism might be warranted: Even though there are some permissible epistemic trade-offs, epistemic trade-offs are quite rare, the epistemic consequentialist should say. Since they're such unusual situations, it's not surprising that our intuitions might not track them very well.

Why should we think that epistemic trade-off situations are so unusual? The reason is that, for agents like us, having a true belief about any given topic is almost always what best conduces to agents like us maximizing our overall accuracy. Let's call that claim TRUTH BEGETS TRUTH:

> TRUTH BEGETS TRUTH As a general rule, for agents like us, having a true belief about any given proposition is the best way for us to promote the overall accuracy of our epistemic states.

To see why TRUTH BEGETS TRUTH is true, let's consider the possible veritistic consequences of an agent A believing that *P* for the rest of A's doxastic state. Consider some other belief the agent might have, and let's call it *Q*. For most possible *Q*s, whether A has a true belief about *P* in no way influences whether A has a true belief about *Q*. My belief that I had cereal for breakfast, for example, is not veritistically connected to my belief that it will rain next week or my belief that turkey vultures use projectile defecation to defend themselves. In these cases, I'll say that the beliefs are veritistically independent:

> INDEPENDENCE An agent's belief that *P* and belief that *Q* are *independent* when whether the agent has a true belief about *P* does not affect whether the agent has a true belief about *Q* or vice versa.

Many, if not most, pairs of our beliefs are independent in this sense, I claim. Whether that's true is a contingent matter, and one that should be verified by empirical research. But if it's true, it would mean that for many collections of beliefs we might have, the best way to maximize the amount of true beliefs in the collection overall is to make each individual belief in the collection true.

Not all of our beliefs are independent from our other beliefs, though. Paradigmatic cases of dependence of beliefs include beliefs that are used in reasoning and scientific inquiry, since those are cases where the beliefs we already have affect which beliefs we'll form, maintain, or abandon. Consider some cases of reasoning, like doing a deduction or an argument to the best explanation. In those cases, having true beliefs generally conduces to producing more true beliefs. In fact, we often conceive of good reasoning in just this way (as reasoning that always leads or is very likely to lead to true conclusions if the premises are true). The same is true of scientific inquiry: Generally speaking, scientific inquiry tends to produce true beliefs when other true beliefs are used in doing the inquiry. When our beliefs are connected in this way, let's call them 'positively dependent':

> POSITIVE DEPENDENCE An agent's belief that *Q* is *positively dependent* on their belief that *P* when the agent having a true belief that *P* conduces to them having a true belief that *Q*.

For agents like us, it seems plausible that when the truth or falsity of some of our beliefs influences the truth of falsity of others, having true beliefs is typically what's best for creating and having other true beliefs. Combining that with our observations about independence above, we should think that for agents like us, in almost all pairs of beliefs either the beliefs independent or one is positively dependent on the other.

Trade-off cases are situations where our beliefs are neither positively dependent on each other nor independent from each other. In trade-off cases, our beliefs are what we might call 'negatively dependent' on each other. So if the observations above are right, we should think that, for agents like us, trade-off cases are quite unusual—they're not the kind of thing we're likely to come across on a regular basis. What this means is that truth-loving epistemic consequentialists should agree with skeptics of permissible trade-offs that, *as a general rule*, we shouldn't have false beliefs in trying to promote having true beliefs. But that's not because accepting trade-offs is epistemically forbidden. It's really because, for agents like us, cases of permissible trade-offs are rare.

2.5 Some Benefits of Accepting Some Trade-Offs

The permissibility of accepting some epistemic trade-offs shows that opponents of epistemic consequentialism are wrong to reject the view on the basis that it admits of *any* trade-offs. Epistemic normativity, contra Berker, doesn't respect a complete separateness of propositions. Given everything I've said so far, though, opponents of consequentialism could still reject the view on the basis that it admits of certain particularly problematic trade offs. That will be the focus of the next chapter. Before that, though, I'll argue that, beyond getting cases like those above right, consequentialism's ability to countenance trade-offs has some theoretical benefits. Countenancing trade offs allows the theory to take advantage of some natural explanations of common epistemic practices that rival theories cannot.

First consider what I call 'positive arguments by supposition.' Here is an example: You're having lunch with your colleague from cognitive science. Unlike your colleague, you doubt the existence of cognitive states, and she is trying to convince you they exist. Your colleague starts by asking you to suppose that there are such states. "Let's see what follows if there are cognitive states," your colleague might say. She then goes on to show you many theoretical benefits of accepting that supposition. "It would allow us to account for the apparent non-reducibility of truths about mental states to truths about neuronal states," she might say. If she offers you enough benefits of accepting the supposition and you don't take the supposition to be too wild, you might be inclined to accept the supposition. That is a positive argument by supposition.

I take this kind of argument to be a dime a dozen in academic discussions. How do these arguments work, though? If you accept epistemic consequentialism, you have a natural explanation of what's going on: The arguments show you the epistemic goods that come from accepting the supposed proposition. Since rightness is explained in terms of goodness on this account, making salient the epistemic goods that come from accepting the supposition can convince you that it's right to accept the proposition. If you reject the permissibility of epistemic trade-offs, you can't accept this simple story about how these arguments work, since you'd have to deny that learning about these kinds of epistemic goods can make a belief right.

In response, rejectors of trade-offs might claim that by offering benefits of accepting the supposition, your colleague is showing that your evidence already supports the supposed proposition. But this move doesn't explain the difference in argumentative force between positive arguments by supposition and straightforward arguments from evidence. For one, arguments by supposition can sometimes work, not because the hearer already accepts entailments of the supposed proposition (as she must do were it just an argument from the hearer's evidence) but because the hearer finds the full package of views plausible despite formerly rejecting individual pieces of that package. (The reader is encouraged to notice the similarity between this and the cases of changes of worldview above.) Epistemic consequentialists have a straightforward explanation of that phenomenon: The supposed proposition is right to believe in virtue of its role in generating the whole package of beliefs. If you reject trade-offs, you can't have a similarly straightforward account of those arguments.[16]

Something else that consequentialists (but not rejectors of trade-offs) can easily explain is the common view that something like modesty, humility, or open-mindedness is epistemically good. This assumption plays different roles (and goes under different headings) in different literatures. In the literature on peer disagreement, for example, it's the main motivator for conciliatory views (see Christensen 2013). In the formal epistemology literature, the view is proposed as a constraint on rational credences known as 'regularity,' which requires agents to not assign extremal probabilities (0 or 1) to contingent propositions (see Lewis 1980, Hájek 2012, sec. 3.3.4).

If we grant that something like this is epistemically virtuous, what might explain it? It's not enough to say just that we might be wrong if we have too strong beliefs on a topic. After all, we might also be right. A more plausible explanation of the requirement to be modest can be seen in Lewis's (1980, p. 268) discussion of regularity for credences:

> [Regularity] is required as a condition of reasonableness: one who started out with an irregular credence function (and who then learned from experience by conditionalizing) would stubbornly refuse to believe some propositions no matter what the evidence in their favor.

[16] Notice also that the consequentialist has a neat story about why we have arguments by supposition: These arguments are tools that allow us to avoid the transparency phenomenon while coming to believe something because of the benefits that holding that belief has. Compare how a moral consequentialist might use a tool to kill a dying animal. Most of us could not help an animal that is dying a slow, gruesome death by killing it with our hands. But killing it might be the right thing to do, so to overcome our inability to do it manually, we might use a tool. Arguments by supposition play a similar role in our mental economy, the consequentialist should say: They allow us to overcome our deliberative inability to accept a belief on the basis of the doxastic benefits that it brings about.

Skyrms (1980, p. 74) gives a similar argument. The idea behind these arguments is that being doxastically stubborn would make us miss out on good beliefs we could have in the future, whereas being open-minded allows us to have those beliefs. These "arguments from stubbornness" are forward-looking: The rightness of having a certain doxastic feature comes from its epistemic benefits down the line. Consequentialists can easily endorse these arguments. Those who reject all trade-offs cannot. If one accepts that the prospect of future epistemic goods can impact the rightness of an attitude now, one will be forced to countenance trade-offs that exploit that forward-lookingness.

Consequentialism's ability to make sense of these phenomena show that the view's propensity to accept trade-offs isn't just a quirk to be explained away. Countenancing trade-offs is theoretically useful in understanding our epistemic practices. Views that reject the possibility of permissible epistemic trade-offs cannot offer similarly straightforward and natural explanations of these phenomena, so consequentialism's acceptance of some trade-offs should count as a mark in its favor.

2.6 Moving Toward More Discussion of Trade-Offs

What we've seen so far is that the existence and theoretical usefulness of permissible trade-offs, although they're rare, shows against the universal rejections of trade-offs that Berker (2013a,b) and Greaves (2013, p. 950) want to give. Previous responses to these arguments have tried to show that particular consequentialist views, like process reliabilism, don't in fact countenance any trade-offs. Both Ahlstrom-Vij and Dunn (2014) and Goldman (2015), for example, argue that on the process reliabilist picture, justification does have the backward-looking structure that Berker thinks is characteristic of epistemically normative notions, despite reliabilism also having some forward-looking elements. If those responses to Berker are right, process reliabilism won't be able to account for the permissible epistemic trade-offs that I brought out here, nor will they be able to take advantage of the theoretical benefits of accepting trade-offs. So they avoid Berker's objections only to be subject to new ones.

The picture of epistemic normativity that will be developed in the rest of this book will involve both backward-looking and forward-looking elements, and it will admit of trade-offs in epistemic rightness. In the next chapter, we'll consider a different trade-off objection. Unlike the objection considered here, the objection in the next chapter will accuse truth-loving epistemic consequentialism of accepting specific, particularly objectionable trade-offs, rather than objecting to the view on the basis that it licenses any trade-offs at all. The next chapter will be the first of several chapters that are structured primarily by objections to truth-loving epistemic consequentialism. The argument in those chapters is primarily defensive, since what I hope to have shown in the first half of this chapter is that truth-loving epistemic consequentialism is naturally and intuitively supported by both mundane cases of right belief and many sophisticated commitments we have about right belief. It also is the most natural and intuitive way of making sense of the idea that epistemic norms are primarily about having true beliefs and not having false beliefs, an idea that is ubiquitous in the history of epistemology. The hope is that if this view can be convincingly defended from the most compelling reasons to reject it, we'll have no reason not to accept it as the most natural, simple, and intuitive view.

3
On Specific Trade-Off Objections

3.1 More Trade-Off Objections

The last chapter introduced truth-loving epistemic consequentialism, a theory of epistemic rightness that says that a belief that *P* is right for an agent to have if and only if among the available options for belief, believing *P* promotes the greatest overall balance of believing truths and not believing falsehoods. As we began discussing there, it is popular to reject truth-loving epistemic consequentialism on the basis that it sanctions trade-offs of epistemic goodness. I argued in the last chapter that it's wrong to reject the view on the basis that it admits of *any* trade-offs, since any view must account for the permissible epistemic trade-offs and views that admit of trade-offs can explain more than their competitors.

Here the focus will be on whether truth-loving epistemic consequentialism is problematic because it admits of certain particularly objectionable trade-offs, rather than whether it's problematic because it admits of any trade-offs at all. I'll argue that truth-loving epistemic consequentialists (and epistemic consequentialists more generally) should borrow three lessons from ethical consequentialists to respond to purported counterexamples involving trade-offs. The first lesson is that, just as it's essential to understanding the ethical consequentialist view that we construe it as an account of right action, which we distinguish from moral responsibility (e.g., praise and blame), so too is it essential to the epistemic consequentialist view that we construe it as an account of right belief, which we distinguish from other epistemic notions like rational and justified belief. This move allows the epistemic consequentialist to escape many of the particular trade-off objections in the literature. But even when the view is construed as a view of right belief, there are still some trade-off objections that might seem worrisome. The second and third lessons are that to respond to these objections, epistemic consequentialists should make their view 'sophisticated' and 'global' in the same way that Railton (1984)

Right Belief and True Belief. Daniel J. Singer, Oxford University Press. © Oxford University Press 2023.
DOI: 10.1093/oso/9780197660386.003.0004

argues that ethical consequentialists should be sophisticated and extend their criterion of evaluation beyond its traditional boundaries. The upshot is that truth-loving epistemic consequentialism is best construed as a view that shares much of its structure with prominent act-consequentialist views in ethics. It's a view about right belief, but not justified or rational belief. It doesn't say that agents ought to explicitly aim to maximize the epistemic good they produce. Rather, it says they should foster the kinds of dispositions and practices that conduce to the epistemic good.

I'll focus on the view that says that having accurate belief is the unique epistemic good (since it's the aim of the book to defend truth-loving epistemic consequentialism), but the lessons I draw out here can be used by other kinds of epistemic consequentialists as well. I'll also focus on objections to epistemic consequentialism formulated in traditional epistemic terms (with a categorical notion of belief), but everything I say here translates naturally to formal versions of epistemic consequentialism (with a degreed notion of belief, e.g., Joyce (2013)) and analogous trade-off worries, like the ones from Greaves (2013).

The primary goal of this chapter is to defend the truth-loving epistemic consequentialist view from specific trade-off objections. It's not to defend truth-loving epistemic consequentialism against other theories of epistemic normativity, like knowledge-first, reasons-first, or virtue-theoretic accounts, or even other epistemic consequentialist views, like ones that take knowledge as the epistemic end. In the last part of the argument, though, I will offer a reason to think that the view I develop has an advantage over its ethical cousins: I'll argue that the most central claim of the consequentialist view I develop is already universally accepted.

3.2 The Target of Epistemic and Ethical Consequentialisms

As I discussed earlier, consequentialists aim to understand what makes an object of evaluation (such as a belief or action) the right one in terms of what best conduces to the good. *Epistemic* consequentialists have the view that "the epistemically right ... is to be understood in terms of conduciveness to the epistemic good" (Ahlstrom-Vij and Dunn 2014, p. 1). There are many different ways of fleshing this out: Epistemic consequentialists differ on what epistemic goodness is (popular options include true belief and knowledge, and less-popular ones are justified belief and understanding), what epistemic rightness is (e.g., justification, rationality, warrant, what one epistemically ought to believe/do), and what the conduciveness relation is (e.g., maximizing over the long term, indirectly promoting). As we know, truth-loving epistemic consequentialism is a simple consequentialist view that says a belief is right when having it best promotes having true beliefs and not having false beliefs. And as we discussed before, process reliabilism (Goldman 1979) is a more intricate example. It says that a belief is justified when it is the product of a process that reliably produces true beliefs (and as such, it is a form of *indirect* consequentialism).

Among *ethical* consequentialists, moral rightness is usually seen as distinct from moral responsibility. Consider these two examples:

> WALLET Last week, my eight-year-old son stole the neighbor's wallet. He did it because the neighbor was a "meany," he said. I tried to teach him why he should return the wallet and apologize, but he refused to listen. I forced him to return the wallet and apologize anyway.

> MEDICINE At the urgent care center, a doctor cleaned Sally's skateboarding wound using one of the standard sterilizing solutions available in the center. There is no way the doctor could have known this, but Sally has an incredibly rare allergy to that particular sterilizing fluid. Because of that, Sally will experience long-term serious negative effects of the allergic reaction.

In these cases, the rightness/wrongness of the agents' actions come apart from their praiseworthiness/blameworthiness: In WALLET, my son did the right thing by returning the wallet, but he is not praiseworthy for it. In MEDICINE, although the doctor was well-intentioned, she did the wrong thing by cleaning the wound with that sterilizing fluid. The doctor isn't blameworthy for doing that, though, since it was standard procedure and she couldn't have possibly known there would have been a problem.

Ethical consequentialists typically take cases like these to show that there are two distinct *kinds* of ethical normative notions. Terms like 'good,' 'right,' 'ought,' 'should,' and 'must' (along with their negations and duals), which I'll call 'deontic terms,' tell us something about the rightness or wrongness of an action. Terms like 'praise,' 'blame,' and 'fault,' which I'll call 'responsibility terms,' tell us something about whether the agent is responsible for the action, not whether it was right or wrong. Ethical act consequentialism is typically construed as a theory of deontic notions, not a theory about responsibility (Hooker 2015). Even though many consequentialists take there to be some link between deontic and responsibility notions (e.g., that blameworthiness requires wrongdoing), it's open to consequentialists to reject all such links (see Capes 2012).

I'll argue below that epistemic consequentialists should think that epistemic terms admit of a distinction that's similar to the one between ethical deontic and responsibility terms. Here are some examples to help motivate that:

> BROKEN MICROWAVE Today, just as he has done at lunch for years, Justin put a Hot Pocket in the microwave and set it for two minutes. Just before he reached in to grab the Hot Pocket, he believed it was hot. There had never been a problem before, but despite everything appearing normal, the microwave was broken today. So in fact, the Hot Pocket was not hot.

> MISLEADING FINGERPRINTS Detective Dustin was dusting the crime scene for fingerprints. After finding the butler's prints all over the scene and the murder weapon, Dustin had sufficient evidence to conclude that the butler did it (in the study with the candlestick). Despite that, purely on a whim and with no evidence or reason, Dustin concluded that the maid did it, not the butler. In fact, the maid did do it and set up the butler.

In BROKEN MICROWAVE, Justin was *justified* in believing that the Hot Pocket was hot, but his belief was *wrong*, since the Hot Pocket was not, in fact, hot. In MISLEADING FINGERPRINTS, it was *irrational* for Dustin to believe that the maid did it, but nonetheless that belief was *right*.

Like in the ethical case, the fact that our judgments come apart like this points toward there being two classes of epistemic notions. How exactly to divide the epistemic terms into the two camps is a hairy question that I won't fully answer here. For this discussion, it will be sufficient to take 'right' and 'wrong' as paradigmatic examples of what I'll call 'epistemic deontic terms.' This camp also includes most uses of 'correct (belief)' and the epistemic 'ought' (although we'll see below that some cases of 'ought' are less clear). In the second camp of terms, paradigm examples will include '(epistemic) justification' and '(epistemic) rationality.'[1] This camp likely also

[1] It's important that the justification here is epistemic, since moral justification is likely an ethical deontic notion.

includes 'warrant' and 'knowledge,' although I won't complete the argument for that here. Perhaps unsurprisingly, I'll call the second class 'epistemic responsibility terms.'

3.3 The Specific Trade-Off Objections

As we began discussing in the previous chapter, trade-off objections to epistemic consequentialism mirror trade-off objections to ethical consequentialism. On the ethical side, objectors claim that consequentialists incorrectly sanction sacrificing the ethical good of some for the overall greater good. A well-known example of this is the organ harvesting case (Foot 1967; Thomson 1976), in which a consequentialist doctor is supposedly committed to trading off the life of one patient to save five others.

In epistemology, trade-off objections say that consequentialists wrongly sanction trading off the epistemic goodness of some of one's beliefs for the overall goodness of their doxastic state.[2] These objections can be found in Firth (1998), Fumerton (1995, p. 12), Jenkins (2007), and Berker (2013a,b). Recall TRUTH FAIRY, the trade-off objection from Jenkins (2007) as formulated by Andow (2017):

> TRUTH FAIRY Suppose you start with no reason to believe that *P* is true and no reason to believe that it is false. The Truth Fairy is a very powerful being, and she makes you the following credible offer: You accept *P* as true, and she will make your epistemic situation very, very good overall. She will arrange for you to have many, many true, justified, knowledgeable beliefs and very, very few false, unjustified, or unknowledgeable ones. However, she does not guarantee that your trust in *P* itself will have any particular epistemic status as a result of her actions.

In TRUTH FAIRY, it's obvious that you're not justified (or rational or warranted) in believing *P*, but according to consequentialist accounts of justification (or rationality or warrant), you are justified (rational, warranted), since believing *P* best conduces to the epistemic good.

[2] There could be other forms of trade-off objections, such as trading off the goodness of one person's doxastic state for the goodness of others' doxastic states. Because these aren't commonly discussed in the literature though, I'll focus only on these kinds of cases here. Examples of other types of trade-offs can be found in Littlejohn (2012, pp. 47 & 81).

Berker (2013b, p. 373) formulates more complex trade-off cases to skirt moves consequentialists might try to make to avoid the trade-off objections. He shows that there are apparently problematic trade-offs that occur completely inside an agent and where the belief that is sacrificed is a direct constitutive means to having the beliefs with epistemic value:

> INTROSPECTIVE FELLOW Anytime Ignacio forms a belief, he also forms beliefs about that belief. So when Ignacio comes to believe *P*—e.g., that grass is green—he also comes to believe that he believes *P*, believe that he believes that he believes *P*, and onward (although we can say that the process stops at some finite level). Ignacio is incredibly bad at forming the first-order beliefs, since he only forms those beliefs by reading tea leaves. But Ignacio is incredibly good at introspection, so he is overwhelmingly likely to be right in his higher-order beliefs.

In this case, as Berker says, it's "obvious that [the] first-order belief ... is unjustified," but consequentialism about justification looks committed to the opposite result, since, as Berker says, the "belief was a constitutive means of, at the same time, acquiring an immense number of true beliefs" (2013b, p. 373).

As we discussed in the last chapter, Berker and Greaves (2013, p. 918) both take consequentialism's propensity for trade-offs to expose a deeper problem with the view. Greaves thinks it shows that consequentialists are open to accepting "epistemic bribe[s]." Berker (2013a) says that consequentialism ignores the "separateness of propositions" (a notion that is meant to be analogous to the "separateness of persons" worry for ethical consequentialism).[3] Berker (2013b) later argues that the real problem is that consequentialism tries to understand epistemic rightness in terms of a promoting or conducing relation. Berker thinks this causes a directionality mismatch with our intuitions: Whether an agent is justified or rational is usually viewed as a question of whether she *responded to* or *respected* her evidence, and these are essentially backward-looking notions. On the consequentialist picture, epistemic rightness is forward-looking, since it's about *bringing about* epistemic consequences. For that reason, the

[3] For more on the worry for ethical consequentialism, see Brink (1993). I won't address the "separateness of propositions" diagnosis of trade-off objections here, both because Berker himself moves on to the latter diagnosis and because Sharadin (2018) already shows how the "separateness" metaphor isn't as compelling as it might seem.

view can't account for the structure of justification and rationality, Berker claims.

The last chapter showed that these general arguments against trade-offs must be wrong, since there are some epistemically permissible trade-offs. Here we'll dig deeper into the specific trade-off objections and ask whether we should be concerned about specific cases involving trade-offs like those mentioned above, rather than the mere existence of trade-offs.

3.4 Responding to Specific Trade-Off Objections, Round 1

The trade-off objections I cited above are all formulated against consequentialist views of justification (or rationality or warrant). Because we should construe epistemic consequentialism as a view of epistemic rightness, not justification, those objections aren't aimed at the best versions of epistemic consequentialism, I'll argue. To do that, I'll first draw out what I see as the analogy between ethical and epistemic normative notions, which helps us see that terms like 'justification' and 'rationality' play a role in epistemic evaluations that is similar to the role that ethical responsibility terms play in ethical evaluations.[4] I'll argue that epistemic consequentialists should cleave deontic from responsibility terms in epistemology, just as ethical consequentialists do in ethics. We saw in the previous chapter that truth-loving epistemic consequentialism gets right many paradigmatic epistemic deontic judgments. So, together with the fact that the trade-off objections show against consequentialist accounts of responsibility notions, we should think that epistemic consequentialism is best construed as a theory of deontic notions, not responsibility notions.

3.4.1 The Analogy

Why should the consequentialist think there is a divide in epistemic normative terms that's analogous to the divide in ethical normative terms? In earlier work, I argued that it's because epistemic responsibility notions share key distinctive features of ethical responsibility notions that deontic

[4] Here when I talk about 'justification,' I'll be focusing on *ex post* (also known as 'doxastic') justification. As I'll point out in a note below, much of what I'll say here doesn't apply directly to *ex ante* (also known as 'propositional') justification, even though there is probably a translation of the ideas that still applies.

notions in both areas lack (Singer 2018a). I now think there's something deeper tying together these camps of notions.

What's common to responsibility terms in both ethics and epistemology is that responsibility terms primarily serve to evaluate the agent with respect to the relevant action or belief. Deontic terms do the opposite—they primarily serve to evaluate the action or belief with respect to the agent. The idea is easier to understand on the ethical side, where we're more used to making this kind of distinction. Consider WALLET again. There, when we said that the right action was returning the wallet, what we seemed to be doing was saying something about the action, namely that *it* was right. Remember, though, that WALLET was a case where the agent did the right thing by returning the wallet, but he wasn't praiseworthy for it (because I had to force him to do it). When we said that my son wasn't praiseworthy for the action, what we seemed to be doing is saying something about my son, namely that *he* wasn't worthy of a positive responsibility assessment for the action. In this way, responsibility terms are primarily about evaluating the agent in a particular respect—i.e., with respect to the particular action or belief in play.

Deontic terms evaluate certain actions or beliefs as right or wrong to have. So deontic terms seem to be primarily about actions or beliefs, not the agent who performs the action or has the belief. Deontic notions are still relative to agents though, since an action that's right for one agent might not be right for another. It might be the right thing to do for a wealthy person to donate $500 to charity, but that same action might not be right for someone who needs that money to survive. So deontic notions are agent-relative—i.e., deontic notions evaluate actions and beliefs *with respect to agents*. But even though the agent is involved in the evaluation, deontic notions do not primarily serve to evaluate the agent. They evaluate the action or belief in a way that involves the agent. So we should see responsibility terms and deontic terms as importantly distinct kinds of notions. Responsibility terms primarily serve to evaluate agents, whereas deontic terms primarily serve to evaluate actions or beliefs.

I take it that one of the main motivating ideas in the literature on virtue theoretic accounts of justification and knowledge is that 'justification' and 'knowledge' act like responsibility terms, in the sense just described. The virtue-epistemic tradition is highly varied, but a common theme is that virtue epistemologists see knowledge, justified belief, rational belief, etc. as instances of successful performances, achievements, or expressions of intellectual virtues (see, e.g., Code 1987, Miracchi 2015, Sosa 1991, Zagzebski 1996; and, for an overview, Turri et al. 2019).[5] For example, on the view of knowledge argued for by Sosa (1991, 2007), knowledge is seen as a kind of true belief that's due to the intellectual virtues of the knower and for which the knower is due credit. So here the term 'knowledge' is seen as primarily evaluating the agent: It's about the true belief being a product of the agent's intellectual virtues and it ascribes credit to the agent for that achievement.

But one need not be a virtue epistemologist to think that epistemic terms like 'justification' and 'rationality' act like ethical responsibility terms in primarily being about evaluating the agent. We can also see this by noting that terms like 'justified belief' and 'rational belief' have some distinctive features of responsibility terms, ones that make them more about evaluating agents than actions or beliefs, and that moral and epistemic deontic terms lack these features.

One distinctive feature of ethical responsibility notions (e.g., moral blameworthiness and praiseworthiness) is how strongly we pretheoretically take these to depend on agent-internal features, such as the agent's beliefs (or what they should have believed) or their intentions. Whether the doctor is blameworthy for using the sterilizing fluid seems to depend, for example, on whether the doctor believed (or should have believed) it might cause a problem. The same sort of connections between agent-internal features seems to occur in evaluations of epistemic rationality: Whether it was rational for you to believe the results of a deduction might seem to depend, for example, on whether you believed the premises (or should have so believed). This happens with justification too: Of course, internalists think that justification depends on agent-internal features, but even most externalists accept that whether one is justified is partially a function of what

[5] Virtue-theoretical views of justification are most naturally construed as views of *ex post* justification. It's less plausible that we should see someone being *ex ante* justified as a success, achievement, etc. As Errol Lord pointed out to me, it seems like we can even think of cases where someone might be *ex ante* justified but not exhibit any kind of success, achievement, etc.—e.g., if they believe the opposite of what they're *ex ante* justified in believing in a blameworthy way. How to connect *ex ante* and *ex post* justification is controversial (see, e.g., Turri 2010), but many accept something like the following: If one is *ex ante* justified in believing *P*, there is a (right kind of) way for them to be *ex post* justified on that basis. If that's right, it suggests a way of translating claims about the successes, achievements, etc. of *ex post* justification into claims about *ex ante* justification—i.e., that if one is *ex ante* justified in believing *P*, then there is a (right kind of) way for them to succeed, achieve, etc. In the rest of the book, I'll focus exclusively on *ex post* justification when I'm talking about justification. See Kvanvig (2000) for more discussion of connecting the two kinds of justification on virtue-theoretic views.

that person believes.[6] And as we saw above, this is a defining feature of virtue-epistemological accounts of justification and rationality. In contrast, consider epistemic deontic terms: Whether a belief that *P* is right or wrong does not usually depend on agent-internal features. To decide that, we typically only need to know whether *P*.

Another connection between moral responsibility notions and epistemic notions like justification and rationality is that we usually think it's a requirement of attributing these evaluations to agents that they deserve that evaluation. On the ethical side, for example, we think it's only appropriate to blame someone if that person deserves that rebuke (Tognazzini and Coates 2014). We typically signal this in attributions of moral responsibility by saying that the agent is blameworthy (praiseworthy, etc.) *because of something they believed, intended, or did (or should have believed, intended, or done)*. E.g., the babysitter is blameworthy for the baby getting hurt, because he didn't pay attention to where the baby was going (but he should have). Non-agents, such as natural disasters, cannot be to blame (in a moral sense) because they aren't proper objects of desert (even when they causally effect some negative outcome).

Attributions of epistemic justification and rationality also have this desert requirement. If we say that someone is justified in having a belief, we typically think that their justification must stem from something they did or a state they were in, like if they based their belief on their evidence or used a reliable belief-forming process. If we accuse an agent of having an unjustified belief, we also usually think it is because of something the agent did or something they negligently didn't do, like if they used wishful thinking, failed to base their belief on their evidence, failed to be sensitive to the implications of their other beliefs, or failed to use a reliable belief-forming process. The same holds for rationality: When we attribute ir/rationality, we might take a stand on whether the agent formed the belief in a way that coheres with the rest of their beliefs or whether the agent formed it in response to their epistemic reasons. So, attributions of justification and rationality are tied to desert in the same way moral responsibility notions are.

Attributions of deontic terms don't have this desert requirement: There's no tension in thinking that someone did the morally right thing but that they only did it by accident, and there's no tension in thinking that they did

[6] Most reliabilist theories, for example, at least require that the agent not believe that the process that generated the relevant belief is unreliable.

the wrong thing even though they had the right intentions. The same holds true of our judgments of a belief being right or wrong: There's no tension in thinking that Joe believes the right thing but only by accident (perhaps by getting the right result after faulty reasoning) or that Jake has the wrong belief but didn't do any faulty reasoning to get there. So, desert seems relevant in our attributions of justification and rationality but not in our attributions of deontic notions. This is another reason to think justification and rationality act like responsibility notions and unlike deontic notions.

A third distinctive feature of moral responsibility notions that epistemic justification and rationality share is that we pretheoretically assume that each requires free will. Pretheoretically, it doesn't seem to make sense to apply terms of moral responsibility to someone unless we take that person to have acted freely. This fact about moral responsibility is often used as a motivation for discussions of free will in introductory philosophy courses. As Tognazzini and Coates (2014) put it, excuses like "I couldn't help it" or "I was forced to do it" are "often enough to render blame inappropriate, so it's a natural thought that someone can only be blamed for those things that he could have helped, or wasn't forced into."

Our pretheoretic intuitions about justification and rationality share this feature: Many of us have persistent fears and biases that force beliefs upon us, even though we might explicitly disavow them. We might, for example, find ourselves regularly convinced there's an intruder in the house when we hear noises downstairs, and in cases where those beliefs are formed by uncontrollable fear, we're inclined to see those beliefs as outside the scope of rationality and justification. We're naturally inclined to treat uncontrollable beliefs as arational, rather than irrational, since we lack the requisite control over them. Alston (1988, p. 259) famously makes this conception of justification explicit. "The natural way to use 'justification,'" he says, "is viable only if beliefs are sufficiently under voluntary control." Alston goes on to argue against this conception of justification by arguing that we lack the required degree of control. Although Alston offers a revisionary account of justification, Alston's claim that the "natural" conception of justification requires voluntary control only goes to support my claim—i.e., that the pretheoretic notion of justification looks similar to pretheoretic notions of moral responsibility.

Again here, deontic terms in both subdisciplines lack this feature: There's no pretheoretic tension in thinking that my son did the right thing in returning the wallet, even though I forced him to return it. And knowing that

Samuel's belief was caused by his psychosis is no guide to whether the belief is right. So a belief being epistemically right or wrong doesn't seem to pretheoretically presuppose that the belief was freely formed.

Overall, then, when we look at epistemic justification and rationality, it seems like those notions share distinctive features of moral responsibility notions, and deontic notions in both epistemology and ethics lack those distinctive features. This should make us think that there are two kinds of epistemic notions, and those kinds are analogous to the two kinds of ethical notions. Epistemic responsibility terms including 'justification' and 'rationality,' like moral responsibility terms, primarily serve to evaluate the agent with respect to the belief in question. Epistemic deontic terms like 'right belief' primarily serve to evaluate the belief with respect to the agent.[7]

Does this commit me to thinking that justification, rationality, and epistemic responsibility are all basically the same thing? It looks like justification and rationality come apart from epistemic responsibility, for example, in cases of higher-order defeat: Suppose you're justified (or rational) in believing *P*, perhaps because you have sufficient evidence for it. If you later find out that you were drugged and would have believed *P* even if it weren't supported by your evidence, it seems like you're epistemically blameworthy if you don't suspend your belief. *Steadfasters*, like Lasonen-Aarnio (2014) and Weatherson (ms), say that if you do maintain your belief, it is still justified (or rational), since the higher-order evidence doesn't undermine the first-order evidence's support of *P*. Similar cases arise when agents don't fully execute their epistemic duties, like if a researcher believes a key claim about their research on the basis of a non-expert friend's testimony rather than on the basis of the research. The belief might be justified on the basis of the testimony, but the researcher is being epistemically irresponsible in believing it.[8] These cases seem to show that justification, rationality, and perhaps other forms of epistemic responsibility notions can push in different ways. How can my view make sense of what's going on in these cases?

My claim is that epistemic justification, rationality, etc. are all one *type* of notion, and it's a type of notion that's analogous to ethical responsibility.

[7] As mentioned above, Alston (1988) explicitly denies that justification has much in common with moral responsibility notions. Alston's argument has been undermined by Vahid (1998), though, and many have come out in support of viewing justification or rationality as epistemic responsibility notions, including Weatherson (2008), Booth and Peels (2010), and Peels (2017).

[8] Thanks to an anonymous reviewer for pointing out these kinds of cases.

This doesn't require thinking there is only one token epistemic responsibility notion. Perhaps the right way to understand these cases is as showing that there are, in fact, many different kinds of epistemic responsibility notions that can push in different ways. When we say that the researcher has a justified irresponsible belief, we're saying that they're epistemically responsible in one respect but not in another. On this way of fleshing it out, there would be different sub-kinds of epistemic responsibility. This is all compatible with thinking that we can break the normative notions in epistemology down into two high-level kinds, the responsibility notions and the deontic notions. That's what I've argued we should do, and as I'll argue in the next section, drawing that distinction will help the truth-loving epistemic consequentialist avoid some of the trade-off objections.

3.4.2 Epistemic Consequentialism as a Theory of Deontic Notions

Like paradigmatic ethical consequentialist views, I'll argue that truth-loving epistemic consequentialism is best construed as a theory of deontic terms rather than responsibility terms. As we saw in the last chapter, truth-loving epistemic consequentialism makes the right predictions about a wide variety of our uses of epistemic deontic terms. Trade-off objections, when formulated as being about responsibility terms, show that the same is not true for consequentialist accounts of responsibility terms. So, as I'll flesh out further in this section, it's best to construe consequentialism as a theory of and only of deontic terms.

Let's start by thinking about some of our most common uses of epistemic deontic terms. As noted in the last chapter, in everyday speech, we regularly switch between talk of a belief 'being true' ('false') and it 'being right' ('wrong'). In the first chapter, I rejected the view of epistemic rightness that said a belief is right iff it's true (the view that's often put in terms of beliefs being 'correct'). That view could easily make sense of why we commonly switch between 'true' and 'right' when talking about a belief, but it wasn't a plausible view of what we should believe, since it required us to believe truths even when we couldn't. Unlike that competitor view, epistemic consequentialists can't predict that true beliefs are always right, since having a false belief can sometimes conduce to the greatest overall epistemic good (like in trade-off cases). That said, consequentialists have a different explanation of why we so easily switch between talk of a belief being true and it being right.

As I argued in the previous chapter, as a general rule for agents like us, having a true belief about any given proposition is what best promotes the overall accuracy of our epistemic states. This was the claim I called TRUTH BEGETS TRUTH. But if TRUTH BEGETS TRUTH is true, the truth-loving epistemic consequentialist will predict that as a general rule for agents like us, the right belief will be a true belief and vice versa. This is why we so easily move from thinking about a belief as being right and thinking about it as being true, the truth-loving epistemic consequentialist should say—it's because as a general rule, the two are the same.

Of course, the truth-loving epistemic consequentialist will say it's not true that *all* right beliefs are true beliefs. Recall the case involving a trade-off in pedagogy from the last chapter. There, your seven-year-old daughter Samantha was showing interest in spacecraft design, but she was not advanced enough to understand general relativity. You decided that the right thing to do was teach her about Newtonian mechanics, since teaching her the simpler (but false) theory would enable her to later come to have true beliefs about how spacecraft really move (either by approximation to the truth or by serving as a stepping stone to learning about relativity). In that case, Samantha's beliefs about spacecraft movement and her future beliefs about relativity were, in the terminology of the previous chapter, 'negatively dependent' on her beliefs about Newtonian mechanics. That is, in that case, her having a false belief about the theory is what would best conduce to her having more true beliefs. So even though Newtonian mechanics was false, the consequentialist would still predict that it was the right thing for her to believe. As I argued in the previous chapter, though, this is the right result, so even in unusual cases like this, consequentialism does well as a theory of epistemic rightness.

The upshot is a continuation of a point of the previous chapter, that truth-loving epistemic consequentialism makes the right prediction about the vast majority of cases involving epistemic deontic notions. These include everyday cases of right and wrong belief, reasoning and inference cases, and pedagogical and permissible trade-off cases. That epistemic consequentialism seems to get these cases right counts as a reason to see it as a theory of deontic terms. Since the above trade-off objections show that consequentialism formulated as a theory of responsibility terms doesn't fare as well, we should see epistemic consequentialism as making a claim about and only about epistemic deontic notions: Whether a belief is right is determined by whether having it best conduces to having the most true beliefs overall. By formulating the view this way, the best versions of consequentialism won't be subject to the trade-off objections discussed above; they instead take those objections into account by formulating the view to be only about deontic terms.

One might worry that the consequentialist is ignoring the fact that we sometimes use the terms 'ought (to believe)' and 'right belief' to talk about responsibility notions. Consider MISLEADING FINGERPRINTS from above: Detective Dustin's evidence (misleadingly) pointed toward it being the butler who did it. Along with thinking that the detective is *justified* in believing that the butler did it, might not we also think that he *ought* to believe it or that it is the *right* thing for him to believe? If so, doesn't this show that consequentialists cannot cleave responsibility notions from deontic notions, as I claimed they should? You might think it at least shows that consequentialists can't predict that the right belief is usually the true one, since this kind of case is common and a counterexample to that claim.

To evaluate this worry, let's consider the analogous worry as it might be leveled against ethical consequentialism. An opponent of ethical consequentialism might accuse ethical consequentialists of getting it wrong since we sometimes use the term 'right (action)' to talk about what an agent is responsible for. We might say things like "Even though ϕing would have saved more people, the train engineer's evidence strongly supported thinking that he would have saved more people by ψing, so ψing was the right thing for him to do." One move in response to this is for the ethical consequentialist to limit the consequences that matter in their theory to the expected or foreseeable consequences, and thereby become a form of *subjective consequentialism* (Railton 1984). More commonly, though, ethical consequentialists hold that these are loose uses of the term 'right' and that, strictly speaking, ψing was not the right thing to do (Sinnott-Armstrong 2015). So, assuming that the epistemic consequentialist wants to hold on to it being true belief (not merely apparently true belief or foreseeable true belief) that is epistemically good (per the motivating intuition for the view), the epistemic consequentialist should follow ethical consequentialists and hold that we sometimes speak loosely in our use of 'right (belief).'

The case of 'ought' is slightly more complicated. There, it's more natural to assume that there are different senses of the term (see, for example, Wedgwood 2016). The 'ought' in the objection is most naturally construed as the subjective 'ought.' But all the consequentialist needs is that there is some sense of 'ought' that is not about responsibility. That's compatible with there being a sense of 'ought' that is a responsibility notion, as the objector argues. So there is no problem for the consequentialist here either.

3.4.3 An Explanation of the Directionality of Epistemic Notions

One benefit of construing the analogy between epistemic and ethical notions the way I do is it allows the consequentialist to explain what Berker took to be the problematic feature of epistemic consequentialism—i.e., its incorrect prediction about the directionality of justification and rationality. Epistemic consequentialists about deontic terms can give an explanation of why justification and rationality would be backward-looking even if epistemic rightness notions are forward-looking.

As I argued above, as responsibility terms, 'justification' and 'rationality' primarily serve to evaluate the agent with respect to the belief. As epistemic responsibility terms, they share some distinctive features with ethical responsibility terms, including (1) that whether they apply is partially a function of agent-internal features, (2) that we should ascribe them to an agent only when the agent deserves the evaluation, and (3) that their attribution pretheoretically presupposes that the agent had some control over the formation of the state. What all of these features get at is that responsibility notions broadly assess whether the agent is due credit or blame for the value that the belief has or lacks.

To explain Berker's observation about the directionality of justification and rationality, the consequentialist should point to the general nature of responsibility terms. An agent who is due credit (or blame) for the value that the belief has (or lacks) must have had access to and control over certain features of the world and herself *before* the belief was formed. Part of the human condition is that we're limited in important ways: (1) as Hume pointed out, we only have access to and control over the future via interacting with the present and remembering the past, and (2) we don't have access to all of the facts of the world (or even all the present or past ones)—we only have access to a small collection of the facts (via our evidence about and memories of those facts). What those limitations entail is that the only way agents like us could be proper objects of responsibility terms is if we're appropriately situated *historically*. Agents cannot be due credit or blame for anything that they aren't historically connected to in the right way. That's where the backward-looking directionality of notions like justification and rationality comes from on this picture. They're backward-looking because they're responsibility notions, not because all epistemic evaluations are backward-looking. So, by treating justification and rationality as responsibility terms, the epistemic consequentialist predicts exactly what Berker took to be the theory's Achilles heel.

Altogether, then, the first move that epistemic consequentialists should make in response to the apparent counterexamples to the view involving trade-offs is to highlight that the theory, properly construed, is a theory of epistemic deontic terms, not epistemic responsibility terms. Doing this avoids most of the specific trade-off objections in the literature, since those are formulated as objections to consequentialist theories of justification or rationality. Doing this also lets the consequentialist explain why Berker's directionality objection misses the mark, since there are good reasons to think that epistemic responsibility terms would be backward-looking even if epistemic rightness, the target of epistemic consequentialist theories, is not.

3.5 Deontic Trade-Offs

That first move saves epistemic consequentialists from trade-off objections formulated in terms of what is justified or rational, but there is still a kind of trade-off worry epistemic consequentialists face. This worry takes aim at consequentialist views of deontic terms. Consider this example, which is a modified version of an example from Fumerton (1995, p. 12):

> GOD GRANT I am a scientist interested in getting a grant from a religious organization. I don't have sufficient evidence to believe in God, I think that belief in God is manifestly irrational, and it's in fact true that there is no God. Despite that, I discover that this organization will give me the grant only if it concludes that I am religious. Further, I am such a terrible liar that unless I actually get myself to believe in God they will discover that I am an atheist. Having the grant will enable me to come to have many, many important and true beliefs that I wouldn't otherwise be able to have.

In GOD GRANT, the epistemic consequentialist looks committed to a belief in God being right, despite the lack of evidence, its irrationality, and it being false. So, it's another case where the consequentialist appears to incorrectly predict that the good of one belief ought to be sacrificed for the overall epistemic good—but this time, it's about what the agent should believe (a deontic notion), rather than what they would be justified or rational in believing.

As we discussed in the last chapter, the first-personal framing of cases like this might be doing some work toward convincing us that these cases are problematic. From Shah (2003) we know that when we deliberate about what to believe, our deliberations exhibit the phenomenon of *transparency*, that "when asking oneself *whether to believe that p*, [one must] immediately recognize that this question is settled by, and only by, answering the question *whether p is true*" (2003, p. 447). What this means is that in first-personal cases, questions of what we ought to believe will appear to be settled only by the truth of the matter. So, it's no surprise that when we consider cases described in the first person, we're inclined to think the belief is right only if its true. Moreover, if we're trying to decide the truth of some matter from the first-person perspective, all we have access to is the information we have, not all the truths. Thus it's natural to interpret the relevant 'ought' as a subjective 'ought,' which is not the one the epistemic consequentialist is after. Even though this objection is purportedly formulated in deontic terms, when it is presented in the first person, I worry it can elicit our intuitions about something other than rightness. So the first-personal framing of these deontic trade-off cases might be misleading.

We can avoid this worry by reformulating it in the third person:

> THIRD-PERSONAL GOD GRANT Tony is a scientist interested in getting a grant from a religious organization. Tony doesn't have sufficient evidence to believe in God, Tony thinks that belief in God is manifestly irrational, and it's in fact true that there is no God. Despite that, Tony discovers that this organization will give him the grant only if it concludes that he is religious. Further, Tony is such a terrible liar that unless he actually gets himself to believe in God they will discover that he is an atheist. Having the grant will enable Tony to come to have many, many important and true beliefs that he wouldn't otherwise be able to have.

The spirit of the objection remains: In cases like this, the objector claims, the right thing for Tony to do is not believe in God, despite the fact that believing in God will best conduce to the epistemic good. The consequentialist looks committed to the opposite result.

3.6 Responding to the Deontic Trade-Offs

Some consequentialists might try to avoid deontic trade-off objections by going in for an *indirect* consequentialism. According to indirect consequentialists, the rightness of a belief depends not on the epistemic consequences of holding the belief but instead on the consequences of something else, like the consequences of following a particular epistemic rule. Ahlstrom-Vij and Dunn (2014) take this route and argue that we should view reliabilists as endorsing a version of indirect consequentialism, where the consequences in question are the consequences of using certain belief-forming processes.

The problem with indirect consequentialism is that the indirect consequentialist can't capture the original motivations we had for going in for this view. The veritist intuition was that having true beliefs and not having false beliefs is what is of ultimate value in epistemology. Indirect consequentialists can't vindicate that. On the indirect account, something other than the truth of beliefs is what really matters, like using a reliable process (even when that process produces false beliefs).[9] The direct epistemic consequentialist doesn't face this problem.

As long as it counts the long-term epistemic consequences as mattering, any direct consequentialist view must bite the bullet on cases like Tony's. But some versions of direct consequentialism can explain why Tony and we (the evaluators of his case) would incorrectly have the intuition that Tony shouldn't believe in God. In fact, the best view not only predicts that we will have such an intuition. It also endorses that intuition as a good one to have. Like above, fleshing this out will involve the epistemic consequentialist taking some cues from ethical consequentialists.

In describing his ethical consequentialism, Sidgwick (1907, p. 413) says, "It is not necessary that the end which gives the criterion of rightness should always be the end at which we consciously aim." The idea is that even though ethical consequentialism is a view about what actions are right, its commitments don't entail that agents ought to think or make

[9] Notice that this is an instance of the more general 'rule worship' objection to rule consequentialist views discussed by Smart (1973, pp. 9–12).

decisions in consequentialist terms. Modern ethical consequentialists almost universally endorse this, but even early ethical consequentialists had this in mind (Bales 1971, Sinnott-Armstrong 2015).[10] As Railton (1984) points out, insomuch as consequentialism says that agents ought to reason in ways that conduce to the good, it should actually say that, most of the time, agents like us ought *not* reason in consequentialist ways. In many cases, like the kinds of cases typically used to motivate the paradox of hedonism, reasoning in consequentialist ways fails to conduce to the good.[11] Real people like us tend to produce the best consequences more often by following our hunches, relying on dispositions we've fostered, and acting quickly, not by carefully working out the details of the consequentialist calculus in every case. Following Railton, let's call a consequentialist view *sophisticated* if it both says that whether an act is right is a question of whether it best conduces to the good and does *not* say that agents ought to aim to produce the good in their decision-making.

Railton (1984, p. 157) calls attention to the fact that on sophisticated consequentialist views, there is a complicated interplay between how agents ought to act and what dispositions they ought to foster, how they ought to make decisions, etc.:

> A sophisticated act-consequentialist may recognize that if he were to develop a standing disposition to render prompt assistance in emergencies without going through elaborate act-consequentialist deliberation, there would almost certainly be cases in which he would perform acts worse than those he would have performed had he stopped to deliberate.... It may still be right for him to develop this disposition, for without it he would act rightly in emergencies still less often.

To understand what's going on here, it's important to notice two distinct aspects of this kind of consequentialist view.

The first aspect of the view is thinking that we can use the consequentialist criterion of rightness to evaluate not only actions but also other features of agents, including their dispositions, decision-making procedures,

[10] See for examples Railton (1984), Hare (1981, pp. 46–47), Bentham (1780, chap. IV, sec. VI), and Mill (1863, chap. II, par. 19).

[11] For readers who might not be familiar with this, the so-called paradox of hedonism is the fact that consciously aiming at one's own pleasure is often self-undermining. Most real people end up happier by focusing on projects and endeavors that bring them pleasure, rather than focusing on pleasure itself. One canonical source for the paradox is Sidgwick (1907, p. 136).

motivational schema, etc. On views like this, agents' dispositions, decision-making procedures, and motivational schema are evaluated in the same way that actions are: Of the ones available, the right ones are the ones that best conduce to the good. Consequentialists who take this move to the extreme by applying the consequentialist criterion of evaluation to everything are *global* consequentialists (Driver 2011, Pettit and Smith 2000), an idea we'll revisit in Chapter 7.

The second aspect of the view is the sophisticated aspect, which both says that whether an act (or other object of evaluation) is right is a question of whether it best conduces to the good and does not say that agents ought to explicitly aim at producing the good in their decision-making. Importantly, views that have both of these aspects leave open the possibility that an act might be wrong (because it doesn't conduce to the best outcome) despite it being motivated by the right dispositions (where a disposition is right to have when, of the available dispositions, having that disposition leads to better overall outcomes than having any other).

There are many reasons to go in for ethical consequentialist views with both global and sophisticated aspects, including that such views can avoid the paradox of hedonism, give neat explanations of how agents should act in emergencies, and avoid worries about alienation from both people and ethical principles (see Railton 1984; Norcross 1997; and Driver 2005). I'll claim that epistemic consequentialists too should be sophisticated and extend the consequentialist criterion of rightness to apply to things other than beliefs. One reason is that situations analogous to Railton's ethical emergencies often happen in the epistemic domain as well. Almost all the time, we rely on our standing doxastic dispositions to regulate our beliefs, including in mundane cases (like our beliefs about whether a car is coming before we cross the street) as well as in more complex cases (like in the 1964 U.S. Supreme Court "I know it when I see it" test for obscenity, *Jacobellis v. Ohio*). In many cases, if we lacked standing doxastic dispositions and tried to explicitly consider what to believe, we'd miss out on true beliefs we would otherwise have. Trying to calculate what is best to believe would often lead us to running out of time (like in making a quick judgment before crossing the street), running out of mental resources (like in considering cases where the intuitions come easily but the arguments are hard to produce), getting the wrong answer in cases where the reasons for our beliefs are inaccessible to us (like in cases where our belief-forming processes are creating true beliefs but we're not sure how), and missing out on the other true beliefs we could have quickly formed if we had not used our time and mental resources focusing on a single issue. So if the epistemic consequentialist is really motivated by the idea that what we ought to do is believe the truth and shun error, they should want us to foster good belief-forming dispositions and practices too.[12]

If I'm right about the structure of the best epistemic consequentialist views, then part of the consequentialist project becomes figuring out which belief-forming dispositions and processes we ought to foster. The full story will have to be sensitive to the psychological peculiarities of real humans and the particular facts of the world we occupy, so we shouldn't expect a simple answer. Again see Bishop and Trout (2004) for a way to start fleshing this out by appeal to empirical psychology. Luckily, appeals to general facts about human dispositions will be enough to explain our intuitions in cases like THIRD-PERSONAL GOD GRANT. As I argued above, one such general fact is that being disposed to believe the truth about every particular proposition we consider is often the best way for us to maximize the accuracy of our full set of beliefs. THIRD-PERSONAL GOD GRANT is a weird case where this usually helpful disposition leads us astray. So, our mistaken intuition that Tony should not believe in God is explained by our non-mistaken intuition about what dispositions Tony ought to have, the sophisticated consequentialist should say.

One way to support the idea that it's our intuitions about right *human* dispositions that are generating our intuitive judgments in THIRD-PERSONAL GOD GRANT is to compare what we think Tony should do to what we would program an ideal scientific robot to do. Ideal scientific robots, unlike real humans, can escape some of the limitations of human agents that make reliance on dispositions and standing commitments necessary to maximize accuracy. So, suppose we were building a robot to study marine biology, and suppose that the only way for the robot to complete the task is to temporarily represent the world as having a God as a stepping-stone to getting a grant. This robot, unlike Tony, wouldn't be subject to our contingent human memory, attention, and processing limitations. Is it permissible for the robot to temporarily believe in God? The consequentialist should say yes. The consequentialist can still maintain that the robot is neither justified nor rational in believing in God, since that's not the question. The question

[12] I'll return to this kind of argument in Chapter 7. Here, I'm going to drop 'global' from the description of the view and just call it 'sophisticated epistemic consequentialism.' I do this for brevity but also because the view need not extend consequentialist evaluation to *all* things to employ the moves I give in this chapter.

is one of what the robot ought to believe, all (epistemic) things considered. The robot's only (epistemic) aim is to get a correct theory of marine biology, so to do that, the robot should temporarily take on the belief in God. The difference between Tony and the robot is that Tony is human, and like us, he is subject to natural human memory, attention, and processing limitations. Because of those limitations, the best way for Tony to promote the epistemic good is to foster and act on the set of dispositions that lead him qua real human to promote the good.

Sophisticated epistemic consequentialism does not predict that the beliefs produced by the best dispositions are always right (unlike the nearby rule-consequentialist view). Just as in the moral case, acting on the right dispositions can sometimes lead us astray, the consequentialist should say.[13] In this way, the epistemic consequentialist bites the bullet in deontic trade-off cases like THIRD-PERSONAL GOD GRANT. But I've tried to convince you that the bullet isn't a particularly hard one to bite, since sophisticated consequentialists have a natural story about why we would have misleading intuitions in those cases. As discussed above and in the previous chapter, consequentialists also get right many paradigmatic cases, including mundane day-to-day beliefs and beliefs in permissible trade-off cases (like the case of Samantha), that have the same formal structure as the purportedly problematic cases. So, sophisticated consequentialists should think that the deontic trade-off objections only show that in some cases there is a gap between what the best set of dispositions would have us believe and what the right belief actually is, not that there is some deeper problem with consequentialism or the structure of epistemic normativity it proposes.

It's worth noting that bullet-biting is not as attractive an option for consequentialists about epistemic responsibility terms. For one, consequentialists about responsibility terms would have to give up on Berker's intuition that responsibility terms have a backward-looking directionality, whereas consequentialists about deontic terms can explain it. The consequentialist about responsibility terms would also need a story to explain the intuition that right belief and justified belief regularly come apart. As I argued above, consequentialists about deontic terms correctly predict that the right belief and the true belief are almost always the same. Consequentialists about responsibility terms would have to predict that justified beliefs are almost

[13] Note that rule consequentialists cannot give an analogous argument, since they must hold that the right rules can never lead us astray (in terms of believing rightly). They must therefore say that right belief and the most truth-conducive belief can be different, thereby giving up on the original motivation for the view.

always true, but of course, justified beliefs are often false. So bullet-biting is really only a good option for consequentialists about deontic terms.

A worry you might have about sophisticated epistemic consequentialism is that it might seem hypocritical or self-undermining. How can the sophisticated consequentialist hold both (1) that it's right for Tony to believe in God and (2) that it's right for Tony to have and act on a disposition to not believe in God? If Tony is a sophisticated consequentialist, shouldn't he try to not believe in God (as his dispositions would require) but also view that as the wrong doxastic state to be in (by his consequentialist commitments)?

The answer is that, in their day-to-day lives, sophisticated epistemic consequentialists maintain a commitment to, but are not directly motivated by, the truth goal. As Railton (1984, p. 153) puts it in the ethical case, the sophisticated consequentialist maintains "a standing commitment" to living a life that best conduces to the good. The majority of the time, sophisticated epistemic consequentialists rely on their already formed dispositions to do things like base their beliefs on their evidence, not be confused by common reasoning mistakes or fallacies, and mitigate biases in their belief-forming processes. Having a standing commitment to the truth goal means that the consequentialist will try to develop and maintain the sorts of dispositions that will help them best pursue the truth. This gives the consequentialist a motivation to base their beliefs on their evidence, for example, since doing that will help them get true beliefs. The sophisticated epistemic consequentialist also recognizes that there may be times when that disposition will temporarily lead them astray from their goal, but they should foster it anyway because doing so is the best way to pursue the goal overall. In this way, the sophisticated consequentialist is not acting toward incompatible goals, nor is their view self-undermining. The sophisticated consequentialist is simply pursuing their goal in a sophisticated way.[14]

3.7 Accounts of Justification and Rationality

Let's take stock of the discussion. In this chapter and the last one, I've aimed to construct a version of truth-loving epistemic consequentialism that avoids trade-off objections while maintaining the intuitive appeal of the view. To do that, I suggested that the epistemic consequentialist

[14] Compare this to the ethical version of this idea from Railton (1984).

take three cues from ethical consequentialists. The best versions of epistemic consequentialism are accounts of epistemic deontic notions like belief rightness, not responsibility notions like justification or rationality, I argued. Since the bulk of specific trade-off objections are formulated against consequentialist views of responsibility notions, by making their view about deontic notions, consequentialists don't respond to those objections so much as circumvent them. But consequentialist views of deontic notions are still subject to some trade-off objections. Rather than go in for an indirect consequentialism, which cannot capture the motivating intuition, I suggested that the consequentialist bite the bullet on the apparently counterintuitive results and explain away the intuitions as misleading. That explanation comes naturally for global, sophisticated consequentialists, and if it's right, it shows that trade-off objections don't expose a deeper flaw in the view, as its critics claim. That's why this version of epistemic consequentialism is the best version of epistemic consequentialism for avoiding trade-off objections.

Consider, by way of contrast, the view of epistemic normativity argued for by Wedgwood (2002). According to Wedgwood, there is a fundamental norm of belief that says that true beliefs are correct and false beliefs are incorrect. On this view, the other epistemic norms, like norms of rational belief and knowledge, are 'explained' by the fundamental norm. One norm is explained by another when the first is entailed by the second combined with certain other facts, like facts about what's involved in trying to achieve some end. In that respect, Wedgwood's account is quite similar to the view I claim consequentialists should adopt. True belief is seen as the ultimate end (thereby determining what is 'correct,' in Wedgwood's terminology), and we aim to understand all epistemic norms in terms of that end.

The similarities end there, though. Consider Wedgwood's explanation of norms of rational belief. Rational belief, Wedgwood tells us, is a kind of means we use to get correct belief. On Wedgwood's view, you have a rational belief when you follow a collection of rules that reliably produce true beliefs for you, since this is how you aim to satisfy the fundamental norm of belief. On this picture, a belief can be rational (because it was produced by properly following the right rules) but incorrect. The rationality of your belief, on this picture, is a question of how aptly you pursued the aim of having true beliefs. In my terms, Wedgwood is best seen as giving an account of an epistemic responsibility notion, not a deontic notion.

This example is instructive for two reasons. First, it shows that there can be accounts of epistemic responsibility notions that share their high-level structure (and even some of their elements) with consequentialist accounts of deontic notions. On consequentialist accounts of deontic notions, rightness is understood in terms of conduciveness to epistemic goodness. Similarly, on Wedgwood's view of rationality, rationality is understood as a kind of means to true belief. The conception of means in play for Wedgwood's account of rationality is not the same as the consequentialist's conception of conduciveness to goodness, but they share the idea that the evaluative notion in play is to be understood in terms of promoting true belief.

Second, this example brings out that, like its ethical counterpart, being a consequentialist about belief rightness doesn't commit one to any particular view about the nature of epistemic responsibility. It's a natural option for sophisticated consequentialists to follow Wedgwood and think that being epistemically responsible is about pursuing the means to having true beliefs. This could be understood in terms of trying to foster the best dispositions to help us get true beliefs, as I discussed it above, or it could be understood in terms of following a set of rules that reliably produce true belief, as Wedgwood describes it. In the second case, the consequentialist will end up with an account of responsibility notions that fits neatly with contemporary reliabilist accounts of justification. If instead the consequentialist thinks the correct dispositions are ones that appeal only to internally accessible features of the agent, that view would fit naturally with access-internalist views of justification.

Importantly, though, it's open to the consequentialist to deny that there are any connections between the dispositions one ought to have and epistemic responsibility. Capturing the motivating intuition for epistemic consequentialism while avoiding the trade-off objections only requires going in for a view about deontic terms. It's open to consequentialists to plump for many different accounts of responsibility notions, even those that aren't consequentialist at all, either because they are only 'explained' by consequentialist commitments at the deontic level (in the sense of Wedgwood 2002) or because they're seen as completely independent of deontic notions for other reasons. I'll return to this issue in Chapter 7, where I'll discuss how truth-loving epistemic consequentialists should see theories of responsibility fitting into a broader conception of truth-loving epistemology, but for now, what's important to note is that many different theories of epistemic responsibility notions are compatible with the truth-loving epistemic consequentialist picture.

3.8 How Plausible Is the Sophisticated View?

So far, I've argued that we should think of truth-loving epistemic consequentialism as a global, sophisticated theory of deontic epistemic notions. Truth-loving epistemic consequentialists say that we should maintain a standing commitment to the truth goal but not always appeal to consequentialist reasoning in our day-to-day lives. Instead, truth-loving epistemic consequentialists say we should foster the dispositions, decision-making procedures, motivational schema, etc. that conduce to us most effectively pursuing the truth. In this last section, let's revisit how plausible this view should seem in light of the modifications made to it in this chapter.

What I'll argue here is that, in addition to matching our intuitions in the vast majority of cases of right belief and being able to avoid the trade-off objections, there's another reason to think the sophisticated conception of the view is right. We all typically assume, at least implicitly, that everyone we meet will regulate their epistemic lives exactly as the sophisticated epistemic consequentialist says we should. We assume that they'll maintain a standing commitment to the truth goal and that they aim to foster in themselves ways of thinking that conduce to that goal. In that sense, we're all already treating each other as sophisticated epistemic consequentialists.

To see this, recall the example of critical thinking classes discussed in the last chapter: In critical thinking classes, when we teach students that affirming the consequent is not conducive to the truth goal (i.e., that it's invalid), students immediately treat that reasoning as failed and try to understand why it fails. Similarly, when we show students how their natural tendencies lead to false beliefs in the Wason selection (card-flipping) task, students immediately ask themselves where they went wrong and reevaluate their belief-forming dispositions. We don't have to first convince the students not to use methods that aren't truth-conducive. Why don't we have to tell students to focus on truth-conduciveness? Why do they immediately jump from a method being not truth-conducive to it being wrong to use? The best explanation is that our students have a standing commitment to the truth goal and they aim to regulate their belief-forming dispositions in accord with it. In their day-to-day normal reasoning, our students use certain belief-forming dispositions that lead them astray in these critical-thinking-textbook examples. When we point out that their dispositions are failing them in these cases, their standing commitment to the truth goal and their aim to regulate their epistemic lives in accord with it motivate them to reconsider their dispositions. This is exactly what the sophisticated epistemic consequentialist predicts they should do.

You might worry that pedagogical cases are misleading since entering the learning environment itself might involve students adopting the truth goal for the relevant material, even if they didn't have it already. The phenomenon isn't limited to pedagogical contexts, though. It happens anytime we explicitly discuss reasoning patterns. For example, with the intention to convince them to abandon such arguments, we might point out to politicians that ad populum arguments for resisting social change are unreliable. This only makes sense if we expect our interlocutors (the politicians, in this case) to be moved by truth-indicating considerations (or at least think they should be so moved). So we're assuming that they already have a standing commitment to the truth goal (or should have one). Of course, politicians often don't respond to these kinds of considerations. But when they don't, we can accuse them of not being good reasoners. So the worry about the misleadingness of pedagogical cases is misplaced; it's standard to assume that when someone is a minimally good reasoner (as we usually assume our interlocutors to be), they'll view having true beliefs and avoiding false beliefs as their epistemic goal and aim to regulate their epistemic lives in accord with it.

We don't assume that the truth goal is at the front of our interlocutors' minds at all times. We don't expect others to walk around explicitly calculating which possible beliefs will best help them reach the goal, like a consequentialist robot might do. In their day-to-day lives, we expect our interlocutors will rely on the belief-forming dispositions they've fostered over their years of practice. But importantly, we also expect our interlocutors to disavow failed belief-forming dispositions, and the faulty beliefs formed with them, when they notice that those dispositions don't conduce to accurate beliefs (like when we teach about fallacies in critical thinking classes). This means we treat our interlocutors as though they have a standing commitment to the truth goal and should regulate their epistemic lives in accord with it. This is exactly what the sophisticated epistemic consequentialist would predict that they should do.[15]

My claim is not that everyone already accepts the truth-loving global sophisticated epistemic consequentialist view of right belief. If that were true, I probably wouldn't need to write this book.[16] The claim here is just that we all already treat those around us as though they're subject to the most central claims of sophisticated truth-loving epistemic consequentialism, namely that they maintain a standing commitment to having accurate beliefs and that they regulate their belief-forming dispositions in accord with that goal.

Notice that we don't assume that those around us share a similar commitment to any analogous kind of ethical goal, even in cases where the only concerns are ethical. It's not uncommon to meet someone who thinks it's permissible not to donate to charity, even after they are convinced that donating conduces to the overall ethical good. If we assumed that the central claims of a global sophisticated ethical consequentialism were as universally accepted as those of the epistemic consequentialist view developed here, we would be surprised to meet such people. But those of us who teach undergraduates regularly meet political libertarians who know that their actions do not maximize the overall good but still think they are permissible. So whereas we always assume that those around us maintain a standing commitment to the truth goal and regulate their epistemic lives in accord with it, we don't assume those around us maintain a standing commitment to any analogous kind of ethical goal. The fact that we all think it's natural to treat those around us as though they're subject to the central claims of truth-loving epistemic consequentialism should make that view seem really quite plausible.

Because it's essentially a veritist idea, other veritist views of right belief might similarly be able to predict that we maintain a standing commitment to the truth goal and regulate our epistemic lives in accord with it.

[15] To get clear on the phenomenon in play here, notice that we don't expect others to regulate their *entire* lives in response to the truth goal. It's OK, we think, for a researcher to leave the lab to take a break, even if doing so would result in them having fewer true beliefs. What's going on here is that the truth goal is what we see as their standing *epistemic* goal. When only epistemic concerns are relevant, we expect others to act like sophisticated epistemic consequentialists—they maintain a standing commitment to the truth goal and regulate their beliefs, dispositions, and belief-forming processes in response to it.

[16] Moreover, the claim is clearly not true: Even if we all already thought that the right belief is the true belief in simple cases (as the sophisticated consequentialist predicts), many would deny that deontic epistemic trade-offs are permissible (contra sophisticated consequentialists).

So I don't take this fact to count decisively in favor of truth-loving epistemic consequentialism. That said, when we combine this fact with the fact that truth-loving epistemic consequentialism is extremely simple, the fact that it makes intuitively right predictions about right belief in the vast majority of cases, the fact that the view can serve as the foundation for an appealing and fecund general conception of epistemology, and the fact that the view can avoid the most prominent objections to it, we're left with a strong holistic defense of the view. Before sketching the general picture of epistemology that's supported by truth-loving epistemic consequentialism in the last chapter, I'll continue the holistic defense of the view in the next three chapters by showing how truth-loving epistemic consequentialism can be further developed to avoid other prominent objections.

4
On Veritism and Promoting the Epistemic Good

4.1 The Truth-Loving Theory of Value

The truth-loving epistemic consequentialist view developed so far is committed to a veritistic conception of epistemic value, which says that (1) all and only true beliefs (or accurate credences) have final epistemic value and (2) all and only false beliefs (inaccurate credences) have final epistemic disvalue. Truth-loving epistemic consequentialists hold that it's only the impact on the truth and falsity of all beliefs that matter for determining whether a particular belief is right; it doesn't treat any particular belief's truth as inherently more important than any other. It's this 'belief impartiality' that gave rise to the trade-off objections discussed in the last two chapters.

In response to the trade-off objections, I first argued that it's important to see truth-loving epistemic consequentialism as an account of right belief, not justified belief, rational belief, or knowledge. I then argued that the consequentialist should be sophisticated in the sense that they should reject the claim that we ought to think in consequentialist terms. The most plausible view is also a global consequentialist view that extends the consequentialist criterion of rightness to evaluate agents' dispositions, decision-making procedures, motivational schema, and the like. As I argued in Chapter 2, this view can make sense of permissible trade-offs in ways better than any trade-off-avoiding view can. And as I argued in Chapter 3, the view can also respond to particular trade-off worries either by not accepting that the view admits of those trade-offs (like when they are trade-offs about justified belief, rather than right belief) or by explaining away the apparent objectionableness of those trade-offs.

As it has been developed so far, the view takes a stand on what constitutes right belief, dispositions, decision-making procedures,

Right Belief and True Belief. Daniel J. Singer, Oxford University Press. © Oxford University Press 2023.
DOI: 10.1093/oso/9780197660386.003.0005

motivational schema, etc., and what is finally epistemically valuable. It hasn't yet taken a stand on whether beliefs (or anything else) might have derivative (non-final) epistemic value. The natural hypothesis is that in addition to the final value (disvalue) a belief has in being true (false), beliefs can also have instrumental derivative value (disvalue) in terms of how well they promote having more true (false) beliefs and fewer false (true) beliefs.[1] On the global consequentialist picture, this kind of instrumental value would also extend to agents' dispositions, decision-making procedures, motivational schema, and the like. It's natural for the truth-loving epistemic consequentialist to stop there and hold that nothing has epistemic (dis)value unless it either has final epistemic (dis)value itself or has instrumental epistemic value by giving rise to final epistemic (dis)value. Let's call this view 'instrumental veritism.'

Sylvan (2018) claims that instrumental veritistic accounts of epistemic value are subject to a generalized version of the swamping problem. To see what that problem is, suppose that, like reliabilists, we wanted to understand a belief being justified in terms of it being the product of a reliable belief-forming process. Also suppose we had a true belief that was produced by a reliable belief-forming process. Then ask whether that true belief could be more valuable in virtue of having been produced by a reliable belief-forming process. If we're veritists who see all epistemic value as consisting in or being derived from true belief (or accurate credences), it doesn't seem like the fact that the belief was reliably produced can *itself* add any value. An analogy from Zagzebski (2000) helps here: Once it exists, a cup of good coffee that was made by a reliably good coffeemaker doesn't seem to gain any additional goodness from the fact that it was made by a reliably good coffeemaker. Once the good coffee exists, its goodness is independent of the process that produced it. Analogously, if we have a belief that is already true, the fact that it was produced by a reliable belief-forming process doesn't seem like it can add any value to the belief, if instrumental veritism is right. So what's the problem? The problem is that justified true belief does seem to be epistemically better than mere true belief, and so, because reliabilists treat justified belief as reliably produced belief, it doesn't

[1] One benefit of this axiology for the truth-loving epistemic consequentialist is that it allows the consequentialist to give a neat story about what's going on in trade-off cases: In trade-off cases, a belief is right despite it being finally disvaluable because its derivative value in producing other true beliefs outweighs its final disvalue.

seem like they can make sense of the additional value a true belief gets from it also being justified.

Sylvan claims that this problem extends to any account of epistemic evaluation that says that the value of a positive evaluand should be understood instrumentally in terms of veritist final value. As Sylvan (2018, p. 390) puts it, the problem extends to any view that holds that being justified (rational, knowledge) is to true belief as being produced by a good coffeemaker is to good coffee. On these views, a justified belief (rational belief, knowledge) is understood as a "mere product of some type of source that is only instrumentally good relative to true belief." Sylvan's solution is not to reject veritism but to deny that all derivative value is to be understood instrumentally. On the veritist view that Sylvan develops, there are fitting ways to value good ends that produce non-instrumental value. Sylvan uses this idea to argue that we can understand the value of rational belief, justified belief, and knowledge in terms of the value of manifesting certain appropriate ways to value accuracy in thought. This avoids the generalized swamping problem because it denies that all epistemic value is to be understood in terms of producing final epistemic value—i.e., it denies instrumentalism about derivative value.

One might think that if Sylvan's generalized swamping problem shows against instrumental veritist views of the value of justified belief, it must also show against the instrumentalist veritist account of epistemic value that fits most naturally with truth-loving epistemic consequentialism. That view says that we should understand the value of a belief being right solely in terms of its truth (i.e., its final value) and its conduciveness to other true beliefs and the lack of false belief (i.e., its instrumental value). So on this view, it might look like the value of right beliefs is understood in the same way that the value of a coffeemaker is understood in terms of it producing good coffee. If so, it's natural to think Sylvan's generalized swamping problem would show against this view.

But that's not right. The truth-loving epistemic consequentialist's particular instrumentalist veritist axiology avoids the generalized swamping problem. For the generalized swamping problem to apply to a view of the value of a belief, the view would need to hold that beliefs receive a positive evaluation because they're mere products of something. Whether a belief is a mere product of something is a question about where the belief came from (in Berker's terms, it's a backward-looking notion). Truth-loving epistemic consequentialism doesn't say that whether a belief is right is a question of where it came from. According to truth-loving epistemic consequentialism, belief rightness is about the final value of the belief itself (i.e., whether it's true) and what other true beliefs it conduces to, not whether the belief was produced a certain way. So Sylvan's problem doesn't apply to truth-loving epistemic consequentialism's account of belief rightness.[2]

More generally, for there to be a swamping problem for a view, the view must say (1) that whether an object of evaluation is valuable is at least partially a function of the history of the object and (2) that the value of the object can be understood solely in terms of its final value and other final value that it gives rise to (currently or in the future). (Claim 2 is instrumentalism.) To see this, let's think about the swamping problem for reliabilism in these terms: Reliabilists say that whether a belief is justified is a function of where the belief came from (i.e., what process produced the belief), and they presumably hold that a belief being justified makes it (more) valuable. That's claim 1. The reliabilist runs into trouble when they combine that with instrumentalism about the value of belief, since instrumentalism says that all of the belief's value must come from the current state of the belief or things it gives rise to. Since objects cannot give rise to their own current histories, these claims are incompatible.

When it comes to the instrumental veritist view that most naturally goes with truth-loving epistemic consequentialism, this problem doesn't arise. According to truth-loving epistemic consequentialism, a belief being right is constituted by it having or conducing to final epistemic value. Importantly, the view doesn't say that whether a belief is right is a function of the history of the belief—it's an exclusively forward-looking view. So the view isn't committed to claim (1) above, and the generalized swamping problem doesn't apply.

What about *global* truth-loving epistemic consequentialism? Doesn't that view treat some objects of evaluation as right in virtue of their history? One might think it does because global epistemic consequentialists sanction certain dispositions, decision-making procedures, motivational schema, etc. as right in virtue of them conducing to the best epistemic outcomes. So mustn't that view also evaluate beliefs as right

[2] As I hinted above, we can reformulate this response to Sylvan in directionality terms. Sylvan's generalized swamping problem only applies to views that understand justification (rationality, etc.) in backward-looking terms (like the consequentialist view given by Ahlstrom-Vij and Dunn 2014). Truth-loving epistemic consequentialism is a forward-looking account, though. Thanks to Nate Sharadin for pointing out this way of expressing the idea.

when they're the products of those right dispositions, decision-making procedures, motivational schema, etc.? No. As I argued in the last chapter, the global consequentialist should think that a belief can be produced by a right belief-forming disposition (for example) and still be wrong. My belief that there's someone behind me might be produced by my right disposition to believe that whenever I hear breathing and don't see someone. But of course it's possible for me to hear breathing and not see someone without there being someone behind me (if, for example, I'm wearing headphones or the sound of my own breathing is reflecting off things). So the global truth-loving epistemic consequentialist also avoids the generalized swamping problem because they don't understand the value of objects in terms of their history.

Where does this leave us in thinking about what the truth-loving epistemic consequentialist should say about epistemic value? The theory of epistemic value that sits most comfortably with the truth-loving epistemic consequentialist picture is an instrumental veritist one. That's one according to which (1) all and only true (false) beliefs and accurate (inaccurate) credences have final epistemic value (disvalue), and (2) other things have derivative epistemic value (disvalue) insomuch as they conduce to beliefs and credences with final epistemic value (disvalue). What I take Sylvan's argument to show is that this theory of value doesn't make sense of the kind of epistemic value associated with justified belief, rational belief, or knowledge. That is, it doesn't account for the value of epistemic responsibility notions. But since the truth-loving epistemic consequentialist aims to give an account of epistemic deontic notions, not responsibility notions, it's no threat to the core of the project that the project's account of epistemic value doesn't work for justified belief, rational belief, and knowledge. As we'll discuss more in Chapter 7, it's open to the defender of truth-loving epistemic consequentialism to accept an instrumental veritist account of the value of epistemic deontic notions and add on whatever account of the value of responsibility notions they'd like as an extension of that theory. Personally, I find Sylvan's non-instrumental veritist account of those notions quite compelling (see also Sylvan 2020), but nothing about truth-loving epistemic consequentialism commits us to that.

In the remainder of this chapter, I'll consider two objections to truth-loving epistemic consequentialism that center on its call for the promotion of epistemic goodness, understood in instrumental veritist terms. According to the objection from Grimm (2009), views that call for the promotion of instrumental veritist value erroneously entail that we should spend our time learning trivial truths by, for example, memorizing entries in a phone book or counting blades of grass. In Section 4.2, I'll argue that there are a few peculiar and misleading elements of these purported counterexamples, and once we nail down exactly what's right about them, we see that they don't really show against consequentialism. In the section after that, I'll consider a promotion-based objection from Littlejohn (2018). Littlejohn argues that there is no sense of 'goodness' in which epistemic goodness is plausibly to be promoted. I'll show that Littlejohn's argument fails in a few places, each of which can be exploited to give an account of the kind of goodness that the consequentialist can appeal to. This not only undermines Littlejohn's objection to epistemic consequentialism but also gives the consequentialist a head start in putting together a metanormative theory to accompany their first-order normative epistemic view. What the failures of these objections bring out is that the simple instrumental veritistic theory of value that the truth-loving epistemic consequentialist would most naturally adopt is a fairly minimal and unobjectionable commitment. And unlike what its opponents claim, these promotion-based objections aren't good reasons to abandon the pretheoretically intuitive view.

4.2 On the Promotion of Phone Book Beliefs

Grimm (2009) poses a problem for what he calls "the unrestricted view" of instrumental veritistic value, which he attributes to Lynch (2004). According to that view, *all* true beliefs (and false beliefs) have value (disvalue). If that view is right, he says, then even true beliefs formed by memorizing the phone book are part of what the view counts as epistemically valuable. This seems like a bad result, Grimm thinks, because it potentially leads to the intuitively unpalatable conclusion that we epistemically ought to be pursuing the value of trivial true beliefs. In most cases, it doesn't make sense to sit down and memorize a phone book, and having a true belief about the 323rd entry in the Wichita phone book doesn't seem to be epistemically valuable (unless, of course, you're a phone book editor). So the problem with the unrestricted view, Grimm thinks, is that it incorrectly predicts that all true beliefs, including true beliefs about total trivia, matter. I'll call this the 'value of trivial true beliefs problem.'

"The restricted view," which Grimm attributes to Goldman (1999, 2001) and Alston (2005), gets around the value of trivial true beliefs problem by restricting what the view counts as epistemically valuable to only true beliefs on certain topics of interest, perhaps including only beliefs that are practically valuable. But, as Grimm (2009, p. 249) points out, the restricted view also has a problem. We're able to epistemically evaluate all beliefs, even when they're not about topics of interest. We can evaluate badly formed beliefs as unjustified, irrational, or wrong, even if they're about the 159th digit of π, the 323rd entry in the Wichita phone book, or the exact time President Obama first tried strawberry cream cheese. On the consequentialist picture, beliefs gain these evaluations only in virtue of how well they promote (or fail to promote) final epistemic value. But if the truth or falsity of these beliefs is not itself epistemically valuable (as the restricted view predicts), how can the consequentialist explain our evaluations of these beliefs? Having a true or false belief that's not about a topic of interest need not promote or inhibit having true beliefs about things that are of interest. So if the truth or falsity of these beliefs themselves doesn't matter, it looks like the consequentialist can't account for our evaluations of them.

I agree with Grimm that the best versions of truth-loving epistemic consequentialism should countenance true beliefs about all topics as finally epistemically valuable and countenance false beliefs about all topics as finally epistemically disvaluable. We shouldn't find this conclusion surprising, though, since the original intuitions motivating the view don't come along with the kind of restrictions the restricted view would put on them. James's oft-repeated quote is "Believe truth! Shun error!" not "Believe truth and shun error only about interesting topics!"

But if we accept the unrestricted view, we must face the value of trivial true beliefs problem. That is what I'll tackle now: According to the unrestricted view, all true beliefs have value, even ones about whether there was an even or odd number of blades of grass on the White House lawn the first time Buddy Clinton, Bill Clinton's dog, pooped on it. On Grimm's view, this is "an absurdity" that "only someone really desperate" would accept (2009, p. 257).

Despite saying that, Grimm goes on to argue for a picture of epistemic normativity that accepts the unrestricted value of true belief. What explains why all true beliefs have value on Grimm's picture is importantly different from the explanation given by the consequentialists that he's arguing against, like Lynch (2004). According to those that Grimm takes to be his opponents, at base there's something like individuals' natural curiosity that explains why all true beliefs matter. In contrast, Grimm argues for a social conception of the value of true belief, one on which we each have an obligation to be good sources of information and true belief is seen as a common good. So, whereas his opponents' views suffer from worries about why true beliefs are valuable if their holders don't care about them, Grimm's view explains the value of true beliefs in terms of a broader moral obligation to "help others carry out their projects and concerns" (2009, p. 262).

In order to defend truth-loving epistemic consequentialism, we need not take a stand on what makes true belief valuable and false belief disvaluable. I find Grimm's answer to that question quite plausible (and for a more recent view with a similar flavor, see Goldberg 2018), but I worry that Grimm's view might also lack a compelling response to the value of trivial true beliefs problem. The unrestricted veritist predicts that having a true belief about any topic is epistemically valuable. As I see it, the value of trivial true beliefs problem is that some of these predictions—i.e., the ones about trivial true beliefs—intuitively appear wrong. Grimm's view seems to be motivated by thinking the problem is something else, namely how the consequentialist might *explain* why trivial true beliefs are valuable. Grimm's social conception of the value of true belief might be well poised to explain *why* true beliefs about trivial matters are valuable. But if the objection is that unrestricted consequentialism is false because it entails that some true beliefs are epistemically valuable when they're not, giving an explanation of that (apparently non-existent) value doesn't fully engage with the objection. So I'll turn now to how I think truth-loving epistemic consequentialists should respond to the value of trivial true beliefs problem.

I take it that the most compelling versions of the value of trivial true beliefs problem point to activities like memorizing the phone book and counting blades of grass, and they ask how epistemically worthwhile those activities really are. The truth-loving epistemic consequentialist seems committed to thinking that activities like that are epistemically valuable (instrumentally), since they're a cheap way of producing things of epistemic value (true beliefs). The objector points to that as an incorrect prediction of the view.

One might think there's an easy response for epistemic consequentialists here. On the standard way of formulating epistemic consequentialist views, they aren't views about what actions an agent should perform. The central claim of truth-loving epistemic consequentialism, as we've been discussing it, is about right belief, not right action. So the "easy" response for the truth-loving consequentialist is to hold that the view makes no predictions about what we should do, so it never instructs us to memorize or count anything. But as we discussed in the last chapter, one compelling way to formulate the truth-loving epistemic consequentialist view is as a global consequentialist view. The global consequentialist holds that the consequentialist evaluation schema extends beyond belief to things like dispositions, decision-making procedures, and motivational schema. We left open there whether the view extends to actions as well, but a natural formulation of it would. (This idea is something we'll take up explicitly in Chapter 7.) So it might not actually be so off-base to think that truth-loving epistemic consequentialism, formulated as a global consequentialist view, would make predictions about what actions are epistemically right.

Let's grant to Grimm that the view under consideration applies to actions and directs us to act so as to achieve the greatest balance of true belief to false belief. Even then, the consequentialist should still think the examples aren't very compelling. One reason is that memorizing the phone book and counting blades of grass are highly inefficient ways of getting true beliefs. Anyone who has tried to memorize several digits of π (or even their own car license plate number) will know that humans are particularly bad at memorizing random series of numbers. Even in contexts that are designed to teach humans complex collections of facts (like in STEM teaching), we know that humans are much worse at gleaning information from textbooks and lectures than from active interaction with the topic. (For a survey of 225 related empirical studies, see Freeman et al. 2014.) Sitting down to memorize the phone book is an extreme form of that traditional learning paradigm. If the goal is just to increase the number of true beliefs you have, you'd be much better off taking an active learning class (about phone numbers or anything else). For most folks, even taking a walk around the neighborhood will likely result in more true beliefs than memorizing the phone book, since when we walk around, we naturally and quickly form true beliefs about all kinds of things (e.g., whether it's raining; the locations of cars, bikes, and other pedestrians; the new color of our neighbor's door; whether trash pickup has happened yet; the peculiar bird sound we don't remember hearing before; the ways the trees are rustling; how the air feels on our skin; etc.). For real humans, memorizing the phone book and counting grass are much slower ways of forming true beliefs than many other mundane things we might otherwise do. So even the epistemic consequentialist view that applies to action won't predict that we ought to spend our time doing those things.

Another complicating factor with these examples is that when we consult our intuitions about how an agent should act, like whether someone should spend time memorizing the phone book or counting blades of grass, it's hard to separate out the epistemic considerations from the other considerations, like the moral and practical considerations, that also bear on the action. Life is short, and for most people, it would be practically impermissible (and possibly even morally wrong) for them to count blades of grass or memorize the phone book in light of their other goals, their contingent positioning in society, and their limited life resources. When we consider questions like whether a certain action is epistemically right, we should be worried that our intuitions will be tainted by what we think is morally or practically required, not just by what we epistemically ought to do.

Altogether, the consequentialist should think that the examples about phone book memorizing and blades-of-grass counting don't present obvious problems for their view. Even if truth-loving epistemic consequentialism does apply to actions, these activities would not be efficient ways of producing epistemic value, and our intuitions about these cases are likely to be influenced by our moral and practical judgments.

In fact, when we focus on what the epistemic consequentialist is committed to about trivial true beliefs, the consequentialist view seems to make the right prediction. Consider a minimal pair of agents: One is a normal undergrad with all of the beliefs that come along with being a normal undergrad. The other is an undergrad with all of the same beliefs as the first plus the true belief that 867-5309 is the 323rd phone number in the Wichita phone book (an issue that the first undergrad has no beliefs about). To make sure that moral and practical considerations don't cloud our judgment here, let's stipulate that the difference in their beliefs is of no practical or moral relevance, so the additional belief will never be distracting or helpful to the second undergrad, nor will the belief affect their interests in any other way. If there were a problem of the value of trivial true beliefs for consequentialism, it would be that the epistemic consequentialist incorrectly predicts that the second undergrad is epistemically better off. But this new 'problem' doesn't strike me as a problem at all—it seems like the right result. If we can get new true beliefs or lose false beliefs *literally for free*, then what reason could there be to think that we wouldn't be epistemically better off doing so?

The objector (now surely annoyed by the failure of the first version of their objection) might stomp their foot and point out that if the consequentialist holds that trivial true beliefs are epistemically valuable, then by consequentialist lights, there must be *some* situation in which the agent ought to pursue that value, since rightness is determined by value on this picture. The now-stomping objector will insist that we find and consider such situations so we can assess the plausibility of the consequentialist view.

The objector is right to insist that there are possible situations in which the value of trivial truths makes it such that we *epistemically* ought to pursue them. That said, the consequentialist should insist that we've already replied to any objection made involving them: Such cases will be weird cases about which we should not trust our intuitions, because for agents that are anything like us, pursuing trivial truths is almost never the most efficient way to get the best epistemic outcomes and our intuitions about those cases are likely to be tainted by our intuitions about the agent's practical and moral circumstances.

Could the objector insist that the epistemic consequentialist is committed to there being cases where we should pursue trivial true beliefs *all things considered*? If the objector insists that the epistemic consequentialist is committed to the existence of such cases, they must be assuming something about the connection between what is epistemically right (or 'epistemic ought's) and what is all-things-considered right (or 'all-things-considered ought's). I'll try not to take a stand on how that connection works in this book, but let's consider how that story would naturally go to explore whether the consequentialist is committed to thinking we should, all things considered, pursue trivial true beliefs.

Perhaps the objector is assuming that epistemic rightness should get some kind of weight in a calculus of different kinds of normativity that apply to an agent, including moral, practical, and possibly other kinds of normativity. On this picture, epistemic norms always get some weight in determining what an agent ought to do, all things considered. The objector could then say that on the consequentialist picture, there must be times when the consequentialist predicts that agents ought to count blades of grass, because the weight of the epistemic 'ought' to pursue trivial beliefs will make the difference in the normative calculus. And the objector would probably be right,[3] but only to a certain extent. In adopting this conception of how epistemic 'ought's factor into all-things-considered 'ought's, the consequentialist should think there are *possible* situations in which the prospect of trivial true beliefs influences what the agent should do, all things considered. The consequentialist need not think that those situations are anything like the kinds of situations that real agents ever face. Real agents (the kind we're familiar with) have severe epistemic and practical limitations, and for real agents, moral and practical concerns almost always play a large role in determining what they should do. So if an agent is anything like real agents, the agent's practical and moral obligations are likely to outweigh any epistemic obligation they have to pursue trivial truths. While the consequentialist might be committed to the *possibility* of agents for whom the value of trivial true beliefs means that they ought to memorize the phone book, such agents should strike us as quite alien.

It's also open to the consequentialist to give a different story about how epistemic and all-things-considered 'ought's interact. At one extreme, the epistemic consequentialist could say that what an agent epistemically ought to do never tells us anything about what an agent ought to do all things considered. On this picture, epistemic 'ought's might be like the 'ought's of being a good assassin—even though we can formulate what one ought to do to be a good assassin, those 'ought's don't bear on what we ought to do all things considered. Of course, this view of epistemic 'ought's is highly implausible, since some epistemic reasons do seem to be good all-things-considered reasons for us. But the consequentialist can give an in-between story of how the 'ought's combine. For example, the consequentialist could say that epistemic 'ought's only get factored into the all-things-considered 'ought' when the beliefs in play are of practical importance to the agent. In that way, genuine epistemic normativity (the kind that influences what an agent ought to do all things considered) would become subsidiary to practical normativity. On neither of these pictures does it follow that the truth-loving epistemic consequentialist is committed to

[3] Actually, it doesn't strictly speaking follow, since one could think that as a matter of necessity, some countervailing moral or practical 'ought's apply to agents anytime an epistemic 'ought' enjoins the agent to pursue a trivial truth. This view strikes me as highly implausible, though, so I don't consider it here.

thinking agents all things considered ought to pursue the value of trivial true beliefs, even though the proponent of that view will still hold that those true beliefs would be epistemically finally valuable, were the agent to have them.

To sum up, we started with the objector claiming that consequentialists are problematically committed to thinking that agents should pursue trivial true beliefs by doing things like memorizing the phone book and counting blades of grass. We saw that this doesn't follow on the truth-loving epistemic consequentialist view, because if the view does apply to action, there are much more efficient ways to get true beliefs. Moreover, as we saw, when we consider these potentially problematic cases, it's hard to separate out the moral and practical aspects of the case from the epistemic ones. So to really figure out whether truth-loving epistemic consequentialists make wrong predictions about what's epistemically valuable, we should compare cases of agents who differ only in whether they have true beliefs (like the two undergrads discussed above). When we do that, we see that agents who have more true beliefs are epistemically better off, which only vindicates the veritistic axiology. The objector might insist that the consequentialist is committed to there being possible situations in which we ought, all things considered, to pursue trivial true beliefs, and the consequentialist can grant that's true in some extreme sense of 'possible.' But agents in those situations would be ones who literally could not be doing better things (epistemically or otherwise) with their time, and agents like that are so dramatically different from limited agents like us that we shouldn't be so worried if the objector's intuitions about those cases don't match the predictions of the theory. That's why truth-loving epistemic consequentialists shouldn't be worried about the problem of trivial true beliefs.

4.3 Littlejohn's Promotion-Based Objection

Littlejohn (2018) has a different worry about whether epistemic goodness is to be promoted in the way the consequentialist claims. Littlejohn considers a number of senses of 'good' in which the consequentialist might hold that epistemic rightness is about promoting the good. For each sense, Littlejohn argues that the consequentialist's claim that epistemic goodness is to be promoted is either implausible or nonsensical when 'good' is understood in that sense.[4] For one sense of 'good,' I agree with Littlejohn that the consequentialist should not hang their hat on true belief *only* being good in that sense. I'll discuss that sense first. I'll then turn to the next two senses, where I disagree with Littlejohn and think there are plausible consequentialist views that use those senses. After rejecting Littlejohn's arguments about those two senses, I introduce another option for the consequentialist that combines two of the senses of 'good.' What I'll show is that there are options open to epistemic consequentialists for how they might understand goodness, which undermines Littlejohn's objection.

4.3.1 Is True Belief Good qua Belief?

If we follow Wedgwood (2002) or Shah (2003), we might think that a belief being true means that the belief satisfies a norm internal to the idea of belief, and true beliefs are good in that sense. In this sense of 'good,' a belief counts as good when it meets the standards of the kind of thing it is. A good (in this sense) toaster, for example, might be one that toasts bread evenly and without burning.

As Littlejohn argues, it doesn't seem like treating true belief as only good in this sense will work for the consequentialist. The problem is that if the only kind of goodness in play is one internal to belief, then we wouldn't have a story about why we should produce more good beliefs. Littlejohn (2018, p. 40) makes this point via the toaster analogy: "If two toasters are good toasters and only one toaster is needed to toast things, the state of affairs that contains two does not seem better than the state of affairs that includes just one. ... If something is good only in the sense that it is a good instance of a

[4] Littlejohn actually first argues that if we're going to be consequentialists, we should be gnostic consequentialists—i.e., consequentialists who value knowledge rather than true belief. Littlejohn then argues against gnostic consequentialism by cases. As Littlejohn himself notes, the second part of the argument can be used directly against veritistic consequentialism (if it works), without gnostic consequentialism as a middleman. Here I'll focus on that version of the argument.

One reason for that is that a key step in Littlejohn's argument for gnostic consequentialism over veritistic consequentialism strikes me as begging the question. Littlejohn says, "There's nothing good about the true beliefs that don't track reality, so there must be more to the fundamental epistemic good than mere accuracy." But true beliefs about oncoming cars and hot teapots prevent me from getting run over and burned, regardless of whether they track the truth. So Littlejohn's claim is best understood as a claim about epistemic goodness. Understood that way, the claim is a straightforward denial of veritism, not an argument against it.

For ease of exposition, I'll consider the proposals in a different order than Littlejohn does. I also do not consider what Littlejohn calls the 'normatively good' sense, since in that sense of 'good,' 'good' is used to mean something like 'ought to be done,' and it's clear that the consequentialist does not mean true belief is good in that sense (just as Littlejohn argues).

kind, it needn't call for promotion." The point is that if the consequentialist says that true beliefs are only good in this internal sense, they cannot explain why we ought to promote there being more true beliefs. I agree with Littlejohn that the consequentialist should not say that true belief is only good in this sense. But, as I'll explore more below, it's open to the consequentialist to argue that beliefs that are good by their own internal standards are also good in some other sense. That could explain why we ought to promote good belief. To do that, we'll need a second sense of 'good' in which good-by-internal-standards beliefs are good. So let's consider Littlejohn's other senses of 'good.'

4.3.2 Is True Belief Good for the Believer?

Having true beliefs is often good for believers, since true beliefs allow us to cross streets without getting hit by cars. This is the second sense of 'good.' It's one in which true belief is seen as *good for* the holder of the belief.

Littlejohn thinks there are two problems for consequentialists who hold that true belief is good for the believer. According to Littlejohn, the bigger problem is that on the consequentialist picture, the rightness of a belief is determined by the total amount of goodness that would be obtained by holding that belief, which means that a belief might be right even though the belief itself doesn't positively contribute to the value of the outcome. That is, it's possible, on the consequentialist account, that some belief can be right despite it being false, since it's possible that holding a false belief can promote the best outcome in terms of achieving the best balance of true and false beliefs. If you read the last two chapters, you'll recognize this as a restatement of the trade-off objections discussed there. But as we saw there, global sophisticated epistemic consequentialist views of right belief can avoid trade-off objections, so the 'bigger' problem Littlejohn sees for thinking of epistemic goodness as good for the believer isn't really a problem.

But, according to Littlejohn (2018, p. 37), there's another problem for consequentialists who say that true belief is good in the sense that it's good for the believer. The second problem is that simply showing that something is good for some agent doesn't mean it is a value that ultimately ought to be promoted. Or as he puts it, the consequentialist would still need a story about why there is any "entailment between claims about the goodness property and a subject's interests" (2018, p. 37). It might promote a subject's epistemic interests to have true beliefs about their likelihood of getting a job, even though it might not be overall good for them to do so (if, for example, the chance that they get the job is low and that would upset them). And it might be good for the job applicant to get the job, but it doesn't follow that it's good that the applicant get the job (if, for example, there are more-qualified applicants).

I agree with Littlejohn that if the consequentialist wants to say that true belief is good for the believer, they must provide some additional story about why that means it's also just plain good. But it's worth pointing out that it's not a particular problem for the epistemic consequentialist to give such a story. Thinking that something being good for agents makes it, in many cases, something to be promoted is a common commitment. This kind of commitment is used in motivating most consequentialist views, not just in epistemology but in ethics too. Consider a generic agent-neutral ethical consequentialist view, which might hold that an action is right when it promotes the greatest overall amount of pleasure, (non-evil) desire satisfaction, or flourishing (perhaps understood in terms of many, possibly incomparable, values). I take it that a motivating idea behind views like this is that what is ultimately good is to be understood partially in terms of what is good *for agents*, and those views take pleasure, desire satisfaction, or flourishing (or whatever) to be what is good for agents. If that's right, then epistemic consequentialists should follow their ethical conspecifics and make the analogous claim about epistemic value: Having true beliefs is good for the agent, and because it's good for the agent (perhaps in the right kind of way), it is just plain good.

In fact, there is a long tradition of epistemic theorists who attempt to ground epistemic norms in the desires of agents in just this way. For example, Stich (1990) and Kornblith (1993) both give accounts of epistemic norms where the source of the norms is in satisfying our desires. More recently, Nolfi (2019) argues for a consequentialist account of epistemic norms where epistemic norms apply to us because of the function beliefs have for us as practically acting agents. On this picture, one's beliefs should be epistemically rational because being that way helps promote the agent's practical ends. Like their ethical cousins, these views will all take certain things being good for a believer to entail that they are also just plain good, in the sense that they ought to be promoted.

Littlejohn's challenge to the epistemic consequentialist at this point in the dialectic is not one about particular commitments or implications of the consequentialist view about right belief. The challenge here is about *why* epistemic consequentialism would be true, if goodness is understood as goodness for the agent. Littlejohn is inviting the reader to think that consequentialists don't give a story about why epistemic goodness being good in the sense that it's good for the agent would mean that the goodness ought to be promoted. But folks like Stitch, Kornblith, and Nolfi aim to do exactly this, and giving a story like this is a foundational task faced by many views of right action. So, I agree with Littlejohn that if the consequentialist wants to understand epistemic goodness in this way, they'll need a story about why it should be promoted, but I see little reason to be suspicious of the possibility of coming up with such a view.

4.3.3 Is True Belief Just Plain Good?

To make sense of the proposal from the last section that true belief being good for an agent (perhaps in the right kind of way) means that it's just plain good or ultimately good, we have to think that there is just plain goodness or ultimate goodness. This is the last sense of 'good' that Littlejohn considers.

Littlejohn's objection to the claim that epistemic goodness is just plain goodness is a reformulation of an objection from Geach (1956) and Thomson (1997, 2008) to understanding ethical consequentialism in terms of plain goodness.[5] Geach's and Thomson's arguments depend on the semantic claim that 'good' only acts like an attributive adjective, never a predicative adjective, in our talk and thought. Borrowing an example from Byrne (2016), 'acidic' is a paradigmatic predicative adjective, since things can be just plain acidic, like lemon juice. On the other hand, 'big' looks like a purely attributive adjective, since nothing can be just plain big; things can be big lemons, big cars, big horses, or big buildings, but they can't just be big *simpliciter*. Geach's and Thomson's idea is that 'good' always acts like 'big' and never like 'acidic,' and that should make us think that there is no property of just plain goodness. Why do Geach and Thomson think 'good' only functions attributively? They think that because, as they claim, we can't infer from 'x is a good F' and 'x is a G' that 'x is a good G.' This shows, they

[5] Littlejohn actually gives two arguments about this sense of 'good.' The first is another repeat of the trade-off worry, so I'll skip discussing it again.

claim, that when something is good, it must be good relative to something, not just plain good.

If this objection succeeds, it shows against all forms of consequentialism, not just epistemic consequentialism. Recently, though, Byrne (2016) has argued that Geach's and Thomson's arguments (and recent more sophisticated versions of that kind of argument) are unsound. What Byrne points out is that for some gradable adjectives like 'flat,' the adjective will fail Geach's and Thompson's test for a predicative adjective (as well as recent sophisticated reformulations of it) but still have a predicative reading. As Byrne explains, it doesn't follow from something being a flat road and it being a man-made object that it is a flat man-made object. That said, because there is an absolute endpoint for the gradability of 'flat,' we can still make sense of something being absolutely flat or just plain flat—i.e., having absolutely no bumps. The point generalizes to all gradable adjectives whose scales have endpoints. For all Geach, Thomson, and their followers say, 'good' might work similarly.

I find Byrne's argument convincing, but I also wonder how worried we should have been about Geach's and Thomson's objection in the first place. I take it that at the heart of the consequentialist's proposal is the idea that there is some property such that more things having that property is better, all things considered. Even if Geach's and Thomson's arguments succeed, all they end up showing is that the English word 'good' (or concept GOOD) doesn't pick out that property. As the sentence before the last one shows, though, we have ways of picking out that property without using that word (or concept). We also have ways of doing it in Philosophers' English—e.g., describing things as 'ultimately valuable,' 'good in themselves,' 'intrinsically valuable,' 'good for their own sake,' 'objectively valuable,' and 'fundamentally valuable.' Of course, some of these terms have been used by various philosophers in technically circumscribed ways that differ from how the consequentialist will want to use them. But philosophers' ability to do just that should help us see the weakness of the original objection. If the natural-language English word 'good' doesn't work, we can still talk about the kind of goodness the consequentialist has in mind either by using one of these other terms or by defining a technical usage of 'good.' So, contra Littlejohn, we shouldn't reject consequentialism (epistemic or otherwise) on the basis that we can't talk or think about the plain goodness the consequentialist claims to be talking about.

4.3.4 Expanding the Roadmap to Understanding Goodness

Littlejohn saw his argument as showing that any way the consequentialist might go in terms of understanding epistemic goodness as something to be promoted, there is a dead end. As I argued above, I don't think Littlejohn has given us sufficiently compelling reasons to reject all of the routes. Instead of a list of dead ends, we should see Littlejohn as giving a roadmap of potential consequentialist views. Before closing, I'll give a sketch of another possible route.

Above, I recounted and agreed with Littlejohn's argument that consequentialists shouldn't see true belief as *only* good qua belief. Doing that would leave the consequentialist with an incomplete story: Something being good for the type of thing it is doesn't mean that it is ultimately good in a sense that producing more of it is better. What would the consequentialist need in order to complete the story? Recall that what makes the view consequentialist is that it says that we should understand what we epistemically ought to believe in terms of what conduces to epistemic goodness. It's epistemic goodness, not all-things-considered goodness, that matters, on this view. So, if we grant that true belief is good qua belief, to complete the story about why true belief ought to be promoted, the consequentialist needs to convince us that more good belief is epistemically better—i.e., that increasing the amount of good belief results in epistemically better situations. I'll argue that convincing us of that should be easy.

Recall the pair of undergraduates from above. In the original example, we compared two undergrads who differed only in that one of them had one more true belief, and we stipulated that the difference in their beliefs was of no practical or moral relevance. What we concluded was that the undergraduate with the additional true belief is (at least marginally) *epistemically* better off. Any reason to think otherwise is likely tainted by our (correct) intuition that for real agents, getting more true beliefs usually has some practical, moral, or other epistemic costs. If we assume the new true belief is literally completely free, then how could someone deny that having it is epistemically better?

To flesh out the general view being proposed here (abstracting away from the particular commitments of truth-loving consequentialism), let's look at an even less committal version of the example. The consequentialist who wants to get epistemic value from the internal standards of belief only needs to hold that having more *good* beliefs is epistemically better. So consider a new example involving two graduate students: They are identical except that one has one more *good* belief than the other. Assuming that there's literally no other difference between the two graduate students, how could the second not be epistemically better than the first? To deny that is to deny that having more good beliefs is epistemically better, which to my ear sounds close to a contradiction.

So the new proposal goes like this: Start with the claim that having more good beliefs is always epistemically better, ceteris paribus. Then we understand what makes a belief good in terms of the standards internal to belief. Suppose we follow Wedgwood (2002) or Shah (2003) and think true belief is good belief (though note that the general strategy I'm sketching here is compatible with many ways of fleshing out the standards internal to belief). Those two claims together get us that true belief is good in a way that epistemically ought to be promoted. This is the conclusion that the epistemic consequentialist needs.

The strategy being proposed here differs from the kind of view gestured at in Section 4.3.2 (though particular versions of the two views may be compatible with each other). In Section 4.3.2, I pointed to views like the one given by Nolfi (2019) that say that certain kinds of beliefs are all-things-considered good for the believer, and in virtue of that, they are all-things-considered good. The alternative view I'm introducing here says that good beliefs are epistemically good and understands good beliefs in terms of the standards internal to belief. This new view avoids having to commit to an account of how epistemic normativity ties into all-things-considered normativity, which the epistemic consequentialist can do because the theory is a theory of epistemic rightness (not all-things-considered rightness).

I've only given a sketch of the proposal here, and doing that was intentional. For one, fully fleshing out what goodness consists in is a project that would require its own book. But also, recall the nature of Littlejohn's worry about the consequentialist's theory of value. Unlike the trade-off objections and the value of trivial true beliefs problem, Littlejohn isn't accusing the consequentialist of making an incorrect prediction. Littlejohn's worry is a metanormative one—it's about whether there is, at a deeper metaphysical level, the kind of epistemic goodness that consequentialists talk about. Littlejohn thinks there's no plausible metanormative account of that kind of epistemic goodness. But as long as we think there's *some* way to make sense of epistemic goodness as a kind of goodness that's to be promoted, we can use the notion in first-order epistemic theorizing; we need not have a fully fleshed-out metanormative view to do that. The main aim of this book is to defend truth-loving epistemic consequentialism as a complete theory of epistemic rightness, so doing so doesn't require taking a stand on what exactly is the metanormative sense in which epistemic goodness is to be promoted. I hope to have convinced you that there are several plausible metanormative views of epistemic goodness that might fit with this first-order view. If I have, that should be sufficient to defuse Littlejohn's concerns about the project.

4.4 Promoting Epistemic Consequentialism

This chapter started with the hypothesis that when it comes to the kind of epistemic value associated with epistemic rightness, truth-loving epistemic consequentialists can (1) treat all and only true (false) beliefs and (in)accurate credences as finally epistemically (dis)valuable and (2) understand the derivative value of epistemically right beliefs, dispositions, etc. instrumentally in terms of producing that final value. The objections considered in the last two sections pushed against truth-loving epistemic consequentialism on the basis that it treats getting true beliefs (and losing more false beliefs) as something to be pursued. There are two distinct aspects of the view that these objections pushed on. First, there is the veritistic aspect of the view, which tells us that final epistemic value consists in true belief and the lack of false belief. Second, there is the consequentialist aspect of the view that says that epistemic value is to be promoted, in the sense that getting more of it is a good thing. As Sylvan (2020) shows, it's possible to go in for the veritist aspect without also going in for the promotion aspect.

What the failure of the objections in the last two sections shows is that these two aspects of the view are pretty minimal and unobjectionable. The central motivating idea of this project is that what we should believe is what helps us get a more accurate picture of the world. The most natural way to make sense of that is by subscribing to a veritistic value theory (and so I encourage the reader to return to the motivation for that in Chapter 2 if they find themselves uncomfortable with that aspect of the view). Along with the veritistic theory of value, the view says that the kind of epistemic value associated with right belief is a kind of thing that is to be promoted. All this means is that we see getting free good beliefs as epistemically good.

Unlike free good toasters, which take up space, use electricity, and might not be wanted, free good beliefs (even ones about the average elevation of bedrooms in Calgary or the airspeed velocity of unladen European swallows) only serve to give us a better picture of the world. How could that not be epistemically good?

5

Consequentialism and Epistemic Utility Theory

The central idea behind truth-loving epistemic consequentialism is that what we should believe is what helps us get a more accurate picture of the world. There's a prominent project in formal epistemology that has the same starting place, called 'epistemic utility theory' or 'accuracy-first epistemology' (see, e.g., Joyce 1998, 2009; Greaves and Wallace 2006; Leitgeb and Pettigrew 2010b; and Pettigrew 2016). Advocates of epistemic utility theory employ a degreed notion of belief ('credences') and model those degreed beliefs with real numbers.[1] Work in epistemic utility theory then uses the tools of rational decision theory (most prominently including dominance arguments and expected utility arguments) to try to derive or explain norms of epistemic rationality from the aim of having accurate credences. Among other things, epistemic utility arguments have been used to defend *probabilism*, the claim that rational sets of credences must be modelable by probability functions (Joyce 1998, 2009), and *conditionalization*, the claim that rational updating on evidence must happen by conditionalizing a prior probability function on new evidence (Greaves and Wallace 2006, Leitgeb and Pettigrew 2010b).

There are two objections to epistemic utility theory in the literature that focus on its ability to derive or explain norms of epistemic rationality from the accuracy aim. Allan Gibbard (2007) argues that aiming at the truth is insufficient to generate a specific requirement of epistemic rationality, namely that rational agents view their own credence function as the one that is prospectively best at getting at the truth. Separately, Caie (2013), Greaves (2013), and Carr (2017) argue that, despite what the theorists claim, epistemic utility theorists can't use the standard tools of decision theory

[1] In this literature, a degree of belief is typically thought of as either the strength of the agent's belief in the proposition or the agent's estimation of the truth-value of the proposition. How exactly it's best to think of degreed belief is a hot-button issue for many formal epistemologists. Nothing I say here will depend on any particular way of thinking about it.

Right Belief and True Belief. Daniel J. Singer, Oxford University Press. © Oxford University Press 2023.
DOI: 10.1093/oso/9780197660386.003.0006

(i.e., the standard dominance and expected utility theory arguments) to justify their conclusions. If these objectors are right, this would undermine the epistemic utility theory's goal of using those tools to extract epistemic norms from the accuracy aim.

Like epistemic utility theory, truth-loving epistemic consequentialism also tries to ground epistemic norms in the search for truth. In this chapter, I'll ask whether either of the worries for epistemic utility theory might also be worries for truth-loving epistemic consequentialism. In Section 5.1, I reconstruct Gibbard's objection. In Section 5.2, I argue (1) that Gibbard's argument doesn't apply to truth-loving epistemic consequentialism because the rule Gibbard focuses on isn't a norm of epistemic rightness and (2) that even if it were a norm of epistemic rightness, truth-loving epistemic consequentialists could give an explanation of that norm. In Section 5.3, I reconstruct Carr's worries about the tools epistemic utility theorists try to use to support their conclusions. In Section 5.4, I argue that Carr's worries (along with the similar worries from Caie and Greaves) don't apply to truth-loving epistemic consequentialism. This brings out an interesting contrast between the two truth-aimed theories of epistemic norms. As I'll argue, truth-loving epistemic consequentialists should disagree with epistemic utility theorists about how to conceptualize and measure veritistic epistemic value. I spell this out in Section 5.5. In the last section, I focus on the disagreement between the two views and argue that despite the apparent tension between them, there's a natural way to accept both.

Epistemic utility theorists' arguments are typically presented as arguments about the requirements of epistemic rationality. I take it that in formulating their arguments this way, the view's proponents had in mind a generic notion of what epistemic norms sanction, not that they were aiming to understand a specific epistemic responsibility notion. When I reconstruct the arguments below, I'll formulate them in terms of epistemic rationality or a generic notion of epistemic permission. When I consider whether the objections might apply to truth-loving epistemic consequentialism, I'll put the arguments in epistemic rightness terms. I'll argue that neither of the objections puts pressure on the truth-loving epistemic consequentialist picture, even when put in rightness terms. In some places, I'll try to show that truth-loving epistemic consequentialism isn't subject to the objection even if epistemic utility theory is (thereby leaving it open whether the objection works against epistemic utility theory), but in other places, I'll argue directly against the objection (effectively defending both truth-loving epistemic consequentialism and epistemic utility theory). So some of what I say below should be interesting to the epistemic utility theorist independently of how plausible they find truth-loving epistemic consequentialism.

Because the literature I'm responding to uses a degreed notion of belief, in most of this chapter I'll do the same. That said, the content of the arguments and my responses will make sense regardless of whether you go in for a degreed notion of belief. And in some places below, I'll switch to using the categorical notion when doing so helps to convey the idea more easily. With those clarifications out of the way, let's now turn to Gibbard's argument.

5.1 Aiming at Truth in Our Beliefs and Credences

In "Rational Credence and the Value of Truth," Allan Gibbard (2007) argues that epistemic norms cannot be explained just by us aiming at the truth. Instead, he claims that the norms are more plausibly explained by us aiming at practical ends. Gibbard's argument can be broken down into two parts. He first argues that epistemic norms cannot be fully understood just in terms of the pursuit of truth because he thinks exhibiting epistemic rationality requires a kind of epistemic immodesty that is not guaranteed simply by valuing true belief and the lack of false belief. Gibbard then argues that the aspect of epistemic rationality that cannot be explained by the pursuit of truth can be explained in terms of a practical aim. Being epistemically rational, Gibbard concludes, should be understood not in terms of the value of true belief but instead in terms of potential guidance value. In this section, I'll spell out how each of the two parts of the argument works.

5.1.1 Gibbard's Argument Part 1: Epistemic Rationality and the Value of Truth

Gibbard's starting place is the idiom that "belief aims at the truth." He takes this to be mostly metaphorical: "Belief ... can't aim literally; it's we who aim," Gibbard (2007, p. 143) tells us. Gibbard takes this to motivate thinking that rational believers must be representable as aiming for truth in their beliefs. Gibbard calls this the 'minimal test for epistemic rationality':

MINIMAL TEST FOR EPISTEMIC RATIONALITY "When a person forms her credences with epistemic rationality, it is as if she were choosing her credences voluntarily, rationally aiming, in light of her credences, at truth in those very credences" (2007, p. 147).

To think of a person as epistemically rational, Gibbard is saying, we must think of that person as pursuing accurate credences by their own lights.

The claim of the first part of Gibbard's argument is that epistemic rationality cannot be understood solely as resulting from an agent purely *valuing* the truth in their beliefs. This is because an agent valuing the truth in her beliefs can't guarantee that she'll pass the MINIMAL TEST FOR EPISTEMIC RATIONALITY, Gibbard argues. Here's how that argument goes:

An agent purely values the truth in her beliefs when the agent prefers her beliefs to be as accurate as possible—that is, when the agent's utility function orders possible situations where she has credences in terms of how accurate they are in that situation. Gibbard has us consider an example of a simple agent who only has beliefs about one proposition, that modern Europeans descended at least in part from the Neanderthals, *S*: Let $g_1(x)$ be how much utility the agent assigns to having credence x in S if S is true, and let $g_0(x)$ be how much utility the agent assigns to having credence x in S if S is false. Then, according to Gibbard, valuing the truth in one's beliefs, consists in satisfying CONDITION T:

CONDITION T Function $g_1(x)$ increases strictly monotonically with x, and function $g_0(x)$ decreases strictly monotonically with x.

CONDITION T tells us that an agent purely values the truth when she prefers having higher credences in S if S is true and she prefers having lower credences in S if S is false (Gibbard 2007, pp. 148–149).

Can valuing the truth, in this sense (i.e., satisfying CONDITION T), guarantee that an agent is epistemically rational? Gibbard doesn't think so. Gibbard thinks that in order to pass the MINIMAL TEST FOR EPISTEMIC RATIONALITY, agents must also be representable as having utility functions that are credence-eliciting:

CREDENCE-ELICITING A utility function is *credence-eliciting* when, in light of some credences *Cr*, the agent's expected utility of adopting

> *Cr* is higher than the expected utility of adopting any other credence function.[2]

That is, Gibbard thinks that, in light of the information they have, epistemically rational agents must prefer to have the credences that they already have.[3]

Gibbard thinks that the requirement that rational agents have a credence-eliciting utility function is generated by the MINIMAL TEST FOR EPISTEMIC RATIONALITY. Here's why: Suppose (for reductio) that there were an ideally epistemically rational agent who, in light of the information she has, has a credence of .5 in *S*, and suppose that, in light of the information she has, the agent prefers, as part of her concern for truth, to have a credence of .7 in *S*. Then the agent can rationally advance her quest for the truth by changing her .5 credence to .7. So, the agent does not view her credences as optimal in the pursuit of her goal of having accurate credences. According to the MINIMAL TEST FOR EPISTEMIC RATIONALITY, for the agent to be epistemically rational, it must be as if she rationally chooses her credences with the goal of maximizing the accuracy of those credences. But our agent is not like that. So, epistemically rational agents must have credence-eliciting utility functions, Gibbard concludes.

Gibbard then points out that there are ways to purely value the truth without having a credence-eliciting utility function. If that's right, it follows by the argument above that there are ways to purely value the truth without satisfying the MINIMAL TEST FOR EPISTEMIC RATIONALITY. To show this, Gibbard shows there are utility functions that satisfy CONDITION T but are not credence-eliciting. The linear score is an example: $g_1(x) = x$ and $g_0(x) = 1-x$ (this score is just a linear measure of how far off the credence is from the truth). If an agent adopts this linear score as her utility function, then she'll satisfy CONDITION T because $g_1(x)$ increases strictly monotonically with x and $g_0(x)$ decreases strictly monotonically with x. So, this agent purely values the truth. But unless her credence is 0, .5, or 1, she'll prefer to have a

[2] Using more standard terminology, we might say that when the utility function views the credences as *at least as good* as any other, then the utility function is *proper*. If a utility function views the credences as strictly the best, then it is strictly proper. By "credence-eliciting," Gibbard means strictly proper. See his footnote 11 on p. 152.

[3] Following Gibbard, I'm assuming that agents' desires and values are representable by a utility function from possible states of the world to how much the agent desires or values that state. Then, following Ramsey (1926), I'm assuming (again with Gibbard) that what agents ought to decide to do is what maximizes their expected utility relative to their credences and utility assignments.

credence that she doesn't have. If her credence is > .5, then she'll view having credence 1 as maximizing her payoff in terms of believing the truth, and if her credence is < .5, she'll view credence 0 as maximizing that payoff. If the agent is purely concerned with the truth, then by her own lights, she can rationally advance that concern my changing her non-extremal credence to an extremal one. But this kind of move would be "epistemically rash" (and a violation of the MINIMAL TEST FOR EPISTEMIC RATIONALITY), so Gibbard concludes that a "pure concern with truth for its own sake [cannot] explain epistemic rationality" (2007, p. 159).

5.1.2 Gibbard's Argument Part 2: Epistemic Rationality as Maximizing Guidance Value

In the first part of the argument, Gibbard argues that epistemic rationality cannot be made sense of in terms of a pure concern for truth. The reason is that an agent can prefer accuracy in her credences without thereby satisfying all of the requirements of epistemic rationality—in particular, without having a credence-eliciting utility function. In the second part of the argument, Gibbard argues that epistemic rationality can more plausibly be made sense of in terms of aiming at prospective guidance value. Requiring an agent to maximize the expected practical payoffs of their beliefs, unlike requiring that they value the truth in their beliefs, does mean that their utility function will be credence-eliciting.

To see why Gibbard thinks this, start by noticing that an agent's utility function being credence-eliciting is a property of the functions $g_1(x)$ (how much utility the agent assigns to having credence x in S when S is true) and $g_0(x)$ (how much utility the agent assigns to having credence x in S when S is false). What makes a pair of these functions credence-eliciting is that the expected utility, when calculated from the perspective of the agent, of having the credence that the agent actually has is higher than the expected utility of having any other credence. We can specify that relationship formally (Gibbard 2007, pp. 152–153), but let's skip that and instead just look at an example: If we let $g_1(x) = -(1-x)^2$ and $g_0(x) = -x^2$, we get the Brier score, a well-studied credence-eliciting utility function. Using this utility function, we can calculate the utility of having some credence c in S is $-(1-x)^2c + -x^2(1-c)$. This quantity is maximized when $x = c$, so if the agent's credence is c and she uses this pair of utility functions to calculate the expected accuracy of other possible credences she could have, she'll view c, the credence she actually has, as maximizing her expected accuracy.

What Gibbard argues is that the collection of pairs of utility functions $g_1(x)$ and $g_0(x)$ that stand in the special relation just mentioned (and are thereby credence-eliciting) is exactly the same as the collection of pairs of utility functions such that if an agent has those utility functions, she views her own credences as maximizing expected guidance value. From this, Gibbard concludes that since epistemic rationality requires agents to be as if they have credence-eliciting utility functions, and this is exactly what is guaranteed by the agent trying to maximize the expected *guidance* value of their credences, we should think that it is maximizing of expected guidance value that best explains epistemic rationality.

Gibbard offers an example of a person trying to avoid a tiger that is behind one of two doors, either the left or the right, one of which he must open. If the tiger is in fact behind the right door, then choosing the right door to open has a utility of -100, let's say, and similarly for the left door. If the tiger is behind the right door, we'll say that the 'guidance value' of the policy to open the right door is -100.[4] Suppose further that the agent has a credence of .4 that the tiger is behind the right door. Then the *actual* guidance value of his credence is also -100. That is, if the agent follows through on the actions that maximize his expected utility, then he'll get -100 utility (since he'll open the door on the right, where the tiger is). In this case, the agent cannot tell that this is the actual guidance value of his credence, since he doesn't know the location of the tiger. (And in general, the actual guidance value of a set of credences will depend on factors not accessible to the agent.) But we can ask what the agent can *expect* the guidance value of his credences to be. In this case, from the agent's perspective, it appears that the guidance value of opening the right door is -40, because he has a .6 credence that the -100 value possibility is on the left side. This is what Gibbard calls the "*prospective* guidance value" of the credence (2007, p. 156).

[4] Gibbard does not give a precise characterization of what constitutes guidance value, but he does give some prototypes: In discussing the possible valuable aspects of beliefs, he says, "Beliefs can be comforting. They can be empowering. They can link one to others in a fellowship of conviction. I'll label all the kinds of value that credences can have apart from their guidance value as *side value*" (2007, p. 155). Guidance value, we might try saying, is the value a belief or policy has in helping us promote our goals, separate from any goals we might have about the belief itself.

Now recall our agent who is trying to pick the most accurate credence she can for S. Gibbard proposes that we can offer her a series of bets $\mathfrak{G}_\beta$ for $0 < \beta < 1$ on whether S such that the payoff of bet G_β is $\overline{\beta} : \beta$. If an agent has a credence x in S, then she'll view all and only the bets G_β such that $\beta > x$ as better than fair (and she'll accept them using standard decision theory). Now ask what credences the agent would choose to have if she were aiming to maximize the expected guidance value of her credences on this series of bets. As long as she has consistent credences, she should expect she can do no better than by acting on the credences she actually has, since having any other credence would have her accept some bets she now takes to be unfair or reject some she now takes to be better than fair. So, from her perspective, the agent aiming to maximize the guidance value of her credences can justify her actual credences, regardless of what those are. That is, an agent aiming to maximize the prospective guidance value of her credences will sanction her own credences as best.

Gibbard extends this basic idea by appeal to a formal result from Schervish (1989). Here is Gibbard's restatement of the result:

> Smooth functions g_1 and g_0 are credence-eliciting if and only if for some possible continuum of bet offers and a policy of accepting any bet offer G_γ exactly when $\gamma < x$, $g_1(x)$ gives the expected payoff of the policy given S, and $g_0(x)$ gives the expected payoff of the policy given $\overline{S}$.[5]

The series of bets $\mathfrak{G}_\beta$ that Gibbard gives is a series that satisfies the right-hand side of this biconditional, so we can conclude that the utility functions g_1 and g_0 of the agent are credence-eliciting.

What Gibbard shows is that the agent having a credence-eliciting utility function, although it is not demanded by having a pure concern for truth, is demanded by the agent maximizing the expected guidance value of their credence on that series of bets. Since epistemic rationality requires being as if one has a credence-eliciting utility function, Gibbard claims, a pure concern for truth doesn't seem well suited to explain epistemic rationality (that's part one of the argument), but a concern for maximizing the expected guidance value of one's credences can explain it (that's part two). So, unless a better epistemic explanation can be had, Gibbard thinks, we must rely on the only available explanation of why agents must be representable as

[5] This is Gibbard's (2007, p. 157) restatement of a formal result gestured at by Schervish (1989, p. 1869). It ignores some minor formal issues that will be irrelevant to the discussion here.

having credence-eliciting utility functions (and hence why they should be epistemically rational), namely the practical one.

5.2 Immodesty and Truth-Based Approaches to Epistemic Normativity

According to the truth-loving epistemic consequentialist, epistemic norms about right belief can be explained in terms of conduciveness to true belief and the lack of false belief. Gibbard's argument purports to show that not all epistemic norms can be explained this way. His argument puts pressure on truth-loving epistemic consequentialism only if it is construed as being about epistemic rightness, rather than rationality. So here, I'll talk as though Gibbard's argument was about epistemic rightness. (That simply amounts to replacing all mentions of 'rationality' above with 'rightness.')

In this section, I'll argue that the truth-loving epistemic consequentialist isn't subject to any version of Gibbard's objection. I'll do this in two steps. I'll first show that if Gibbard's proposed practical explanation of the central epistemic norm works, the truth-loving epistemic consequentialist has an equally compelling purely epistemic (purely 'truthy') explanation of the same norm. I'll do that by showing how Gibbard's proposed practical explanation of the norm can be used as a model to construct an equally plausible epistemic explanation. But, as I'll argue after that, the truth-loving epistemic consequentialist shouldn't endorse that explanation, because truth-loving epistemic consequentialists should deny that the central norm Gibbard considers is one that agents really epistemically ought to follow. What Gibbard describes as the "minimal test for epistemic rationality" (construed as being about epistemic rightness, not rationality) isn't a standard that good epistemic agents should meet, since subjectively aiming at the truth is often not the best way to get to the truth. This gives the truth-loving epistemic consequentialist two independent lines of argument that undermine Gibbard's objection as it might be applied to truth-loving explanations of epistemic deontic norms.

5.2.1 Explaining Immodesty Without the Practical

Gibbard tells us that we can't make sense of epistemic normativity in terms of the aim of truth because epistemic normativity requires agents to pass the MINIMAL TEST FOR EPISTEMIC RATIONALITY, which I repeat here:

> MINIMAL TEST FOR EPISTEMIC RATIONALITY "When a person forms her credences with epistemic rationality, it is as if she were choosing her credences voluntarily, rationally aiming, in light of her credences, at truth in those very credences" (2007, p. 147).

As we saw above, on Gibbard's view, passing this test requires agents to be representable as though they have utility functions that are credence-eliciting, which means that were they sufficiently ideal decision-makers, they would choose the credence function they have as the most accurate function available in light of the information they have. Let's say that an agent who chooses her own credence function as the most accurate available in this sense is *immodest*. Gibbard is not alone in thinking immodesty is a requirement of epistemic rationality (see, e.g., Joyce 2009; Horowitz 2016; Greaves and Wallace 2006; and Oddie 1997; many of them take inspiration from Lewis 1971).

Gibbard argues that truth-loving views of epistemic normativity don't have the resources to explain why we epistemically ought to be immodest, but Gibbard thinks that we can explain why agents are required to be immodest if we appeal to a norm of practical rationality, namely that we ought to maximize the expected practical guidance value of our credences. Gibbard spells out how that explanation would work by appeal to an argument involving an infinite series of bets. What I'll show is that we can transform Gibbard's practical explanation into a purely truth-based explanation, thereby undermining Gibbard's claim that truth-loving views cannot explain why agents ought to be immodest.

Gibbard considers an agent who is gambling on a single contingency and doesn't know at what odds they will be gambling. Gibbard has us consider the full (infinite) set of odds of bets that the agent might face. That's the set of bets $\mathfrak{G}_\beta$ for $0 < \beta < 1$ such that the payoff of bet G_β is $\overline{\beta} : \beta$. If an agent has a credence x in the proposition in play, then she'll view all and only the bets G_β such that $\beta > x$ as better than fair (using standard decision theory). Gibbard then appeals to the result from Schervish (1989) to show that an agent will accept all and only those bets as fair iff their credence function is credence-eliciting (which, along with our other assumptions, entails that they are immodest). Gibbard thinks this shows that the requirement to have a credence-eliciting utility function is best explained by agents trying to maximize the prospective guidance value of their credences, since the agent is best construed as trying to maximize their payoff in a series of bets like this one, where they don't know the odds that they'll face.

Elsewhere, I object to Gibbard's methodology of appealing to a hypothetical infinite series of bets (Singer 2012, chapt. 4).[6] Here I'll take a different tack by questioning why we should think that our agent aiming to maximize the prospective *guidance* value of their beliefs is the best explanation of why they would accept the bets they do in this series of bets. Why couldn't we instead view our agent's fairness-of-bets judgments as a product of them aiming to maximize the expected *epistemic* value of their beliefs?

The idea works like this: To reach his conclusion, Gibbard needs to construe the potential payoffs involved in these bets as being a practical (non-epistemic) kind of payoff. Gibbard concludes that it's the agent trying to maximize that practical payoff that explains why they would choose their own credence to face the potential series of bets. But couldn't we equally plausibly construe the kind of payoffs involved in the potential bets as epistemic? If we did that, we'd be imagining an agent who has a credence in some proposition *S* and is trying to decide what credence to have in *S* to maximize their epistemic payoff on the bets about *S*. Using the same reasoning that Gibbard uses (via Schervish's theorem), we can reach the conclusion that it's the agent trying to maximize the prospective *epistemic* value of their beliefs that explains why their utility function must be credence-eliciting. The thought is that if this alternative framing of the hypothetical agent that Gibbard describes is coherent, then truth-loving views can appeal to this explanation of why we should be immodest, and this explanation should be equally as plausible as Gibbard's explanation involving prospective guidance value. For this to work, we'll need to make sense of the series of 'epistemic bets' that the agent might face. What kind of value is involved in the bets? And, what does it mean for the agent to accept or reject an epistemic bet?

The natural (and correct) answer to the first question is that the value of the potential payoffs in the series of bets is epistemic value. One might worry that when we're considering a unique proposition (as we do the way

[6] In Singer (2012, chapter 4), I argue that Gibbard is left appealing to merely hypothetical bets to explain epistemic rationality even in ideal cases, and I claim that those merely hypothetical bets don't seem to be able to play the role he needs them to play. I then undermine Gibbard's motivation for pursuing such an account in the first place by arguing that Gibbard's argument hinges on a not fully plausible conception of what it is to aim at an end.

Gibbard set up the argument), epistemic value isn't flexible enough to get the argument going. The bets that Gibbard has us consider in the practical version of the argument importantly vary in terms of potential payoff. In the series Gibbard sets up, the odds vary from a guaranteed win (1:0) to a guaranteed loss (0:1) and include every possible odds ratio in between. One might think that epistemic value can't be that flexible, since when we're considering just one proposition, the potential payoffs are limited by the minimum and maximum final epistemic value that a single belief could have.

This is a place where the Truth Fairy can help the truth-loving epistemic consequentialist. Since consequentialist views are open to beliefs having arbitrary amounts of derivative epistemic value by conducing to the final epistemic goodness of other beliefs, the Truth Fairy can offer you bets with arbitrary odds by guaranteeing that your epistemic state will contain certain ratios of true to false beliefs depending on whether you win or lose the bet.[7] So to generate a series of bets $\mathfrak{G}_\beta$ for $0 < \beta < 1$ that's analogous to Gibbard's series, the Truth Fairy guarantees that the *epistemic* payoff of bet G_β is $\overline{\beta} : \beta$. Here, like in Gibbard's series, if an agent has a credence x in the proposition in play, she'll view all and only the bets G_β such that $\beta > x$ as better than fair (using standard decision theory) and accept all and only those.

What would it mean for an agent to accept or reject one of these hypothetical bets? Again here, we'll make the epistemic case analogous to the practical one: We should see accepting a bet as a kind of action, one that's similar to asserting the proposition in play, and rejecting would be doing the opposite action. Notice that the agent need not actually have a full belief in the proposition (let alone absolute certainty in it) to perform this action. Compare Gibbard's setup: There, in each hypothetical bet, the agent chooses a door based on their best judgment about where the tiger is. The agent need not have a full belief (let alone certainty) about where the tiger is to perform this action. Similarly, we can imagine our agent choosing an 'epistemic door' to open as a way of accepting or rejecting the bet.

One might worry that the epistemic version of the argument is really stretching our imaginative abilities. Unlike Gibbard's version of the argument, which simply proliferates cases of real-life betting, the proposed

[7] One worry here: If we're limited to categorical beliefs, this method of producing states with final epistemic value can only produce rationally valued epistemic states, not the full continuum of real valued ones. We should be surprised if anything important hangs on this detail, though, since this method still allows us to get at least arbitrarily close to any odds ratio we'd like.

epistemic analogue is quite fantastical, you might think. I'm not sure we should be worried, though.

The practical formulation of the argument from Gibbard has us consider an agent who is attempting to maximize the prospective guidance value of their doxastic state for an infinite series of bets at literally all possible odds. The epistemic version of the argument copies that setup exactly, and so it shouldn't be objectionable on those grounds. So whatever worries there might be about the fantasticality of the epistemic version of the argument must derive from the idea of the bets being epistemic rather than practical. There are only two differences there: There is a difference in the kind of value in play (epistemic value as opposed to practical), and there is a difference in what it is to accept or reject the bet. A difference in the kind of value could ground an objection to this argument only insomuch as we take issue with the idea of epistemic value. That strikes me as a kind of skeptical worry that's not worth taking up here. So we should consider whether there's an important difference in what's involved in accepting or rejecting the bets. It doesn't seem to me that there is. Above, I described acceptance of the epistemic bets as an action that the agent performs in response to an offer from the Truth Fairy. But we can also construe it in a much more familiar way. Whenever we adopt any belief or credence, we're balancing the potential payoffs and losses of epistemic value that we might receive from that belief or credence. All that we need to get the epistemic version of Gibbard's argument going is that we're unsure in advance what the odds are. Construing epistemic value in the way the truth-loving epistemic consequentialist does allows us to make sense of that in a way that's flexible enough to get Schervish's theorem to apply.

What this shows is that if Gibbard's proposed guidance-centered explanation of why agents should be epistemically immodest works, the truth-loving epistemic consequentialist has an equally compelling epistemic (purely 'truthy') explanation of the same thing. That is enough to undermine any objection to truth-loving epistemic consequentialism that Gibbard's argument brings out. That said, truth-loving epistemic consequentialists should really object to Gibbard's argument at a much earlier step. Even though truth-loving epistemic consequentialists *could* give this explanation of why we should be immodest, truth-loving epistemic consequentialists should deny that immodesty is a genuine requirement of epistemic normativity. So they should deny that providing an explanation is necessary. I'll turn to showing why that's true now.

5.2.2 Why It's OK to Be Epistemically Modest

Being epistemically immodest means that an idealized version of you would view your credences as the most accurate credences you could have in light of the information you have. So if we're epistemically required to be immodest, it must always be the case that, by our own lights, there is no credence function that is more accurate than the one we have. This is not a requirement of epistemic normativity, or so I will argue. Seeing why is easiest when we think about non-ideal agents, so I'll start there. I'll argue later that the result holds for ideal epistemic agents too.

Consider this example:

> Diving Ducks and Ducks that Dive Cory has been regularly bird-watching and cataloguing his bird sightings for about 5 years. In that time, he's seen about 40 different species of ducks. Cory has heard other birders talking about 'dabbling ducks' and 'diving ducks,' and he's been informally classifying his duck sightings in that way on the basis of their behavior. Last week, Cory learned that not all ducks that dive are properly categorized as diving ducks. Whether a duck is truly a diving duck (versus a mere duck that dives) is dependent on whether it is a member of the subfamily Aythyinae or the quite distinct taxonomic tribe Mergini. In the past week, Cory has learned enough about the complex observable characteristics of ducks to determine which taxonomic group a duck species is in, but making that determination in any particular case is hard and requires careful and lengthy reflection. For most species of duck that Cory had previously thought of as a diving duck, he hasn't yet thought about whether it is a true diving duck, so he suspends belief about it.

In this case, Cory has enough information available to him to draw many new conclusions about which taxonomic groups the different kinds of ducks are in, but he hasn't yet put the time and energy into considering that question for most of them. Because of that, Cory couldn't be immodest. To see why, consider a particular kind of duck that Cory hasn't thought about. Suppose it's the long-tailed duck (*Clangula hyemalis*), and let L be the proposition that long-tailed ducks are true diving ducks. By stipulation in the case, Cory suspends belief on L, but were he to put the time and energy into reflecting on it, perhaps reflecting on the facts that long-tailed ducks are overwhelmingly seen in salt water and that they have relatively small feet, he would (correctly) conclude that *L* is false. Since Cory has enough information to conclude that *L* is false, then in light of the information he has, it must be true that a set of beliefs like his but that disbelieved *L* would be more accurate than the set he has. So he is not, in Gibbard's sense, immodest. Nonetheless, I take it that we could easily fill out the details of the case so that it seems like Cory is taking the right kind of epistemic approach to these beliefs. We could stipulate that Cory is busy thinking about other things, for example.

What this case brings out is that if immodesty is epistemically required, then it is never epistemically permissible to be in a position where we haven't worked out the implications of some of our beliefs yet. But real agents are constantly being bombarded with new information and face many processing limitations. So for real agents, it's extremely common to have not worked out the implications of the information we have. In many cases, we intentionally put off thinking about things until a later time (or don't think about them at all) due to more pressing concerns (epistemic, practical, and other). If immodesty were required, then doing this would always be epistemically wrong.

We can see this even more clearly in cases involving competing demands on our epistemic resources:

> LOTS OF BIRDS Cory just arrived at the Forsythe Wildlife Refuge, a huge marshland that is typically populated with a truly overwhelming number of birds. Right after getting out of his car, Cory looks out and everything he sees is completely covered in snow geese. They're in the air, on land, and floating in the water. Everywhere he looks, there are hundreds of birds, each of which is a snow goose. Cory does a quick estimate to jot down in his log book. He estimates that it's about 150,000 snow geese, but given what he's seen, he wouldn't be shocked if it's only 80,000 or as many as 800,000. Cory could think harder about exactly how many snow geese there seems to be (by, for example, mentally breaking down his visual field into smaller parts, counting the geese in one of those, and multiplying by the number of field parts), but if he did, he'd likely miss many of the songbirds and ducks that he is about to scare away. So instead of narrowing down the exact number of snow geese, he turns his attention to the songbirds and ducks.

Here, Cory has credences about the number of snow geese that, by his own lights, could be improved by further reflection. So, Cory is not immodest, in Gibbard's sense. But here, it seems epistemically permissible for Cory not to be immodest, since it seems like it is at least permissible for him to put his effort toward noticing all of the other birds that surround him rather than drawing out the implications of (his beliefs about) his visual perception for his number-of-snow-geese beliefs.

It's easy to exploit the contingent limitations of real epistemic agents to generate other cases where it seems epistemically permissible for agents to be epistemically modest. Real humans are limited in the size of their total memory, the size of their working memory, their ability to recall different pieces of information at the same time, their processing speed, and their ability to reason well and without biases. Each of those can be exploited in their own way to create cases where it would seem epistemically permissible for agents to be epistemically modest.

The truth-loving epistemic consequentialist has a natural story about why this is. What we see from the cases above is that simple direct consequentialist views of epistemic rightness are subject to a 'paradox' that's analogous to the paradox of hedonism. The paradox of hedonism is often cast as a problem for simple hedonistic subjective consequentialist views of moral rightness. What the paradox of hedonism says is that for real agents, directly aiming at pleasure in one's decision-making is self-undermining, since we'll often miss out on pleasurable experiences by subjectively focusing too hard on maximizing the amount of pleasure we receive. An analogous thing happens in our epistemic lives. If Cory were to have focused on getting a more precise estimate of the number of snow geese, he would have missed out on the beliefs he formed about the songbirds and ducks. So by focusing too hard on maximizing the accuracy of our beliefs, we can open ourselves up to missing out on other accurate beliefs, and so being obsessed with the truth in one's thoughts can be self-undermining. Let's call this the 'paradox of truth-seeking.'

As we discussed in Chapter 3, in response to the paradox of hedonism (and for other reasons), it's standard among ethical consequentialists to divorce the consequentialist criterion of right action from the claim that we should consciously aim at maximizing goodness (by, for example, using explicit expected utility calculations). Following Railton, we described a consequentialist view as 'sophisticated' if it says that rightness is a question of whether the object of evaluation best conduces to the good and does *not* say that agents ought to aim to produce the good in their decision-making. In addition to the considerations in favor of epistemic consequentialists being sophisticated discussed in Chapter 3, cases like DIVING DUCKS AND DUCKS THAT DIVE and LOTS OF BIRDS (and the paradox of truth-seeking that they bring out) should also motivate epistemic consequentialists to accept a sophisticated view.

Recall that what makes someone immodest, in the sense that Gibbard thinks is epistemically required, is that she is "as if she were choosing her credences voluntarily, rationally aiming, in light of her credences, at truth in those very credences" (2007, p. 147). If someone is always immodest in that sense, they must always have the credences that are, by their lights, subjectively the most accurate. But not holding that agents ought to be like this is exactly what makes a consequentialist view sophisticated. If maximizing accuracy in our beliefs meant that we must be immodest, then subjectively aiming for the truth in our beliefs must always be the best way for us to pursue that aim. What the paradox of truth-seeking brings out is that for real agents with natural human limitations, subjectively aiming at the truth is not always the best way to maximize accuracy.[8]

So far, the argument I've given depends heavily on the agents involved being limited. But most of the appeals to immodesty in the literature (including those mentioned above) intend it only to apply to sufficiently idealized agents. It's natural to think, for example, that if Cory had free and unlimited memory, infinite processing power and speed, etc., we could expect him to have worked out which of the ducks are true diving ducks. But, as I'll argue, the failure of immodesty as an epistemic requirement isn't limited to non-ideal agents. Truth-loving epistemic consequentialists should think that even ideal agents should sometimes be modest.

The central tenet of truth-loving epistemic consequentialism is that agents epistemically ought to promote accuracy in their beliefs, and there

[8] It's worth noting that what's doing the work here is the *sophisticated* nature of the view, not the *global* nature of the view. According to the global epistemic consequentialist, we ought to have and use heuristics, dispositions, decision-making procedures, etc. that lead to us having more accurate beliefs. As discussed in Chapter 3, on this view, there can be cases where we use a heuristic, disposition, decision-making procedure, etc. (and should have used it) but still get a wrong belief from it. Intuitively, one might think that these will be cases where immodesty fails, since these will be cases where we should be able to see by our own lights that our belief is not best. But this last step doesn't follow. Rightness of a belief is determined by the real consequences of holding it, on this view, not the expected or foreseeable consequences. So a belief being wrong, on this view, doesn't connect up with it being not prospectively best, which is what would be needed for the global aspect of the view to generate cases where immodesty fails.

can be times, even for ideal epistemic agents, where being modest is the best way to promote accuracy. Consider the following case:

> BOOTH FAIRY You walk into a room, and in front of you are 11 booths. Each of the booths has one bird in it. In the first booth, there is a clearly visible piping plover. You know there is one bird in each of the remaining booths, but you cannot see what species of bird is in any of those. The Booth Fairy credibly tells you that if you simply suspend belief on what kind of bird is in the first booth, he'll tell you what birds are in the other 10 booths. He also credibly tells you that he can read your thoughts with a new long-distance fMRI machine. If you stop suspending belief about what bird is in the first booth, he'll instantly swap out the birds in the other ten booths so that you'll no longer have true beliefs about what birds are in those booths.

In this case, if you're an ideal epistemic agent aiming to maximize the accuracy of your beliefs, you'll suspend belief about the piping plover and learn what birds are in the other 10 booths. If you did that, though, you'd still be able to see the piping plover, so presumably you'll still have whatever evidence you previously had for that belief. So after you suspend belief about the piping plover, you'll be in a modest belief state, since by your lights, there will be a more accurate doxastic state than your own (namely the one where you believe there is a piping plover in the first booth and save the rest of your doxastic state). So even ideal epistemic agents sometimes need to be modest to maximize the accuracy of their beliefs.

Notice that this is a trade-off case, like the kinds of cases we considered in Chapters 2 and 3. For trade-off cases like this one to work, the agent's beliefs and the world have to be intermingled in the right kind of way. There has to be an unusual kind of correlation between the agent's doxastic state and the state of the world. I claim that cases like this show that, even for ideal epistemic agents, being modest is sometimes the best path to accuracy. But you might think I've missed the mark, maybe because you think ideal epistemology, analogous perhaps to ideal political theory, involves many idealizing assumptions, not just about the agent but also about the world the agent inhabits. Those idealizing assumptions, you might claim, rule out the nefarious connections between the world and the agent's beliefs needed to generate cases like BOOTH FAIRY.

Put one way, whether this objection is right is primarily a sociological question—one about whether epistemologists doing ideal epistemic theory in fact make those kinds of idealizations. I won't try to answer that empirical question here. But one might wonder, regardless of whether those idealizations are made, whether there are some good theoretical reasons for doing so. Surely ideal theorizing in epistemology will allow that ideal agents might have incomplete and misleading evidence. And surely it would allow that ideal agents could, in theory, be in skeptical scenarios such as a brain-in-a-vat scenario. What might motivate the ideal theorist to countenance those epistemic non-ideal elements in ideal cases but prohibit the kind of connection between an agent's beliefs and the world that is needed to generate cases like BOOTH FAIRY?

I'm suspicious of there being a non-ad-hoc way to carve off the relevant cases because it's unclear that anything all that unusual is going on in BOOTH FAIRY. The only unusual dependence mechanism required to get BOOTH FAIRY going is that the fairy can reliably tell whether the agent believes there is a plover in the first booth. That kind of intermingling is not very implausible. Cases where agents have beliefs about their own beliefs will exhibit the same kind of dependence (since the 'world' in these cases is the agent's beliefs). As we'll see in the next section, there might even be extremely realistic cases like this where agents have beliefs about their own actions.[9]

Overall, then, if we're guided by the idea that what is epistemically required of us is that we pursue accuracy in our beliefs, we shouldn't always expect agents to be immodest, contra what Gibbard thinks. We saw above that for non-ideal agents, being modest is often the best way to deal with having limited epistemic resources. But even for ideal epistemic agents, modesty can be required when an agent's belief is intermingled in the right kind of way with the subject of the belief. So why would Gibbard and so many others have incorrectly thought that immodesty is epistemically required? A natural thought here is that it is the same kind of jump that convinces folks new to moral consequentialism to go in for subjective consequentialism. It's natural to think that if a kind of normativity is centrally

[9] Moreover, notice that the kind of connection between the agent's beliefs and the world needed to get this case going is a simple correlational one and one that could plausibly be produced with extant technology. In that sense, the kind of constitutional connection posited between beliefs and the world by proponents of mental content externalism (e.g., Putnam 1975) should strike the reader as *much* weirder.

guided by producing some good, then agents who are subject to that kind of normativity should subjectively aim to produce that good. But that last step doesn't track how real agents work, nor does it track what consequentialist theorists take the best versions of their view to be. So I don't take that move to be well motivated here. And without that immodesty claim, Gibbard's broader argument doesn't get off the ground.

All together, I've offered two independent responses for the truth-loving epistemic consequentialist to Gibbard's argument that truth-centric views of epistemic normativity can't make sense of epistemic norms. As I argued in this section, truth-loving epistemic consequentialists should hold that the purported epistemic norm that Gibbard's argument hinges on isn't an epistemic norm. It applies neither to ideal nor to non-ideal epistemic agents. But even if that argument fails (as I suspect many theorists will say), the truth-loving epistemic consequentialist can give a truth-based explanation of that norm that should be equally as compelling as the practical one Gibbard gives. Either way, truth-loving epistemic consequentialists shouldn't be worried about this kind of argument against truth-centric views of epistemic normativity.

5.3 Objections to Dominance and Expected Value Arguments

Epistemic utility theorists, like truth-loving epistemic consequentialists, are centrally moved by the idea that epistemology is about getting an accurate picture of the world. So epistemic utility theorists typically agree with truth-loving epistemic consequentialists that all and only accurate doxastic states have final epistemic value. But unlike truth-loving epistemic consequentialists, epistemic utility theorists attempt to understand epistemic norms in terms of the subjectively rational pursuit of final epistemic value. The standard way that epistemic utility theorists do this is by using the tools of rational decision theory.

Joyce (1998, 2009), for example, uses dominance avoidance reasoning to argue that our degreed beliefs should be representable as probability functions. His argument has this form:

1. If an agent's credences violate the probability axioms, then there is a particular probability function such that, in every possible world, it is more accurate than the agent's credences.

2. It is epistemically irrational for an agent to have a set of credences that are less accurate than some other set of credences in every possible world. (Dominance premise)
3. So epistemically rational agents' credences must be probability functions.[10]

The second step of this argument is an appeal to an intuitive principle of rational decision theory: that we should avoid options that necessarily do worse than some other option. The idea of these dominance avoidance arguments is that when we're trying to maximize some quantity and must choose among ways of pursuing it (and there are no other goals in play), we shouldn't choose a way of pursuing the goal when there is another way that does better no matter how the world is. Applied to credences and the pursuit of accuracy, the idea is that a rational agent should not adopt a credence when there is another credence that has higher accuracy at all worlds.[11]

Joyce combines this dominance avoidance argument with an argument for thinking that no probability functions are dominated and that any probability function could be permissible in some context, so he concludes that it can be rational to have any probability function as a credence but it's never rational to have non-probability functions. Greaves and Wallace (2006) and Leitgeb and Pettigrew (2010b) also use the strategy of using principles from rational decision theory applied to the accuracy goal to defend norms of epistemic rationality. Instead of dominance avoidance, they use expected utility maximization arguments to defend both conditionalization and probabilism.

Carr (2017) shows that epistemic utility theorists' arguments like these face a dilemma. The principles epistemic utility theorists use to attempt to vindicate their conclusions assume that what credences the agent has are independent of what the credences are about. But often this isn't true. As Carr (2017, pp. 514–515) explains, the things our doxastic states are about can be causally and evidentially dependent on the doxastic states themselves. These include cases where the doxastic states are self-verifying

[10] Hájek (2008) has argued the the conclusion in this argument doesn't follow without additional premises. I'll ignore that issue here.

[11] See Pettigrew (2019) for further discussion of how these arguments work.

and self-falsifying, cases where the doxastic states directly causally effect what they're about, cases where lower-order doxastic states affect the veracity of higher-order doxastic states, and cases where our doxastic states affect our actions, among others. Carr focuses on the following example:

> HANDSTAND "Suppose your (perfectly reliable) yoga teacher has informed you that the only thing that could inhibit your ability to do a handstand is self-doubt, which can make you unstable or even hamper your ability to kick up into the upside-down position. The more confident you are that you will manage to do a handstand, the more likely it is that you will, and vice versa."
>
> "More precisely: let H be the proposition that you'll successfully do a handstand ... [F]or all n in $[0, 1]$, $Cr(H) = n$ at t_1 will make it the case that $Ch(H) = n$ at the next moment, t_2, and that this will remain the chance of H up to ... when you either do or don't do a successful handstand" (Carr 2017, p. 515).

Carr further specifies that your conditional credence that you'll do a handstand given the information you learned from the yoga teacher is .5. The problem is that if you conditionalize your credences on the information you learned, your credence in whether you'll do a handstand will be .5. But you know in advance that .5 will not maximize the expected accuracy of your credences. Since you know that whether you'll do the handstand is perfectly correlated with your credence, you know that if you had 1 or 0 credence, you would guarantee yourself maximal accuracy. So in this example, conditionalization conflicts with maximizing your expected accuracy, and as such, Carr concludes, maximizing expected accuracy cannot vindicate conditionalization, as Greaves and Wallace (2006) and Leitgeb and Pettigrew (2010b) had hoped to show.

It's natural to read Greaves and Wallace (2006) and Leitgeb and Pettigrew (2010b) as having offered *proofs* of their results, so what went wrong? According to Carr, what went wrong is that these authors used a non-standard conception of maximizing expected utility. They used a version of expected utility maximization that assumes that what credences the agent has are, in an important way, independent of the truth of the propositions they're about. In doing so, they ignored the effects that adopting and having different credences might have on the world. Those effects should be taken into account if we were using the standard conceptions of expected utility maximization from rational decision theory, Carr argues.

Carr (2017, p. 520) also shows that Joyce's accuracy dominance avoidance argument faces a similar problem. The notion of dominance that Joyce uses in the argument above asks how accurate a credence function is at a world without taking into account whether the agent has adopted that credence at the world, thereby ignoring the effects of having the credence on the accuracy of the credence. In HANDSTAND, certain combinations of credences and truth-values about whether you'll perform a handstand are ruled out by the case (e.g., ones where you do the handstand despite having credence 0 that you will). The dominance reasoning Joyce uses treats those combinations as possible. Doing this is essential to Joyce's conclusion that probability functions are not dominated in the same way that non-probability functions are. Were Joyce to have used more standard dominance avoidance reasoning (following rational decision theorists), those possibilities wouldn't have been taken into account and some probabilistic credences would have been ruled irrational.

The important upshot of Carr's argument is that the non-standard decision theoretic rules that epistemic utility theorists use can't be justified by the aim of accuracy, since in some cases they straightforwardly conflict. Caie (2013) and Greaves (2013) also notice this issue and treat it as a problem for epistemic utility theorists. Carr, on the other hand, thinks this is a feature of epistemic utility theory rather than a bug. Carr thinks that epistemic utility theorists should try to justify the non-standard decision rules they appeal to. And while Carr doesn't end up offering a full story about how this justification might work, she does hint at two ideas: (1) that the non-standard rules might make sense because of the direction of fit of belief,—i.e., that belief aims to represent the world rather than merely conform with it (2017, p. 521), and (2) that the non-standard rules might be explained by beliefs aiming at respecting evidence rather than maximizing accuracy (2017, p. 532). Carr leaves the epistemic utility theorist with a dilemma: They must stick with the non-standard rational decision rules and somehow defend them or they must give up on the non-standard rules and give up on their central results.

5.4 Dominance Avoidance and Truth-Loving Epistemic Consequentialism

I won't attempt to settle whether Carr is right or whether there is some way to construe the epistemic utility theorist's project as being motivated by an aim for accuracy. Instead, I'll focus on Carr's objections to the use of expected utility maximization and dominance avoidance arguments to generate the epistemic utility theorist's conclusions. I'll ask about the implications of her arguments for truth-loving epistemic consequentialism's proposal that we can understand right belief and credence in terms of maximizing accuracy. As I'll argue in this section, Carr's arguments about expected utility maximization have no bearing on the truth-loving epistemic consequentialist picture, but when it comes to the dominance avoidance arguments, Carr's argument brings out interesting contrasts between the epistemic utility theorist's and the truth-loving epistemic consequentialist's theories of final value.

As we discussed above, one kind of epistemic utility theory argument appeals to expected utility maximization. Those arguments start with the idea that maximizing accuracy is the goal and then direct agents to do that by maximizing their expected accuracy. Truth-loving epistemic consequentialists hold that the right belief/credence is the one that in fact best conduces to the overall accuracy of the agent's doxastic state. So if we think of epistemic utility theory as offering a theory of right belief/credence, the difference between truth-loving consequentialism and epistemic utility theory would be the same as the difference between consequentialist ethical views that take actual versus expected consequences to matter for action rightness. As I argued in Chapter 3, views that take the actual consequences to matter are the most common in ethics, and those views best capture the intuition that the norms are about promoting the end (rather than what agents take to be the end). Truth-loving epistemic consequentialists should follow their ethical analogues and reject the idea that rightness is to be understood in terms of expected consequences.

That said, I think it would be too quick to just think of epistemic utility theorists as offering a subjective version of the objective truth-loving epistemic consequentialist view. It is more charitable, I propose, to see epistemic utility theorists as taking seriously the idea that their view is about *rational* or *justified* belief/credence, as opposed to *right* belief/credence. The thought might be that what matters for rationality and justification is something like pursuing the end *to the best of one's abilities*. If that's right, then whereas truth-loving epistemic consequentialism is a theory of right belief/credence, epistemic utility theory should be seen as a non-competing theory of rational or justified belief/credence. Regardless of whether we see epistemic utility theory as a subjective consequentialist view of right belief/credence or as a distinct theory of rational or justified belief/credence, concerns about epistemic utility theorists' use of (non-standard) expected utility theory (like the kind Carr offers) won't translate to truth-loving epistemic consequentialism, since truth-loving consequentialism doesn't use the objected-to machinery of expected utility maximization.

It's a different story when it comes to how truth-loving epistemic consequentialists should think about dominance avoidance arguments. Consider the general form of those arguments: They assume there is an exhaustive list of possible states of the world $A_1 \ldots A_n$ and that we're trying to decide which of options $O_\ell \ldots O_m$ for a belief/credence/action is best. They then suppose there is a pair of options O_j and O_k such that, for each A_i, adopting (doing) O_j will result in a worse outcome than adopting (doing) O_k in A_i. From that, they conclude that we should not do O_j, since no matter how the world is, O_k is better. Unlike expected utility arguments, which focus on the consequences an agent should expect, dominance avoidance arguments work via *necessary* claims about which beliefs/credences produce better outcomes. So, since truth-loving epistemic consequentialists care about getting the best outcomes, truth-loving epistemic consequentialists should care whether dominance avoidance arguments stand or fall.

To understand Carr's (2017) concern about epistemic utility theorists' use of dominance avoidance arguments, it's important to notice that the conclusions of dominance avoidance arguments hinge on what set of worlds the arguments take to be possible. O_t might not dominate O_s with respect to one set of worlds, but O_t might dominate O_s if we restrict the set of worlds in play. As Carr (as well as Caie 2013 and Greaves 2013) points out, the standard way for epistemic utility theorists to use dominance avoidance arguments includes all possible worlds, including ones where the beliefs/credences aren't adopted by the agent. Doing this is essential to getting Joyce's (1998, 2009) probabilism result. Carr (2017) (unlike Caie 2013 and Greaves 2013) thinks that epistemic utility theorists are right to use this expansive set of worlds, and she draws out the need for epistemic utility theorists to justify this assumption.

What should the truth-loving epistemic consequentialist think? Truth-loving epistemic consequentialists are centrally concerned with what beliefs/credences best conduce to getting an accurate picture of the world. Dominance avoidance arguments work by telling us something about which options are best in a class of worlds. As long as the class of worlds includes the actual world, dominance avoidance arguments tell us more about which options do better or worse the more they restrict that class. If a belief/credence results in more or less epistemic value (by producing more or less accurate beliefs), the belief/credence must actually be adopted in that world. So truth-loving epistemic consequentialists should be happy to restrict the class of worlds in play in dominance avoidance arguments to only worlds in which the belief/credences under consideration are adopted. That means that truth-loving epistemic consequentialists should share Carr's concern about epistemic utility theorists' use of the broader class of worlds, including worlds in which the agent doesn't adopt the belief/credence.

As Carr shows, this means that truth-loving epistemic consequentialists won't be able to use dominance avoidance arguments to justify probabilism. But this shouldn't be surprising since, as we've seen, truth-loving epistemic consequentialists should be suspicious that there are any perfect and uniform rules about how to govern our doxastic lives, given the particular strengths and limitations of real human beings and the complexities of the environments they inhabit. In fact, the failure of probabilism can be seen as a straightforward consequence of a propensity to accept trade-offs, since, for example, we could imagine the Truth Fairy guaranteeing that our doxastic states are highly accurate in exchange for a minor violation of the probability axioms (e.g., having a .90 credence in rain and a .101 credence in not rain). Even absent a Truth Fairy, it's easy to imagine that realistic agents might do better (in terms of overall accuracy) by being less coherent in their doxastic states than probabilism would require.[12] So, like epistemic utility theorists, truth-loving epistemic consequentialists should be happy to admit dominance avoidance arguments into their argumentative toolbox,

[12] Notice that the general move here can be used to motivate several already existing objections to Bayesianism. For example, the problem of logical omniscience for Bayesianism accuses Bayesians of incorrectly predicting that rationality requires that we have correct extremal credences in all logical and mathematical truths. The consequentialist can explain why the logical omniscience claim seems wrong, even if accuracy is our goal. Real human reasoners would typically do worse in terms of overall accuracy if they met that criterion, the consequentialist should say. So even though the Bayesian picture might be right for a certain idealized kind of reasoner, consequentialists should think the ideal norms have very misleading implications about right belief/credence for real agents.

since they can teach us about what conduces to accurate beliefs/credences for real agents using inferences from facts about what necessarily conduces to (or fails to conduce to) accuracy for a broader class of agents. Using the arguments this way means that truth-loving epistemic consequentialists won't be able to use these arguments to support probabilism, but the consequentialist wouldn't want to endorse that anyway.

5.5 Epistemic Value for Consequentialists and Epistemic Utility Theorists

As I just explained, truth-loving epistemic consequentialists are primarily motivated by the idea that epistemic rightness is about getting at an accurate picture of the world, and because dominance avoidance arguments tell us about what doxastic states do that, truth-loving consequentialists, like epistemic utility theorists, should include those arguments in their argumentative toolbox. That said, there is actually a big difference in how truth-loving epistemic consequentialists and epistemic utility theorists will think about what dominance involves in these arguments. This section will flesh out that difference and ask how much it matters.

Epistemic utility theorists (like Joyce 1998, 2009) measure and compare credences in terms of how close the credences are to (the characteristic function of) the truth-values of the propositions at a world at a time. So, using these measures, if we have two credence functions and one is uniformly closer to the truth on every proposition than the other, then that one will be *better* than the other. The measures used by epistemic utility theorists are, in this sense, 'local'—they take into account only the proximity of the particular credence function to the truth at a time.

Truth-loving epistemic consequentialists are concerned not only with the local accuracy of our doxastic states but also with how having the states influences the accuracy of our other doxastic states (and themselves) through time. By comparing credences in terms of their accuracy at a world at a moment, epistemic utility theorists' measures ignore some important elements of epistemic final value, the truth-loving epistemic consequentialist should say. Consider an example: Suppose there's an agent who is trying to figure out whether *P* because they want to know whether *Q* and they already believe *P* if and only if *Q*. Also suppose that after they form a belief about whether *P*, it will take a moment for them to make the inference to whether *Q*. In this case, it's natural to think the relevant accuracy-involving consequences of the agent's potential belief that *P* include facts about whether a belief that *Q* would be true, even though their belief that *Q* will not be among the beliefs that the agent immediately has upon forming their belief that *P*. So on the most natural truth-loving epistemic consequentialist picture, part of what we want to compare in deciding which beliefs/credences are best is what influence having the beliefs/credences will have on the agent's other (future) beliefs/credences.[13] Epistemic utility theorists' measures of accuracy, which only measure the accuracy of a credence at a world at a time, can't account for that.

As the literature on scoring rules makes clear, saying exactly how we should measure the accuracy of beliefs and credences is complex and controversial (for the tip of the iceberg, see Joyce 1998, 2009, Leitgeb and Pettigrew 2010a). Up to this point, I've tried to avoid taking a stand on how exactly to do that. (A careful reader may have even noticed that up to this point, I haven't even taken a stand on whether the relevant veritistic effects should be restricted only to the relevant belief/credence-holder's other doxastic states or whether they might also include others' doxastic states.) The strategy has been to attempt to defuse potential objections to various ways the consequentialist might flesh out their theory, rather than taking a stand on exactly which way to flesh out the nitty-gritty details of the theory. That said, on the truth-loving epistemic consequentialist picture, credences and beliefs are thought of as real aspects of agents that exist through time, affect other doxastic states (at the same time and other times), and affect the world they inhabit. So on this view, to gauge the goodness of a belief or credence, we should include all the veritistic effects of the doxastic state, not just the accuracy of that particular attitude at a time. The most natural theory would hold that the rightness of a belief or credence for an agent is determined by the consequences of holding that belief or credence for the accuracy of the whole set of the holder's beliefs in their lifetime. In the end, I want to remain agnostic about whether this is the best way to flesh out the theory of value (rather than, say, also including other agents' doxastic states), but let's treat this view as a hypothesis in this section to draw out its implications.

As the example above begins to bring out, if the consequentialist adopts this way of fleshing out their theory of value, they'll think about dominance reasoning in a quite different way from the way epistemic utility theorists

[13] Notice that the examples in Chapter 2 of permissible epistemic trade-offs also had the feature that the rightness of a belief seemed to depend on the accuracy of other *future* beliefs of the agent.

do it. On the epistemic utility theorist's picture, the value of doxastic states is only measured at a time and with respect to some fixed assignment of truth-values to the propositions in play. These local measures of accuracy don't take into account how the credence might interface with the propositions that it's about (Carr's point) or how the credence might interface with the agent's credences at other times. Truth-loving epistemic consequentialists, if they adopt something like the picture I just sketched, will want to compare credences and beliefs in a way that takes into account the full implications of adopting the credence or belief. In addition to the final value of the accuracy of the belief/credence when it is adopted, truth-loving consequentialists should also take into account the veritistic effects of how the credence/belief might interface with the world (as Carr's example brings out) and the veritistic effects of how the credence/belief might interface with the rest of the agent's credences/beliefs through time. In this way, the epistemic consequentialist will think of the relevant consequences of a belief or credence in a way that's more analogous to how the consequences of an action are typically thought of in rational decision theory and ethics, where the consequences are typically thought of as spread through space and time.[14]

How much does this difference in measures matter for how the two views will assess real beliefs and credences? Ultimately, that's a question that can only be answered by careful empirical research that's sensitive to how often there are cases where a belief/credence being 'locally accurate' (in the way epistemic utility theorists think of it) comes apart from it conducing to the overall accuracy of an agent's beliefs through time. In theory, these could dramatically come apart. We could imagine, for example, trade-off cases where the Truth Fairy offers us future accuracy for current inaccuracy. In cases like that, the two views will make opposite predictions about what the right beliefs are.

That said, I expect that for real agents, the two theories of value will likely rank beliefs in the same order most of the time. In Chapter 2, I argued that we should think that, as a general rule, for real agents, having a true belief is the best way for us to maximize the overall accuracy of our beliefs.

[14] As many readers will know, evidential and causal decision theorists disagree about how exactly to measure the consequences of an action that should be relevant for the action's rational status, and that disagreement is hotly debated. That distinction is besides the point I'm making here, though, since both sides there agree that the consequences of actions can generally be spread through space and time.

This was the claim I called TRUTH BEGETS TRUTH. TRUTH BEGETS TRUTH is supported, I argued, by the insight that when it comes to most pairs of beliefs, the two beliefs are either independent (meaning that one being true has no effect on whether the other is true) or positively dependent (meaning that one being true makes it more likely the other is true). It's rare, I argued, for real beliefs to be dependent on each other in the way they are in trade-off cases, where one being false leads to many others being true. This meant that, on the truth-loving epistemic consequentialist view, the right belief to have is almost always the true belief.

The same kind of argument can be used to show that for real agents, there will likely be minimal or no difference in how epistemic utility theorists and consequentialists rank credences for real agents. For there to be cases where a credence being best in the epistemic utility theorist's sense comes apart from it being best in the consequentialist's sense, it would need to be a case where sacrificing the accuracy of the credence at one time improves the overall accuracy of the agent's credences through time.[15] This would have to be a case where our future credences are neither independent nor positively dependent on our past credences, essentially amounting to a trade-off of credential accuracy through time. As I argued in Chapter 2, I think some trade-offs do happen and it can be epistemically permissible to take them, but nonetheless, I hypothesize that for real agents, they're rare. Confirmation of that will come only via careful empirical inquiry, but if it's true, it shows that although epistemic utility theorists and consequentialists conceive of the goodness that's to be produced by epistemic norms quite differently, they'll rarely disagree about how to rank doxastic states in real cases.

5.6 Are Epistemic Utility Theory and Truth-Loving Consequentialism Opposed?

Epistemic utility theorists and truth-loving epistemic consequentialists share a starting place in thinking that epistemic norms are about maximizing accuracy in our doxastic states. The goal of this chapter was to assess whether objections to epistemic utility theory might pose problems for truth-loving epistemic consequentialism. But even though the two views share a starting place, I've argued here that neither Gibbard's nor Carr's

[15] Here I'm assuming that in cases like Carr's Handstand, epistemic utility theorists will measure the accuracy of the credence on the assumption it is adopted, contra Carr's inclinations. Either way, I suspect cases like Carr's are also quite rare.

objections to epistemic utility theory transfer to truth-loving epistemic consequentialism.

The response to Gibbard was two-fold. There, I argued that if Gibbard's proposed practical explanation of immodesty worked, then truth-based views should be able to produce an equally compelling epistemic explanation of immodesty using his model. Epistemic utility theorists generally accept that immodesty is a requirement, so they might be able to mirror this aspect of my response to Gibbard. As we saw above, though, the truth-loving epistemic consequentialist should additionally deny that immodesty is a requirement of epistemic rightness. Epistemic utility theorists cannot mirror this move without giving up on immodesty (of course), but neither can they mirror it without giving up on Joyce's arguments for probabilism, which also use immodesty as a premise.

The response to Carr was also two-fold. I argued that truth-loving epistemic consequentialism isn't subject to the worries about how epistemic utility theorists use expected utility arguments because truth-loving consequentialists shouldn't see expected utility maximization as relevant to understanding right belief. As I suggested above, aiming to maximize expected goodness is more plausibly involved in having a rational or justified belief, not a right belief. When it comes to Carr's worries about dominance avoidance arguments, I argued that truth-loving consequentialists should be happy to sanction those arguments, since they might be able to teach us about what doxastic states in fact conduce to epistemic goodness. But, depending on how epistemic utility theorists respond to Carr's challenge (and similar challenges from Greaves and Caie), they might want to limit their dominance avoidance reasoning to cases that include all possible worlds, including those in which the credences aren't adopted. The consequentialist will be more interested in dominance arguments that use the narrowest available set of worlds, since those have the most potential to teach us about what real agents ought to think. Epistemic utility theorists will be unhappy to follow the truth-loving epistemic consequentialist in these responses, since it would require them to give up on many of their central results, including the most prominent defenses of conditionalization and probabilism.

Focusing on the kind of value involved in dominance avoidance arguments seemed to bring out an even deeper divide between epistemic utility theorists and truth-loving epistemic consequentialists. Epistemic utility theorists measure veritistic value in terms of 'local' accuracy, which is simply a measure of how close the credence or belief is to the truth. Truth-loving epistemic consequentialists should go in for a more holistic measure that takes into account not only the the local accuracy of the doxastic state but also how adopting that state will affect the accuracy of other doxastic states through time.

All of this disagreement between epistemic utility theorists and truth-loving epistemic consequentialists might make us think that the two views are fundamentally at odds with each other. But I think there's a more ecumenical way to understand the situation. As I said at the outset of this chapter, epistemic utility theorists typically cast their views in terms of rational belief, not right belief. In this chapter, I intentionally elided the distinction to better assess whether the objections to epistemic utility theory translate to truth-loving consequentialism. Bringing that distinction back in can help assuage worries about whether the two views really clash. If we take seriously the idea that epistemic utility theorists are after a theory of rational belief, as opposed to a theory of right belief, we might be able to make sense of why defenses of those views might be justified in giving different responses to the objections. There might be rationality-related reasons to go in for a certain way of thinking about dominance avoidance, or there might be reasons to think expected utility maximization is relevant to a norm of rational belief or credence, despite it not being relevant for right belief or credence.

Moreover, even though the views differ at a theoretical level about how to measure veritistic value, as I argued at the end of the last section, for almost all real cases we should expect the two views to rarely disagree about what's best. Whatever disagreement remains might again be explainable in terms of the views having different targets. As we'll discuss more in Chapter 7, there's good reason to think that our best theory of rationality (and other epistemic responsibility notions) might differ dramatically in structure from our best theory of right belief. There's no tension in thinking that there's a kind of value associated with rational doxastic states that's different from the value associated with right doxastic states. The main aim of this book is to flesh out a theory of rightness, so I won't take a stand here on whether epistemic utility theory is well poised to help us understand epistemic responsibility notions. But by distinguishing what we take the targets of epistemic utility theory and truth-loving epistemic consequentialism to be, we can be less worried that these two seemingly allied views are in tension.

6

On Racist Beliefs and Moral Encroachment

6.1 The (Apparent?) Conflict Between Epistemic and Moral Norms

Consider the following case:

> COSMOS CLUB The Cosmos Club has 50 staff, all of whom are Black. The club has 500 members, only 5 of which are Black; the rest are white. Agnes, a new member of the club, doesn't know any of the members or staff yet. In front of her, she sees a Black man who, unbeknownst to her, is noted historian (and member of the club) John Hope Franklin. Agnes knows the statistics about the racial breakdown of the club members and staff, and she knows that the staff can't be identified by their dress, name tags, or anything visible like that. Agnes correctly works out that the probability that a person at the club is staff given that they're Black is over 90 percent. On that basis, Agnes believes that Franklin is staff and asks him to bring her coat. (This is a simplified version of a case from Basu 2021a that is originally from Gendler 2011.)

Gendler (2011) argues that cases like these show that there are epistemic costs to being anti-racist. The reasoning, slightly simplified, goes like this:

1. There are epistemic costs to not taking base rates into account (such as missing out on background statistical information).
2. If we take base rates into account using extant racial categories, we'll encode problematic associations (such as the tight correlation between being Black and being staff in the above example).

Right Belief and True Belief. Daniel J. Singer, Oxford University Press. © Oxford University Press 2023.
DOI: 10.1093/oso/9780197660386.003.0007

3. If we encode those problematic associations, we'll be disposed to act in racist ways (like by treating someone as a staff member because they're Black).
4. Norms of anti-racism require that we not be disposed to act in racist ways.
5. So there are epistemic costs to following the norms of anti-racism.

As presented in my formulation, the argument is obviously not valid without the additional claim that we'll continue using extant racial categories in thought. I don't take this to be very controversial. As Egan (2011) argues, it's difficult to see how we could give them up, and it's unclear that the relevant base rate information could be taken into account with categories that don't lead to the same problem. Moreover, it seems like the extant categories are helpful to anti-racist pursuits, since we must use those concepts to understand and explain the history of racist oppression that has given rise to the unjust social structures that anti-racists aim to overthrow.

As she presents it, Gendler's argument appears to heavily rely on contingent facts about human reasoning. She discusses at length examples of how humans who use extant racial categories suffer epistemic costs like deficiencies in cross-race face identification, stereotype threat, and cognitive depletion following interracial interaction. This might encourage the reader to think that her argument wouldn't apply to ideal epistemic agents. I don't think that is the right lesson to draw, nor is it the lesson she intends. Notice that we need not assume that in the example above Agnes is epistemically limited. We can see this more clearly in the following example adapted from Basu (2019b):

> SUPPOSEDLY RATIONAL RACIST Spencer is a waiter at a restaurant and has served thousands of Black and white customers. Through a careful statistical analysis, he has concluded that his Black customers tip worse than his white ones. Spencer was interested in why, so he researched the leading social systematic explanations of racial disparities and read some of the empirical literature on this (which seems to support his conclusion; e.g., Lynn 2007). On that basis, Spencer believes that Black people have been and are oppressed by racist social institutions, and he doesn't blame Black people for tipping less. That said, he does believe that the Black couple who just sat down will likely tip him worse than the white couple who just sat next to them. Spencer

really needs rent money, so he focuses his service more on the white couple than the Black one.

We need not assume that Spencer is epistemically limited to generate the apparent conflict between epistemic norms and moral norms here. In fact, if Spencer were better at theoretical reasoning, that might seem to make him more justified in his conclusion that Black people on average are worse tippers than white people, since this fact is an unfortunately true byproduct of the unjust social structures of contemporary American society. So, if Gendler is right, then the conclusion of her argument is quite general: In societies that are structured by deep racial disparities, there are epistemic costs of being anti-racist.

One response to Gendler's argument tries to draw a division between accepting a racial generalization and being disposed to act on it, putting pressure on premise 3. That is, one could think that Agnes should believe that the person is staff on the basis of his skin color but not treat him like staff on that basis. And in the other case, the idea would be that Spencer should believe that the Black couple will tip worse but not treat them any differently on that basis. Proponents of this view would hold that the agents could have the beliefs and simply not act in racist ways.

The thought behind this idea is that it's the act, not the belief, that stands to harm others or is racist; the belief itself can't harm or be racist. Treating John Hope Franklin as staff on the basis of his skin color would both harm Franklin directly and perpetuate the unjust racist social structures that gave rise to the racial imbalance in the first place. But simply believing Franklin is staff and keeping one's mouth closed doesn't harm anyone, the proponent of this move would say.

Some might object to this move by questioning whether there's a coherent notion of BELIEF such that the agents in these cases can believe but not act on that belief. It's unclear that real humans could mask the effect of these beliefs on their actions in situations where a lot is at stake for them, like if they're risking being the victim of a violent crime (cf. Gendler's section 6). But I find a different response more compelling.

Marušic and White (2018), Basu (2019b, 2021b), and Basu and Schroeder (2019) convincingly argue that we should see beliefs themselves, independent of what actions they factor in, as capable of wronging. For example, Basu (2021b) argues that "we are, each of us, in virtue of being social beings, vulnerable and we depend upon others for our self-esteem and self-respect. Respect and esteem, however, are not mere matters of how we're treated in word or deed, but also a matter of how we're treated in thought." Marušic and White (2018) flesh this out more generally in Kantian and Strawsonian terms: According to these authors, how we ought to relate to others is fundamentally distinct from how we relate to objects, and when we adopt what Strawson calls 'the participant stance' toward others, our beliefs can fail to show regard for others as much as our actions can. Additionally, as I'll discuss more below, some accounts of racism predict that beliefs themselves can be racist. If these authors are right, we can remove the action-based elements of the argument above and focus directly on the beliefs as things that can be morally problematic. Doing that gives us a simplified version of Gendler's argument, but it also motivates an approach to these cases that's in tension with truth-loving epistemic consequentialism.

In Section 6.2, I'll flesh out the simplified argument for Gendler's conclusion and get clear about the puzzle it generates. In Section 6.3, I'll consider what kinds of responses to the puzzle there could be. One response to the puzzle is to go in for moral encroachment, the view that moral features of a situation can affect epistemic evaluations. According to some defenders of moral encroachment, this view allows us to reject Gendler's conclusion while saving what's important about the premises. But using moral encroachment that way is incompatible with truth-loving epistemic consequentialism. In Section 6.4, I'll argue against moral encroachment as a solution to the puzzle. The view doesn't actually capture everything it purports to, I'll claim. In the final section, I'll argue that it isn't so bad to accept Gendler's main point—i.e., that in societies structured by deep racial disparity, we can't be both epistemically ideal and anti-racist. While this may seem like an unfortunate outcome, I'll argue that its badness is best seen as a product of the racist ills of society, not incorrect theorizing about epistemic norms.

6.2 Irrational or Racist: The Puzzle

To get started simplifying Gendler's puzzle, note two things: First, in the motivating cases above, the agents believing in accord with their evidence and aiming for truth in their beliefs leads them to doing something racist. Agnes concluded that Franklin was staff and treated him as such, and Spencer concluded that the Black couple would tip less and gave them worse service. If we grant that beliefs can wrong on their own, we can leave the actions out of the picture and still generate the apparent conflict between epistemic norms and norms of anti-racism. Second, whereas Gendler's original argument works via problematic associations that would be encoded by taking into account base rates, we can see in SUPPOSEDLY RATIONAL RACIST that the same problem occurs in any society with unjust racial disparities. If there's any racial disparity, evidence can be gathered about that disparity that would seem to justify that person in believing something about someone on the basis of their race, and in many cases (like Agnes's and Spencer's), doing so would be racist. That means we can generalize and simplify the argument like this:

1. Epistemic norms require taking into account information about racial disparities.
2. If we take into account information about racial disparities, we'll believe things about people on the basis of their race.
3. In many cases where we'd believe things about people on the basis of their race, norms of anti-racism require that we not believe those things on the basis of race.
4. So epistemic norms and norms of anti-racism conflict.

A few notes about this version of the argument: First, I put this argument in terms of what is *required* by epistemic norms and norms of anti-racism. I take it that not much hinges on formulating it exactly this way. Much of the literature puts the first idea in terms of epistemic justification instead. We should think that, more generically, what the motivating cases bring out is that there appears to be a tension between what looks good epistemically and what looks good in terms of being anti-racist. Below, I'll be more precise about the different kinds of normative terms, but for now, let's focus on the bigger picture.

Second, one might wonder if premise 3 of this argument could be strengthened to say that anti-racism requires never inferring something about someone on the basis of their race. This seems too strong to me for two reasons: (1) some simple inferences seem fine to make on the basis of someone's race—e.g., inferring from someone being Black that they are a member of a minority group; and (2) sometimes it's required by norms of anti-racism that we do infer things about people on the basis of their race—e.g., a doctor working to minimize healthcare disparities among minority groups probably *should* infer facts about different health risks that individuals face on the basis of their race. So I think the argument is best put in terms of there being *some* cases where these norms conflict.

Third, notice that to give a complete defense of premise 3, we'd need to settle on an account of what the norms of anti-racism require. According to doxastic accounts of racism, being racist simply consists in having a set of racialized beliefs or accepting a certain kind of racialized ideology (e.g., Appiah 1990, Shelby 2002, Souza 1995). If that kind of view is right, it's natural to think that norms of anti-racism will require us to not have certain kinds of beliefs or perform certain kinds of inferences. Other accounts of racism, like behavioral accounts (e.g., Philips 1984) and affective accounts (e.g., Garcia 1996), don't fit as naturally with thinking that norms of anti-racism prohibit certain beliefs or inference patterns, even though they can probably be extended to make sense of a sense in which the beliefs in the motivating cases are problematic. The view I personally find the most compelling is Glasgow's (2009) account of racism as a kind of disrespect for a person as a member of a racialized group. That view can make sense of how certain beliefs and inferences can be racist, and it fits naturally with the accounts of how beliefs can wrong I mentioned above. That said, my goal here is to defend truth-loving consequentialism from a response to Gendler's argument that accepts premise 3. So here I won't take a stand on how best to understand the third premise. For this argument, I will simply grant to my opponent that the relevant kinds of beliefs are problematically racist.

Let's now focus back on the argument as a whole. I imagine that most readers will join me in a sense of dissatisfaction with the conclusion, since it tells us that if we're going to be anti-racist, we must undermine our epistemic position in some way. For one, the conclusion clashes with an idyllic picture of normative philosophy, according to which different normative parts of philosophy (epistemology, ethics, aesthetics, etc.) will end up with compatible theories of what we ought to do in different senses. According to this idyllic picture, what we're epistemically required to do shouldn't conflict with what we're morally required to do. Another concern with the conclusion is that, as Jennifer Saul (2018, p. 238) points out, the conclusion "can be seen as (inadvertently) undermining anti-racism movements, by suggesting that opposition to racism leads one into irrationality," and it "fits exceptionally well with the right-wing narratives of politically correct thought-police attempting to prevent people from facing up to difficult truths; and of the over-emotional left, which really needs to be corrected by the sound common sense of the right." So, if possible, it would be nice to avoid Gendler's conclusion while still explaining how agents are subject to both epistemic norms and norms of anti-racism.

Let's consider what we might ideally like from a compelling response to Gendler's argument. I take it that there are three desiderata we should have for a good response. First, and most obviously, we'd like the proposed response to avoid there being a conflict between epistemic norms and moral norms of anti-racism. "I'll call this the 'No Conflict desideratum.' "

> No Conflict There is no conflict between epistemic norms and moral norms.

Exactly how strong to make this desideratum is up for debate. On the strongest reading of it, it would require that it's impossible for epistemic and moral norms to conflict—i.e., there could never be a situation in which what an agent epistemically ought to do conflicts with what they morally ought to do. A weaker reading might be that moral and epistemic norms don't *actually* conflict (or conflict in nearby worlds)—i.e., there aren't any real situations (or realistic enough situations) in which a conflict occurs, even if a conflict could, in theory, occur. Meeting this weaker requirement would still force the solution to explain what's going on in COSMOS CLUB since that one is based on a true story.

A second desideratum for responses to the argument is that the response maintain that it's wrong to have the racist beliefs in question. Presumably, the account will hold that there are (sufficient) moral reasons not to hold the belief, but the account might also point to other kinds of reasons not to hold the belief. This is the Racist Beliefs Are Wrong desideratum.

> Racist Beliefs Are Wrong Agents like those in COSMOS CLUB and SUPPOSEDLY RATIONAL RACIST are wrong to hold the purportedly racist beliefs.[1]

As we'll see below, there are accounts that will treat this exclusively as a moral requirement, but some will think there is also something epistemically wrong with holding the racist beliefs.

[1] I put this in terms of 'purportedly racist beliefs' to not make the claim a tautology in the eyes of those who think that it's a conceptual truth that we shouldn't hold racist beliefs.

The last desideratum is about what is epistemically required in cases like COSMOS CLUB and SUPPOSEDLY RATIONAL RACIST. When an agent inhabits a society characterized by structurally racist institutions like ours and has evidence of these things, the agent would be epistemically amiss if they didn't take that information into account in some way. If one adopts a traditional evidentialist picture of epistemic justification (e.g., Feldman and Conee 1985), then one would think Agnes's and Spencer's beliefs are justified because they have the beliefs supported by their evidence. I don't want to assume that any response to Gendler's argument must judge Agnes and Spencer to be justified. That said, a response to Gendler that says that these agents should willfully have inaccurate beliefs or ignore their evidence doesn't seem to capture what's required either. Such agents would be missing out on important information about their world, including information that might be helpful in their anti-racist pursuits. So good responses to Gendler should say that agents in cases like those above should take into account the information about racial disparities and the race of the person they're interacting with, and ideally, the response would explain in what way the agents should take that information into account.

> Take Information into Account Agents like those in COSMOS CLUB and SUPPOSEDLY RATIONAL RACIST ought to take into account the information about racial disparities and the races of those they're interacting with.

As we'll see below, a lot will hinge on exactly how to make sense of this epistemic desideratum. In the spirit of being as ecumenical as possible in setting out the desiderata, I won't strengthen it further here, but below I'll argue that some proposed ways of making sense of this desideratum fall short.

By putting the three desiderata like this, we can clarify what's at the heart of Gendler's puzzle: In a world with unjust social structures like ours, the social structures give rise to unjust racial disparities. If a view says that agents epistemically ought to take into account the information about racial disparities and the races of those they're interacting with (to meet the Take Information into Account desideratum), it's hard to see how the view could avoid saying that the agents epistemically ought to have beliefs that wrong others in racist ways. So then if the view satisfies the Racist Beliefs are Wrong desideratum by holding that racist beliefs are at least morally wrong, it must also think that epistemic and moral norms conflict, thereby not satisfying the No Conflict desideratum.

In the next section, I'll canvass some responses to the puzzle and show why truth-loving epistemic consequentialism is in tension with a popular solution, moral encroachment.

6.3 Dilemmism, Moral Encroachment, and Purism

One possible response to the puzzle is simply to accept the conclusion that epistemic norms and norms of anti-racism conflict. Roughly inspired by Basu's terminology, I'll call this the 'dilemmist' position. Basu (2021a) characterizes the dilemmist position as thinking that "we must choose between doing what we epistemically ought (attend and respond to the background statistical information about the race of the staff members) and what we morally ought (not use someone's race to make assumptions about them, such as that they are staff)."[2] How I'll use the term (but not how Basu uses it), being a dilemmist only commits one to thinking there is this conflict. It doesn't commit one to a particular answer to the question of which should win out (or if one should). In other words, there are many ways of being a dilemmist: One could accept that there's a conflict and think that moral norms take precedence over epistemic norms. One could think that the epistemic norms take precedence. One could think there's another kind of norm that will answer the question of which takes precedence in any case, or one could even think there's just a dilemma here and nothing further can be said about what we ought to do. These are all dilemmist positions, in my sense, because they accept there being a conflict between epistemic norms and norms of anti-racism.

How well do dilemmists do with respect to the desiderata? Dilemmists can straightforwardly account for the sense in which the racist beliefs are wrong and the sense in which agents ought to take the information into account, since the view is compatible with any story about how those work.

[2] It's not clear to me that Gendler endorses the dilemmist position, despite that being the standard thing to say in the literature. Her conclusion is that "racially-based inequities—and the psychological processes by which we inevitably encode them—carry not merely moral, but also epistemic, costs" (Gendler 2011, p. 57). It doesn't follow from Gendler's conclusion that the norms conflict. It's only if the norms are determined by the costs—the claim of the consequentialist—that they would necessarily conflict.

What the dilemmist gives up on is the No Conflict desideratum. So dilemmists only get two of the three desiderata.

Some defenders of moral encroachment views think they can do better. They claim to be able to explain all the desiderata with one view that allows the moral features of situations to impact the epistemic status of a belief. According to defenders of this view, when we do this, moral and epistemic norms don't clash, and we can save all the desiderata.

Moral encroachment is often understood by analogy to pragmatic encroachment, the view that practical stakes can affect the epistemic status of a belief. The standard kind of motivation for pragmatic encroachment uses pairs of cases that go like this: Sarah has her paycheck in hand and is deciding whether to go wait in line to deposit it today, which is a Friday. In the first case, nothing hinges on whether the deposit gets done today. In the second case, if she doesn't deposit the check by the end of tomorrow, her mortgage payment will bounce and she might lose her house. Sarah asks her wife whether the bank is open on Saturdays. Sarah's wife says she thinks it is. According to the defender of pragmatic encroachment, in the first case, Sarah might come to know or have a justified belief that the bank is open on Saturday on the basis of her wife's testimony. In the second case, she might not (or at least it is harder). What explains the difference in epistemic status can't be a difference in the evidence Sarah has, since she has the same evidence in both cases. So it must be the practical stakes themselves that change the epistemic status. (For more on pragmatic encroachment, see Fantl and McGrath 2002, 2009; Stanley 2005; and Schroeder 2012.)

Defenders of moral encroachment think something similar happens with moral stakes. In COSMOS CLUB, for example, a defender of moral encroachment might hold that since believing Franklin to be staff risks doing something morally wrong, Agnes must have more evidence to be justified in believing it. Were the stakes lower, such as if it were about believing that Franklin likes martinis on the basis of him holding one, the justification hurdle would be lower.[3]

How do moral encroachment views fare with respect to the puzzle about racist beliefs? According to some proponents of these views, they're able to meet all three of the desiderata. Basu (2021a), for example, claims that moral encroachment can solve the puzzle because the moral and epistemic

[3] I won't flesh out the motivation for moral encroachment views more here, since I don't challenge the motivation. For further development of different motivations for the view, see Bolinger (2020b).

"considerations work together to determine what you should believe and what you should do." So Basu thinks moral encroachers can account for the No Conflict desideratum. Moral encroachment is also compatible with basically any view of how to explain the Racist Beliefs Are Wrong desideratum. So they don't have a problem there. Lastly, defenders of moral encroachment hold that their view explains the Take Information into Account desideratum since any moral encroachment view will give an account of how the traditional truth-indicative features of beliefs (evidence, being the product of a reliable belief-forming process, etc.) work together with moral features of situations to give rise to epistemic statuses. Different defenders of moral encroachment will tell different stories about exactly how this works (see Bolinger 2020a for an overview), but the general theme is that agents take the information into account because the traditionally epistemic features of the situation play into what the agent should believe. So moral encroachment views, at least by some of their proponents' lights, are able to meet all three desiderata on a response to Gendler.

You might have noticed that I said that *some* defenders of moral encroachment might take their view to be a response to Gendler's puzzle. In the next section, I'll argue that moral encroachment cannot solve the puzzle. One key piece of that argument will be the claim that if moral encroachment views can solve the puzzle, their view will have to say that moral features of situations can affect epistemic *permissibility*, not just any epistemic status. In the literature on moral encroachment, the view is rarely put as being about epistemic permissibility. It's most commonly discussed as a view of epistemic justification (e.g., Basu 2019b; Fritz 2017; Pace 2011), epistemic rationality (e.g., Bolinger 2020a), or knowledge (e.g., Moss 2018). It's compatible with everything I'll argue below that a defender of moral encroachment could maintain that their view is merely about justification, rationality, etc. but not epistemic permissibility. If they do that, though, as I'll argue, they'll give up on their view being a viable solution to the puzzle. I'll turn to that argument in the next section.

Before that, let's consider how truth-loving epistemic consequentialism and pragmatic/moral encroachment interact. Both kinds of encroachment are often defined in contrast to 'purism' about epistemic statuses. Purism is standardly understood as the view that the only thing relevant to determining the epistemic status of a belief is the holder's evidence (e.g., Bolinger 2020b and Basu 2021b). In the bank cases, defenders of pragmatic encroachment deny this by holding that the practical stakes are also relevant. In COSMOS CLUB, defenders of moral encroachment deny this by holding that the moral risks of holding the belief about Franklin are also relevant. As Bolinger (2020b) argues, purism isn't the same thing as evidentialism. Evidentialism is typically construed as the view that one's belief is justified only if it's the belief supported by one's evidence (e.g., Feldman and Conee 1985). Bolinger shows us that evidentialism is consistent with thinking that practical or moral stakes matter for justification, just not that they *directly* matter. There are various ways of fleshing out how practical and moral stakes might indirectly matter for justification that are consistent with evidentialism. One natural one is thinking that the stakes affect how much evidence one must have for one's evidence to support a particular belief. The evidentialist can get on board with that picture, because the evidentialist can hold that fit with evidence determines whether a belief is justified but also think that stakes determine whether a particular content fits with a particular collection of evidence.

Truth-loving epistemic consequentialism holds that epistemic rightness is determined by true belief and the lack of false belief. So it is not a purist view in the way purist views are typically cast—it doesn't hold that the only thing relevant to determining the epistemic status of a belief is the holder's evidence. But if purism is supposed to be the natural competitor to encroachment, the standard way to understand purism is overly narrow. Consider a simple reliabilist about justification who holds that a belief is justified iff it was formed by a reliable belief-forming process. Further suppose that this reliabilist individuates the belief-forming processes in ways that are insensitive to moral and practical stakes. For example, suppose that this reliabilist holds that the belief-forming process in the bank cases is something like *trusting one's partner about mundane issues when one has no reason to suspect they're mistaken*. This reliabilist will hold that Sarah is either justified in both cases or unjustified in both cases, since it's the same process being used and the reliability of it doesn't change between cases. So this reliabilist will have to deny pragmatic and moral encroachment. But the simple reliabilist view doesn't fit the standard conception of purism, since the simple reliabilist denies that the only thing relevant to determining the epistemic status of a belief is the holder's evidence—reliability of processes also matters.

But I take it that we want to count the simple reliabilist as a purist, at least insomuch as we use the concept PURISM to pick out the natural alternative to encroachment views. There's a natural sense in which this view is 'pure'—whether a belief is justified according to it depends only on factors that have traditionally been construed as relevant for justification. What are the factors that have traditionally been construed as relevant for justification? They include things like evidence, coherence, and the reliability of belief-forming processes, but they do not include the practical and moral stakes of a situation. More substantively, they're all factors that are (or their proponents take to be) directly relevant to the truth of propositions. Evidence is typically construed as a guide to truth. Reliabilists care about reliable processes because they're a guide to truth. And proponents of coherence being relevant for justification typically see it as being indicative of truth as well (e.g., BonJour 1985, p. 153). Moral and practical features of situations aren't like this: Whether Sarah's mortgage payment will bounce if she doesn't deposit the check doesn't tell us anything about whether the bank is open on Saturday. And similarly, whether treating Franklin as staff on the basis of his skin color would wrong him and perpetuate unjust social structures doesn't tell us anything about whether he is staff.[4]

So a better way to understand what the encroachment views deny and what purists accept is that the only things that are relevant to determining the epistemic status of a belief are truth-indicative features of beliefs. Different purists will disagree about which truth-indicative features are the important ones (evidence, coherence, being the product of a reliable belief-forming process, etc.), but what these views have in common is they agree that epistemic statuses are determined exclusively by truth-indicative features of beliefs.

On this way of understanding purism, many forms of epistemic consequentialism do turn out to be purist views, even though they wouldn't count as purist views in the way they're conceived of by Bolinger (2020b) and Basu (2021b). For example, Ahlstrom-Vij and Dunn (2014) construe reliabilism about justification as a purist rule-consequentialist view. That view is purist because on that view, a belief is justified "if and only if it is the direct product of a belief forming process whose direct products tend to be true" (2014, p. 542). So, like the simple reliabilist above, that

[4] The reader might be inclined to think that Franklin wouldn't be wronged by this if he were staff (i.e., if the believed proposition were true), so then knowing whether he would be wronged would be indicative of the truth of the proposition. Thinking this incorrectly assumes that true racist beliefs can't wrong people. See Basu (2019b, sec. 4).

view holds that justification depends only on a truth-indicative features of beliefs.[5]

Truth-loving epistemic consequentialism is also a purist view on this more inclusive conception of purism. Like other purist views, truth-loving epistemic consequentialism holds that it's only truth-indicative features of beliefs that matter for the epistemic status under consideration. That said, there is an important structural difference between truth-loving epistemic consequentialism and most other purist views. According to most purist views, whether a belief that *P* is justified is only a question about the truth-indicative features of that particular belief. According to the truth-loving epistemic consequentialist, whether a belief is right depends not only on the truth-indicative features of that belief but also on the truth-indicative features of other beliefs. Despite that difference, truth-loving epistemic consequentialism is still a purist view, since it says that epistemic evaluation is only about stuff that relates to the truth of beliefs, and with other purist views, it denies that moral and pragmatic factors have any effect on the relevant epistemic status. So if moral encroachment is right, the truth-loving epistemic consequentialist might be in trouble.

But is there really a conflict? Recall that truth-loving epistemic consequentialism is a view about right belief (and credence). Moral encroachment, as it's typically construed, is a view about justification, rationality, or knowledge, not rightness. So, in theory, the two views might seem compatible. But as I'll argue in the next section, moral encroachment views can't explain all three desiderata unless they also hold that moral encroachment occurs on rightness. This means we can't simply avoid the conflict between consequentialism and encroachment by holding that they're views of different things. Instead, I'll argue that no version of encroachment can in fact give a satisfying account of all three desiderata. This means that we should give up on moral encroachment trying to solve Gendler's puzzle.

6.4 Why Moral Encroachment Doesn't Solve the Puzzle

In this section I'll argue that moral encroachment views can't satisfy all three desiderata on a solution to Gendler's puzzle, contra what some of its

[5] There might be some room to sneak pragmatic and moral elements into the way that processes are individuated for this reliabilist view. I take it that's not the intended reading of the view, though.

defenders claim. I'll use '𝔑' (for '𝔑acist proposition') to refer to the proposition in cases like COSMOS CLUB and SUPPOSEDLY RATIONAL RACIST that moral encroachment purportedly applies to. In COSMOS CLUB, this is the proposition that Franklin is a staff member, and in SUPPOSEDLY RATIONAL RACIST, it's the proposition that the Black couple will tip worse than the white one.

Let's start by thinking about a very simple moral encroachment view. According to the simple kind of moral encroachment view discussed by Basu (2021a), moral elements of situations affect the amount of evidence that one needs in order to have a justified belief about a proposition—i.e., moral stakes raise the threshold of evidence needed for justification. This version of moral encroachment is about justified belief (rather than knowledge or what we ought to believe), and it takes the mechanism of encroachment to be threshold-raising. This view also takes encroachment to apply to full belief, rather than credences. For simplicity, let's also (temporarily) assume that full beliefs are the only doxastic states agents have (no credences or anything else). Let's call this 'simple moral encroachment.'

Advocates of simple moral encroachment hold that the agents in COSMOS CLUB and SUPPOSEDLY RATIONAL RACIST aren't justified in believing 𝔑 because the stakes make it too morally risky to justifiedly believe given their evidence. The problem for this view comes in trying to understand how the view meets the Take Information into Account desideratum, and why we should think the view isn't simply telling agents to ignore the relevant information. We're supposing that in cases like COSMOS CLUB, the agent's evidence supports 𝔑, at least with high probability, so if the agent's belief in the proposition wouldn't be justified, how should they take the information into account?

To meet the Take Information into Account desideratum, the simple moral encroachment defender might try to say that the agents ought to believe 𝔑 even though that belief would be unjustified. But this idea doesn't get simple moral encroachment very far. If defenders of simple encroachment say that the agents epistemically ought to believe 𝔑 even though that belief is unjustified, they'd be unable to meet the No Conflict desideratum, since the epistemic norms would make believing 𝔑 required, which would conflict with the anti-racist moral norm not to believe 𝔑. So for the simple moral encroachment view to capture all three desiderata on responses to Gendler, it must go a step past thinking that believing 𝔑 is unjustified.

It must additionally say that the agents epistemically ought not believe it. That is, the view must accept something like the following:

> UNJUSTIFIED → IMPERMISSIBLE Doxastic states are epistemically impermissible if they are unjustified.

Of course, if the view under consideration were about rationality, knowledge, or another epistemic state, it would need to accept an analogous principle to meet the No Conflict desideratum. This is why, as I mentioned above, moral encroachment views cannot be only about justification, rationality, knowledge, etc. if they're going to work as a response to Gendler; they must also be about epistemic permissibility or rightness. In cases like COSMOS CLUB and SUPPOSEDLY RATIONAL RACIST, the simple moral encroachment view must hold that the agents epistemically ought not believe $\mathfrak{R}$.

But then, if the simple moral encroacher accepts UNJUSTIFIED → IMPERMISSIBLE, they can't say that agents ought to take the racial information into account by having an unjustified belief. So we're back to the central problem for simple moral encroachment: If the agents in these cases ought not believe $\mathfrak{R}$, in what sense are these agents taking into account the information that bears on $\mathfrak{R}$—i.e., in what sense could these agents be satisfying the Take Information into Account desideratum?

As we'll see, I don't think simple moral encroachment views can answer this question, and I think this problem generalizes to more complex moral encroachment views. The problem, in brief, is that moral encroachment views require agents to act (doxastically) like they're ignorant of the racial information, so they fail to meet the Take Information into Account desideratum. To see this problem, it will be helpful to compare what views say about the agents in COSMOS CLUB and SUPPOSEDLY RATIONAL RACIST to what the view says about agents who actually are ignorant of the background racial information or the information about the races of those they're interacting with.[6] For brevity, let's call the first kind of agent (the kind in the motivating cases above) 'informed' and the second kind of agent 'ignorant'.

[6] I'll also suppose that it's not the case that these agents should have had the relevant information or evidence, to avoid concerns that these things can impact the epistemic statuses of beliefs (cf. Goldberg 2017).

To meet the Take Information into Account desideratum, moral encroachment views must think there should be a difference between informed and ignorant agents. What kind of difference should there be? It's not enough for the defender of moral encroachment to say that the informed agent will have more evidence about $\mathfrak{R}$ than the ignorant agent. This is true by stipulation in the cases and definitions, but pointing out the evidential difference doesn't tell us enough about in what sense the informed agent is taking the information into account. If the informed agent is taking the information into account, there should be some difference in how the two agents represent the world to themselves—i.e., there should be a difference in the *doxastic states* of the agents.[7] What should this difference be?

The defender of simple moral encroachment might point to one obvious doxastic difference between the two agents: The informed agent should believe all of the facts about the background unjust racial disparities that the ignorant agent will not. In COSMOS CLUB, for example, the defender of moral encroachment can point out that the informed agent, but not the ignorant agent, will believe that all of the staff at the club are Black, that almost all of the members are not Black, etc. So one doxastic difference here is that the informed agent will take into account the background and base rate information in a way that the ignorant agent wouldn't be justified in doing, since they lack the relevant evidence.

Is this enough of a doxastic difference between the informed and ignorant agents for the defender of moral encroachment to meet the Take Information into Account desideratum on responses to Gendler? I don't think it is. Let's suppose that the simple view said this was enough and consider what it would be committed to. Such a view would say that the agent in COSMOS CLUB should (1) believe that there's over a 90 percent chance that a Black person who is in the club is staff, (2) believe that the person in front of her in the club is Black, (3) have no reason to doubt that the person in front of her is staff, but (4) suspend belief on whether the person in front of her is staff. As I will argue, such a person is failing to take all of their information into account.

[7] It might seem like I'm committed to an objectionable kind of evidential or mental content internalism here, but I take the premise I'm using here to be much more narrow. The claim is simply that in cases like cosmos club and SUPPOSEDLY RATIONAL RACIST, the informed agent isn't taking the information into account if they have the same doxastic states as the ignorant agent, not that there can't be an evidential or mental content difference between two internally identical agents.

To see why I think such an agent isn't taking all their information into account, let's compare the agent in COSMOS CLUB with a particular ignorant agent in a new case that I'll call GALAXY CLUB. GALAXY CLUB is the same as COSMOS CLUB except that just as she is looking up, Agnes gets an eyelash in her eye that prevents her from discerning the race of the person in front of her. So in GALAXY CLUB, Agnes is unsure if the person in front of her is Black or white. Importantly, in GALAXY CLUB, Agnes knows that if the person in front of her is white, as 90 percent of the people in the club are, that would *guarantee* that they're not staff (since we stipulated that all the staff are Black). So in GALAXY CLUB, Agnes has much more reason to be unsure whether the person is staff than she does in COSMOS CLUB. That means that Agnes in GALAXY CLUB ought to be less sure that the person in front of her is staff than Agnes in COSMOS CLUB. But advocates of simple moral encroachment must hold that Agnes should be equally sure in both cases. That's because simple moral encroachment countenances only three doxastic attitudes Agnes could have about whether the person in front of her is staff, namely belief, disbelief, and suspension of belief. There is no room for a degreed difference in doxastic states between the cases. So defenders of this view must say that in COSMOS CLUB and GALAXY CLUB, Agnes should have *the exact same doxastic attitude* about whether the person is staff. Because simple moral encroachment can't explain the doxastic difference between the ignorant and the informed agent in these cases, it doesn't meet the Take Information into Account desideratum.

The obvious next move for moral encroachers is to add in credences or degrees of beliefs to the possible doxastic states Agnes can have. This way, they can make sense of how Agnes should be more certain of $\mathfrak{R}$ in COSMOS CLUB than in GALAXY CLUB while not fully believing in either case. The natural idea would be that Agnes should have credences in all of the relevant propositions (including $\mathfrak{R}$) that match their evidential probabilities (or at least that correlate in the right kind of way with her evidence), but Agnes should not have a full belief in $\mathfrak{R}$ (because it is not justified given the moral stakes). Adding in credences in this way would make the simple moral encroachment view match closely the views from Pace (2011) and Bolinger (2020a). I'll call this view 'simple moral encroachment with credences.'

Adding credences doesn't solve the problem, though. Were Agnes to have formed a high credence in COSMOS CLUB rather than a full belief, she could have acted exactly the same, and her doxastic states and actions would be equally racistly problematic. To see this, look at what simple moral encroachment with credences says about Agnes in COSMOS CLUB and GALAXY CLUB. In GALAXY CLUB, Agnes's evidence will make it about 10 percent probable that the person in front of her is staff, so according to the view, she should have a 10 percent credence in $\mathfrak{R}$ and not believe it. In COSMOS CLUB, Agnes's evidence will make it about 91 percent probable that the person in front of her is staff, so according to the view, she should have a 91 percent credence in $\mathfrak{R}$ and still not believe it.

The only evidential difference in Agnes's evidence between COSMOS CLUB and GALAXY CLUB is that in the former, Agnes sees that the person in front of her is Black. According to this new view, that should cause a change in credence in $\mathfrak{R}$ from close to 0 to close to 1. We took it for granted that *believing* $\mathfrak{R}$ on the basis of race was racist in the original case and ruled out by the second desideratum. How could it not be similarly wrong to so drastically increase one's credence on that basis? It seems that if Agnes increases her credence at all in $\mathfrak{R}$ upon learning the person's race, then she's transgressing in the same way she did when she changed her belief (though perhaps the magnitude of the wrong is smaller). While it may not be a racist *belief* now, surely there's something equally problematic about Agnes going from being almost certain Franklin is not staff to being almost certain he is staff because of his race.[8] So if simple moral encroachment with credences holds that the agents in the above cases should have credences in propositions that match their evidential probabilities, they'll either run afoul of the Racist Beliefs Are Wrong desideratum (if they incorrectly predict that the change in credence is not racist) or the No Conflict desideratum (if they predict that the credences are racist and epistemically required).

An important part of this argument is thinking that insomuch as one thinks that moral encroachment applies to belief because of cases like COSMOS CLUB, one should equally think that moral encroachment applies to credences and other doxastic states. Moss (2018, pp. 184–185) has already defended this claim by showing that the reasons for thinking that moral encroachment apply to full belief translate naturally to thinking that moral encroachment applies to credences (and other kinds of degreed beliefs). This shouldn't be surprising either. If you thought the relevant beliefs in

[8] Recall that I'm granting to my opponent for dialectical reasons that Agnes's belief was problematically racist in the original case. So the only additional claim that I'm making here is that if the belief was racist, then so is the credence.

the motivating cases were racist because you accepted a doxastic theory of racism, for example, you should equally see credences and other ways we represent the world to ourselves as open to being racist too. If instead you thought moral encroachment arose from cases of doxastic wronging, there are good reasons for you to think moral encroachment can arise from high credences wronging as well. Recall Basu's idea that doxastic wronging can happen because we, as social beings, can be disrespected in thought just as much as we can in action. Why think that disrespect in thought can only come via full belief? In Basu's and Schroeder's (2019) Wounded by Belief case, for example, why think that my partner's mistaken full belief that I've broken my resolution to not drink wounds me any less than her inaccurate strong suspicion? And recall the idea from Marušic and White (2018) that doxastic wronging occurs because we should relate differently to objects than to others. This applies equally well to degreed beliefs about others as it does to full beliefs. So insomuch as we thought moral encroachment happens on full belief because of the ability of beliefs to wrong or because beliefs can be racist in the way that doxastic theories of racism predict, we should equally think that moral encroachment happens on credences for the same reasons.

The point applies even if we reject doxastic theories of racism and the idea that beliefs can wrong, since our credences are often as intimately connected to our actions as our beliefs are. A small difference in whether we're in danger might rationalize taking a different route home from work, for example. So, if we thought that moral encroachment happens to belief because of belief's intimate connection to morally evaluable action (i.e., if we thought that Agnes's belief was epistemically defective because it led to the morally objectionable action of asking Franklin for her coat), then again we should think that moral encroachment applies to credences for the same reason.[9] We can also see this with behavioral theories of racism: If you thought that the beliefs in the motivating cases were racist because of their connection to racist actions, the same can be said for the credences in the new cases. So for whatever reason you might have thought

[9] I learned after writing this that Jackson and Fritz (2021) recently argue that radical moral encroachment applies to credences if it applies to beliefs, but they don't take the argument to apply to moderate moral encroachment views. The difference between the radical and moderate views is that the radical views take moral features of the belief itself to play into the epistemic status of the belief, whereas moderate views only allow the agent's actions or options to do that. The second argument I give here is meant to motivate the idea that moderate moral encroachment views should also think moral encroachment happens to credences.

that the full beliefs in the motivating cases were racistly problematic, you should equally think that the credences in the new cases are problematic. This means that advocates of simple moral encroachment with credences can't solve the problem by holding that our credences should reflect the evidential probabilities.

We're back, then, to asking what the doxastic difference between Agnes in COSMOS CLUB and Agnes in GALAXY CLUB should be. We saw that the moral encroacher can't say that the difference should be in the agents' credences. But remember that credences were introduced into the simple moral encroachment picture purely for the purpose of being the element of Agnes's doxastic state that encodes the difference in her information in the two cases. Without a difference in credences, simple moral encroachment with credences faces the same problem as simple moral encroachment without credences. The problem is that it fails to explain the Take Information into Account desideratum, since it must hold that there should be no doxastic difference between the informed Agnes in COSMOS CLUB and ignorant Agnes in GALAXY CLUB.

So when we look at simple moral encroachment with credences, what we see play out is a dilemma that shares its structure with the problem for moral encroachment without credences: If the view holds that having the racist belief (changing one's credence) is epistemically required, it runs afoul of the No Conflict desideratum or incorrectly predicts that the belief (credence change) is not racist. If the view instead says that suspension (same credence) is required, it fails to account for the sense in which agents ought to take the information into account.

Recently, Moss (2018) offered a view similar to simple moral encroachment with credences that says that the agents in COSMOS CLUB and SUPPOSEDLY RATIONAL RACIST should have credences in $\mathfrak{R}$ that match its evidential probability. On this view, though, the credences would be justified but they'd fail to be knowledge. Could this view avoid the problem?

One thing this view gets right, I think, is that it marks down the credences themselves, not just the beliefs, in light of the moral stakes. If the view aims to be a solution to Gendler's puzzle that captures all three desiderata, it doesn't go far enough, though. The view would need to hold that Agnes is justified in changing her credence in $\mathfrak{R}$ from near 0 to near 1 when she learns the race of the person in front of her (but that her new credence doesn't constitute knowledge). If the defender of this view additionally held that Agnes epistemically ought to change her credence (not just that the change would be justified), then the view would run afoul of the No Conflicts desideratum. As I argued above, insomuch as we find believing $\mathfrak{R}$ on the basis of race morally objectionable, we should equally find changing one's credence like this objectionable. So if this view were to hold that Agnes epistemically ought to change her credence from near 0 to near 1 on the basis of learning Franklin's race, it won't be able to account for the No Conflict desideratum. On the other hand, if the view were to say that Agnes changing her credence is justified but not required, then it can't explain the Take Information into Account desideratum, because Agnes is not required to take the information into account on this view (even though her credence would be justified were she to do so).

I hope that we can now start to see that this general form of argument can be given against any moral encroachment view, not just the particular ones I considered here. If a moral encroachment view purports to meet all three desiderata on responses to Gendler's puzzle, it will need to simultaneously hold that we morally must not hold the racist beliefs (or credences), that we epistemically must take the racial information into account, and that moral and epistemic norms don't conflict in these cases. What I've argued here is that, in cases like COSMOS CLUB and SUPPOSEDLY RATIONAL RACIST, if an agent is taking the information into account, then we should see some change in their doxastic state about the objectionable belief content when they learn the race of the person they're interacting with. But that change in the agent's doxastic state about the objectionable content on the basis of the person's race is exactly what is morally objectionable. So in order to meet the Take the Information into Account desideratum and the Racist Beliefs Are Wrong desideratum, the view must give up on No Conflicts.

This argument doesn't hinge on any of the simplifications used in the toy moral encroachment views discussed above. I focused on views that take threshold-raising for the epistemic status to be the central mechanism for moral encroachment, but the argument works equally well against views that take the mechanism to be sphere-expanding in the sense described by Bolinger (2020b), like those discussed by Moss (2018) and Gardiner (2020), and those that think moral considerations can directly influence epistemic statuses, like the view strongly suggested by Basu (2019b). Moreover, the argument doesn't depend on what epistemic status is in play, since as I discussed above, whatever the status is, if the view makes sense of the No Conflicts desideratum, it will have to hold that lacking the epistemic status will make the doxastic state epistemically impermissible. So this argument works against moral encroachment views that take the relevant epistemic status to be any status, including justification, epistemic rationality, and knowledge.

The argument does depend on thinking that in cases like COSMOS CLUB and SUPPOSEDLY RATIONAL RACIST, there epistemically ought to be a change in the agents' doxastic states about the objectionable content when they learn the racial information in the situation—i.e., that a change in doxastic state about $\mathfrak{R}$ is required for agents to meet the Take Information into Account desideratum. My argument for this above centered on there being a difference in what informed Agnes should think about the person in front of her in COSMOS CLUB versus what ignorant Agnes should think in GALAXY CLUB. Even though many defenders of moral encroachment will think there should be that difference,[10] I take this to be the most natural place to push back on the argument. So let's consider an alternative.

An alternative moral encroachment view might say that the agents ought not change their doxastic state about $\mathfrak{R}$ in learning the racial information, but rather, they merely ought to be disposed to change their doxastic state more easily. To flesh this out more, let's consider Agnes in COSMOS CLUB versus Agnes in GALAXY CLUB again. Recall that the only evidential difference between them is that in COSMOS CLUB, Agnes has the information that the person in front of her is Black, which she lacks in GALAXY CLUB. According to the disposition-based view, Agnes ought to have the same doxastic states (either beliefs or credences) about $\mathfrak{R}$ in both COSMOS CLUB and GALAXY CLUB. The difference, this view says, between the cases is that in COSMOS CLUB, Agnes takes the racial information into account by being disposed to more easily come to believe $\mathfrak{R}$ upon receiving further supporting evidence. In this way, Agnes doesn't have the objectionable belief, but she still takes the information into account in some broader sense.

I'm skeptical that this approach to moral encroachment gives a more satisfying response to Gendler than the other moral encroachment views. First, it's difficult to see how the defender of this view could craft the disposition in such a way to avoid it being, for all intents and purposes, a doxastic state of the agent that represents $\mathfrak{R}$ as more likely in the COSMOS CLUB case. If you go in for thinking that the agent can take the information about $\mathfrak{R}$

[10] The most popular versions of moral encroachment generally seem to have the same structure as simple moral encroachment with credences, where there is some element of the doxastic state of the agent that is supposed to track the evidential probability of $\mathfrak{R}$. See Bolinger (2020b) for more discussion of the particular versions.

into account by having a disposition to change their doxastic state about 𝔑, you must think that having the disposition is how they should represent the information about 𝔑 to themself. But the ways by which we represent the world to ourselves in this evidentially responsive way just are our doxastic states. So it seems like it will be hard to make sense of how this view could go in for a difference in dispositions being a way for the agent to take the information into account in COSMOS CLUB without there also being a difference in doxastic state.

Another way to get at this point is to consider what it would be like if someone *only* had a new or stronger disposition to change their doxastic state in COSMOS CLUB as compared to GALAXY CLUB (and did not have a different doxastic state). It seems like the mere disposition wouldn't be sufficient for meeting the Take Information into Account desideratum. It would need to be literally true that the agent in GALAXY CLUB should represent the 𝔑-ness of the world to herself in exactly the same way as the agent in COSMOS CLUB, despite the fact that the agent in GALAXY CLUB knows that it's overwhelmingly likely that the person in front of her is white, which would entail that they're not staff. Merely having a disposition to more easily change one's view about 𝔑, without actually thinking that 𝔑 is more likely in the one case, doesn't seem to capture what's epistemically required. So if the view said that there was no doxastic state that accompanied the disposition, it couldn't meet the Take Information into Account desideratum.

But even if the view could make sense of how having a disposition could be a way to take the information into account without there being an accompanying doxastic state, the view would still face another worry. This worry is that having the disposition to more easily believe or raise one's credence in 𝔑 based on race seems to be as problematic as having the belief or credence on that basis is. If the disposition-based view is right, we should be able to construct cases similar to COSMOS CLUB in which (1) the agent has the disposition, (2) the agent comes to believe the person is staff after receiving some new evidence, but also (3) were the agent not to have the racial information (and so lack the disposition), they would not have believed the person is staff even after gaining the new evidence. In a case like that, the agent still ends up believing 𝔑 because of the information they have about the person's race. It's hard to see how that's not as morally objectionable as the belief in the original COSMOS CLUB case, and so the puzzle can be recreated for this view. Again here, like with the addition of credences to simple moral encroachment above, we could run though the various reasons to think the belief in the original case is problematic, and we'd see that they all apply equally well to this disposition. So, what we see then is that even if the disposition-based moral encroachment view could be made sense of without doxastic states, it doesn't look like it can square the three desiderata any more than the other views can.[11]

Overall, then, there's a general problem for using moral encroachment as a response to Gendler that aims to account for all three desiderata. If such a view can make sense of the way that Agnes in COSMOS CLUB epistemically ought to represent the world to herself differently than Agnes in GALAXY CLUB, it will be committed to Agnes having an objectionable doxastic state and so either run afoul of the Racist Beliefs Are Wrong desideratum or the No Conflict desideratum. But if it gives up on there being a difference in how informed Agnes and ignorant Agnes should represent the world, the view isn't able to explain the Take Information into Account desideratum. Either way, moral encroachment views fail to capture all three desiderata, and so the views aren't the compelling responses to Gendler that some of their proponents purport them to be. In the next section, I'll argue that if we're going to give up on a desideratum, we should give up on the No Conflicts desideratum and be dilemmists.

6.5 How to Be a Dilemmist

In the previous section, I argued that moral encroachment views can't meet all three of the desiderata for a response to Gendler. One of the key steps in that argument held that if a moral encroachment view could satisfy the No Conflicts desideratum, it must be a view about epistemic permissibility or rightness, not only justification or another epistemic status. The reason for that is that if there are going to be conflicts between moral and epistemic norms, the conflict must be about what is permissible or right, since

[11] You might think another way to hold that the information shouldn't be represented in agents' doxastic states is to follow Munton (2019) who argues that some statistical generalizations of the relevant kind are epistemically objectionable because of how they project to new cases. While I'm skeptical of there being an epistemic flaw in Munton's central cases, that's irrelevant here since we're assuming that the moral encroachment theorist grants that the information should be taken into account in some way. Munton's argument, even if it's right, only gives us a way of not taking the information into account. Moreover, even if Munton is right about some statistical generalizations, it seems like it should be possible to build a case like cosmos club and SUPPOSEDLY RATIONAL RACIST that avoids the projectability problems that Munton brings out.

that is what the relevent moral norms govern. As I mentioned above, very few defenders of moral encroachment put the view in terms of epistemic permissibility or rightness. They instead opt for talk of justification, rationality, or knowledge. As we've discussed, it's possible to be a truth-loving epistemic consequentialist (or other kind of purist) about epistemic rightness and still predict moral encroachment on justification, rationality, or another epistemic status. Doing this won't further moral encroachment's ability to respond to Gendler, but it will allow the purist about rightness to save many of the judgments the moral encroacher would like to make. In this section, I'll further plump for being a dilemmist about rightness. I'll argue that being a dilemmist doesn't have many of the disadvantages that it might appear to have, and what disadvantages it might appear to have turn out to be problems of racist societies, not problems of the view itself. Dilemmism, I'll conclude, is the most promising response to Gendler, which works out well, since it's exactly what the truth-loving epistemic consequentialist would predict.

The main motivation for going in for dilemmism is that the view can accept the intuitive premises of Gendler's argument. The dilemmist can hold that epistemic norms require us to take into account information about racial disparities. It can also hold that having racist beliefs and performing racist actions are morally wrong. And it can hold both of those even though doing the former might either constitute having racist beliefs or give rise to us performing racist actions. In saving those two desiderata, one might worry that a problem with the view becomes immediately obvious: Mustn't the dilemmist hold (seemingly incorrectly) that the agents in COSMOS CLUB and SUPPOSEDLY RATIONAL RACIST are doing something right, at least in some sense?

To answer that, we should be very careful about what the dilemmist is committed to. Because the dilemmist can disconnect epistemic rightness from other epistemic statuses, the dilemmist need not think that Agnes's or Spencer's beliefs are justified, rational, warranted, etc. This allows the dilemmist to agree with many of the judgments of moral encroachment views. Moreover, the dilemmist can explain our reluctance to describe those beliefs as 'right' in any sense. Since dilemmists will hold that the racist beliefs are morally wrong (and presumably all-things-considered wrong), dilemmists can hold that, even though the beliefs are epistemically right, describing them as 'right' (in any sense) is itself morally wrong because doing so might encourage us to think in ways that give rise to them, which is morally wrong. Cases like this arise for ethical consequentialism as well. Consider a sniper who has someone in his sights that, unbeknownst to anyone, will be a future evil dictator. Shooting the future dictator can be the right thing to do morally (and all things considered), according to the ethical consequentialist, but even so, the consequentialist won't condone us encouraging snipers to shoot people who are, unbeknownst to them, future evil dictators. The moral risks of thinking like that are too high. Similarly, even though the dilemmist is committed to thinking that Agnes's and Spencer's beliefs are epistemically right, the dilemmist has a good story about why we'd be uneasy describing them as such (because doing so is morally, and presumably all-things-considered, wrong).

I imagine that the objector might still worry that the dilemmist being committed to the beliefs being epistemically right is problematic. The objector might insist, after all, that the point of epistemic normativity is to guide us on what to think and how to reason, so mustn't the dilemmist be committed to thinking there's an interesting sense of 'right' according to which Agnes's and Spencer's beliefs are right? And if so, doesn't that incorrectly suggest approval for their beliefs, at least in some sense?

The objector might be motivated to accept this kind of reasoning because they accept the conception of ethical and epistemic normativity discussed in Chapter 1 that holds that all norms of belief are epistemic norms and that ethical norms don't apply to beliefs. If that conception of the kinds of normativity were right, it would follow that Agnes's and Spencer's beliefs would be just plain right, since them being epistemically right would be sufficient for that. But notice that in a lot of this discussion, we've been granting to proponents of moral encroachment that beliefs can be morally wrong. That assumption is incompatible with the traditional picture of ethical and epistemic normativity. And as I'll argue in the next chapter, for the global epistemic consequentialist, epistemic normativity is best conceived of as normativity that's in service of the epistemic end, rather than the normativity of belief. As such, the truth-loving epistemic consequentialist should think that epistemic normativity applies not only to beliefs and reasoning but also to the use of statistical tests, the setup of experiments, and (as I'll argue in the next chapter) even actions. It's natural to accept a similar story about ethical normativity on the global consequentialist picture. If we do, we'll see ethical normativity as applying not only to action but also to other things like what dispositions one should have, how one thinks about others, and, importantly, beliefs and reasoning. Using that more general sense of ethical normativity allows the dilemmist to respond to the above worries: The dilemmist need not hold that Agnes's and Spencer's beliefs are right in any sense beyond a quite deflated and deficient one.

The idea is that while the dilemmist must hold that the beliefs are epistemically right, it's open to the dilemmist to think that isn't saying much since the beliefs are morally (and all-things-considered) very wrong. Compare a case of someone suffering from a social anxiety disorder that causes them to be dysfunctionally shy in large crowds. Let's suppose it's Sven. Suppose Sven's therapist suggests that Sven try speaking with three new people at a party because doing so will help him overcome his fear. Now suppose Sven goes to a party and is gripped by fear. In an attempt to work through it, he yells a slur at someone. What should we think of what Sven did? If we contort our intuitions enough, we might say that what he did was right in some respect (since he interacted with someone) and wrong in another (since he called someone a slur), but doing so would strongly go against what we're inclined to say here (that what he did was just wrong). Whatever sense in which Sven did something right in this situation is deeply deficient because it's strongly overridden by the moral considerations against calling someone a slur. In fact, the sense in which Sven did something right is so deeply deficient that we find it misleading to even talk or think that way. Nonetheless, we might not be surprised if Sven's therapist thinks at least *some* progress was made in the incident. In Agnes's case, like in Sven's, the moral considerations strongly override the epistemic ones. In the epistemic case, the dilemmist should hold that while the agents' beliefs are epistemically right in these cases, that only makes them right in a deeply deficient sense of the term—one that's so deficient that it's not even worth considering in normal thought and talk. So it's not a major problem for the dilemmist, I take it, that they're committed to thinking there's something right, in a very weak sense, going on with the agents in the motivating cases.

A related worry about dilemmism is one that was mentioned in the introduction to this chapter. As Saul (2018, p. 238) argues, a commitment to dilemmism "can be seen as (inadvertently) undermining anti-racism movements, by suggesting that opposition to racism leads one into irrationality." Why would the dilemmist be committed to this? The idea is that the dilemmist will say that following anti-racist moral norms forces us to violate epistemic norms, because the two kinds of norms conflict in cases like this. As Saul further points out, this conclusion is itself not helpful to anti-racist efforts since it "fits exceptionally well with the right-wing narratives of politically correct thought-police attempting to prevent people from facing up to difficult truths; and of the over-emotional left, which really needs to be corrected by the sound common sense of the right."

Saul is right that the dilemmist is committed to thinking that following anti-racist norms forces us to violate epistemic norms and that this picture fits squarely into the right-wing narrative she mentions. That said, as I just argued, the dilemmist is only committed to thinking that being anti-racist in these cases is a merely technical violation of epistemic norms, not that it's a violation that should hold any real normative weight for us. And while the dilemmist might be committed to something that looks like the literal truth of the right-wing narrative, the dilemmist ought to deny the implication of that narrative that agents ought to care about that form of 'irrationality.' Again here, compare cases where other kinds of normativity conflict: In Peter Singer's pond case, we should reject the argument that we shouldn't save the drowning child because doing so would leave us smelly and so be aesthetically irrational. Similarly, the dilemmist can (and should, I think) hold that the fear of epistemic irrationality should not dissuade us from being anti-racist. Moreover, the dilemmist should also say that we have a moral obligation to reject discussions of anti-racism in the terms of the right-wing narrative, since doing so has clear moral risks. It's no objection to the dilemmist here that their view makes certain versions of that narrative literally true, since we often have moral reasons not to say things that are literally true.[12]

Another worry about dilemmism mentioned in the introduction to this chapter is that dilemmism is in conflict with what I called the 'idyllic' picture of normative philosophy, in which different parts of normative philosophy like ethics, decision theory, epistemology, etc. will end up producing correct theories of different kinds of normativity that don't conflict with each other. As the reader can probably discern from how I describe this picture, I'm worried that it's motivated by an overly utopian and unrealistic picture of normative philosophy. Conflicts of norms appear to be present in lots of areas of normative work. The norms of being a professor can commit us

[12] There are easy cases here like the oft-repeated case of the person who asks their partner how they look in their new dress. But there are also cases more analogous to what's going on with anti-racism and the right wing: If you're a doctor who's running short on time to give an order to save someone's life, making random true claims about history of medicine is not morally permitted—you must say what is needed to save the person's life. Similarly, in societies with deeply racist social structures, employing the right-wing narrative Saul mentions is not morally permitted—we must focus on how to dismantle those structures and protect those targeted by them.

to having office hours at the same time that the norms of being a parent commit us to picking up our kids from soccer practice. Sometimes norms of being healthy conflict with norms of being social, when, for example, an alcoholic is having a night out with friends. And aesthetic norms can conflict with child-saving norms, like in the pond example just discussed. The dilemmist (as I use the term) need not think these conflicts are genuine dilemmas where there is no further fact about what we should do (like the kind discussed by Williams and Atkinson 1965). All the dilemmist needs is that there is both a norm that approves of the belief and another one that disapproves of it, which is compatible with thinking one norm should win out. Cases like these are commonplace, so the idyllic picture, insomuch as it rejects the possibility of that kind of conflict, is overly idealistic.

Also notice that, in many situations, what explains these apparent normative conflicts is disadvantageous facts in the world, not bad theorizing about the norms. Suppose you promise to go see your neighbor's art show, but as you're going out the door, your partner calls to say they're sick and need you to go to the hospital with them. In this situation, you have a strong moral obligation to go to the hospital with your partner. That's not the only norm in play here, though, which we can see by noting that you owe an apology (or at least an explanation) to your neighbor and they could reasonably be disappointed that you didn't attend the art show. What this suggests is that there was also a norm that you attend the art show. But notice that if you did go to the art show, even though you'd be keeping your promissory obligation, you would be doing something morally (and all-things-considered) wrong and you certainly wouldn't be praiseworthy for it. So in this case, there are two norms, they conflict, and one overrides the other. What explains why the norms conflict? It's that you had an obligation to both your neighbor and your partner, and the facts of the situation made it such that it was impossible to satisfy both. Situations like these are extremely common and are at the heart of pretty much every romantic comedy and sitcom episode.

The dilemmist should think that something similar is going on in cases like COSMOS CLUB and SUPPOSEDLY RATIONAL RACIST. In cases like those, moral and epistemic norms conflict because the racist social structures make it such that pursuing the truth (using reliable belief-forming processes, believing what your evidence supports, etc.) leads you to having racist beliefs. In these cases, the moral norm to be anti-racist overrides what would otherwise be your all-things-considered obligation. And here, like above, the dilemmist should say that if you did have the racist belief, even though you'd be fulfilling an epistemic obligation, you'd be doing something that is morally and all-things-considered wrong. Also like above, the dilemmist should see the source of the norm conflict as being the facts in the world, not poor theorizing about norms. It's the racist social system itself that explains the conflict, and it's that system that makes it impossible to satisfy both the epistemic and moral demands in COSMOS CLUB and SUPPOSEDLY RATIONAL RACIST. So if the reader is still uncomfortable with the idea that epistemic and moral norms can conflict, the dilemmist has a response for you: You should be uncomfortable with it, but not because it's bad normative theorizing. You should be uncomfortable with it because it's another negative byproduct of the racist social systems that structure much of contemporary society.

Before closing, let's consider one more tool that the dilemmist can use to explain our intuitions about COSMOS CLUB and SUPPOSEDLY RATIONAL RACIST. According to the dilemmist, the agent's beliefs in those cases are both epistemically right and morally wrong. So far, I've focused on the ways the dilemmist can gain traction in explaining our intuitions by holding that the beliefs are morally (and perhaps all-things-considered) wrong. In addition to holding that the beliefs are morally wrong, though, the dilemmist can also hold that the fact that the epistemic norms say we should have some racist beliefs is itself morally bad. On this proposal, not only would the dilemmist be claiming that the beliefs are morally bad; they'd also be claiming that a feature of epistemic norms (namely that they instruct agents to have certain beliefs in certain cases) is itself morally bad.

By making this meta normative claim about the moral badness of a feature of epistemic norms, the dilemmist can agree with even more of what their opponents want to say. Those who support moral encroachment on epistemic rightness want to hold that epistemic norms do not require agents to have the racist beliefs in the motivating cases. While the dilemmist has to disagree with them on that, the dilemmist can at least agree with their opponents that epistemic norms *shouldn't* require agents to have racist beliefs.

Claims about what the epistemic norms should or shouldn't be might strike the reader as odd, so let's think about them by way of an analogy to other kinds of norms. At one point, the norms of polite society in the United States required that people meeting each other for the first time shake hands. Moral norms also required that we not potentially expose ourselves or new people we meet to potentially deadly pathogens. At the onset of the COVID-19 pandemic, these norms came into conflict. What's going on with the norms in this situation? The natural view is that not only did the pandemic make it such that we shouldn't shake hands, but it also made it such that we should give up on the hand-shaking norm. The pandemic made the hand-shaking norm morally wrong to hold on to. The situation here is symmetrical to how the dilemmist should think of epistemic and moral norms: They should think that the norms do conflict (just as the norms of polite society and moral norms conflicted at the onset of the pandemic), and they should think that in these cases, the moral norms should override the epistemic ones. The novel point here is that they should also think that epistemic norms shouldn't conflict with the moral norms in these cases (just as we all think that norms of polite society shouldn't conflict with the moral norm not to spread disease), and so the epistemic norm is morally deficient.

It's important to be clear that by making these claims, the dilemmist is distinguishing what the norms in fact *are* from what they *should be*. What the dilemmist disagrees with the moral encroacher about is whether the epistemic norms do in fact make it right to have the racist beliefs. But just as we think that the hand-shaking norm became morally problematic at the beginning of the pandemic, the dilemmist should agree with the moral encroacher that epistemic norms shouldn't condone racist beliefs, regardless of whether they do. Recall that in the example above, we thought that what explained the badness of the hand-shaking norm and why it conflicted with the moral norm was the pandemic, not a misunderstanding of what the norms are. Analogously, the dilemmist should hold that what explains the badness of the epistemic norms in these cases and why they come into conflict with the moral norms is the facts about racial disparities that have been given rise to by our deeply racist social structure. It is racism that is the source of the issue here, not bad theorizing or mistaken intuitions about norms.[13]

[13] Another benefit of the dilemmist holding that these cases show that features of epistemic norms are morally problematic is that it allows the dilemmist to explain what is wrong with someone who tries to defend their racist belief by appeal to those norms. The dilemmist can hold that arguments like that are defective because they appeal to false premises about what norms one should follow. The analogy to shaking hands works here too: Someone would be wrong to defend a handshake in pandemic times by saying that a norm of polite society makes it right. The reason why is that that norm itself is defective, even if it still exists.

There is, of course, a difference between norms of polite society and epistemic norms. When it comes to norms of polite society, it's easier to understand what we should do when we discover that one of the norms is bad, since we at least have a vague idea of what would be involved in changing the norms of polite society. When it comes to epistemic norms, it's less clear what the implications might be of holding that a norm is bad. Can we, for example, change the epistemic norms? And if so, should we, and what factors should bear on that? My inclination is to think that we should alleviate the moral badness of the epistemic norms by targeting its source (racism), not the norm. But to fully answer these questions, we'd need a better understanding of exactly what constitutes epistemic norms and what grounds their normative force. Answering these metaepistemic and metanormative questions is beyond the scope of this book. So, unfortunately, I won't provide those answers here. I hope the upshot of the discussion is clear, though: We should think the problems there are with conflicting norms in these cases are problems of racism, not bad theorizing about norms.

Where does this leave the dilemmist? Dilemmists about epistemic rightness can save both the Take Information into Account and the Racist Beliefs Are Wrong desiderata for responses to Gendler's puzzle. The dilemmist cannot, of course, save the No Conflicts desideratum. What I've argued above is that dilemmists can agree with many of the key judgments that their opponents make about the motivating cases, including the judgments that the agents aren't justified, rational, warranted, etc. What they can't agree with their opponents about is whether the agents' beliefs in those cases are epistemically right. The dilemmist must hold that the beliefs are epistemically right at least in a technical sense. But the dilemmist can also explain our reluctance to accept that the beliefs are epistemically right in terms of it being highly morally risky to assert that (or even think it). They can also insist that mere epistemic rightness in these cases is a deficient sense of rightness, one that can't ultimately justify any beliefs or action, since what is epistemically right in these cases is overridden by what's morally required. Finally, by conceiving of the epistemic norms themselves along with the beliefs they condone as morally problematic, the dilemmist can help us understand the source of the normative conflict we see. On this view, the conflict in norms is explained by the non-normative facts. Just as the sudden sickness of your partner explains why your promissory obligations to your neighbor conflict with your obligations to your partner, and just as the pandemic explains the conflict between the hand-shaking norms and the moral norm not to spread disease, the dilemmist should hold that it's the existence of racism that explains why epistemic and moral norms conflict in cases like those we started with. So the dilemmist shares their opponent's concern about not satisfying the No Conflicts desideratum. But unlike their opponents, dilemmists need not attribute their failure to satisfy all the desiderata to a failure of normative theorizing. On the dilemmist's view, the problem of normative conflict is a (relatively very minor) symptom of having deeply racist social systems.

On a high level, the concern that started this chapter was that it looked like cases like COSMOS CLUB and SUPPOSEDLY RATIONAL RACIST should push us toward thinking that moral features of situations can affect what it's right for us to believe in those situations.[14] But moral encroachment about epistemic rightness is incompatible with the truth-loving epistemic consequentialist view I've defended in the rest of this book. As we saw, moral encroachment about rightness can't meet the natural desiderata we had on responses to Gendler's puzzle. When it comes to solutions to that puzzle, the dilemmist solution looks more promising even though it too can't satisfy all the desiderata. Dilemmism about epistemic rightness is exactly what the truth-loving epistemic consequentialist (and other purists about epistemic rightness) would predict, so truth-loving epistemic consequentiaists should go in for dilemmism to avoid the threat from moral encroachment motivated by Gendler's puzzle.

[14] For all I've said here, there could be other reasons to go in for moral encroachment about epistemic rightness, rather than moral encroachment about justification, rationality, knowledge, or some other epistemic status. Arguments from minimal pairs of cases like the arguments for pragmatic encroachment mentioned above are usually presented as arguments for moral encroachment about justification, rationality, or some other non-rightness status. (Again, see Bolinger 2020b for a more comprehensive list of moral encroachment defenders.) And as I've argued, moral encroachment about justification, rationality, knowledge, and similar epistemic statuses is compatible with truth-loving epistemic consequentialism.

7
Consequentialist Epistemology

The main goal of Chapters 2 through 6 was to develop and defend an account of normative epistemology that's centrally guided by the idea that epistemic norms are about getting at the truth and avoiding falsehoods. The view developed, truth-loving epistemic consequentialism, says that a belief (credence) is epistemically right iff, among the available options, it's the belief (credence) that maximally conduces to true belief and lack of false belief (accurate credences). I used the methodology sketched in Chapter 1 to defend the view by drawing out how it's supported by our pretheoretic intuitions (first half of Chapter 2) and showing how defenders of the view can respond to objections (second half of Chapter 2 to Chapter 6). In doing that, I argued that the best version of the view has the following features:

BIPARTITE The view distinguishes two kinds of epistemic normative notions. Epistemic deontic notions (like 'right belief') evaluate beliefs and other evaluands as epistemically right or wrong, and they are the main target of the view I give. Epistemic responsibility notions (like 'epistemic rationality' and 'epistemic justification') primarily serve to evaluate agents with respect to their beliefs, rather than the beliefs themselves, and these notions are not the target of the theory. (See Chapter 3 and below.)

SOPHISTICATED The view is sophisticated, in the sense described by Railton (1984)—i.e., it says that a belief (credence) is right iff it does in fact best conduce to epistemic goodness, and it does not say that agents ought always think in terms of conducing to goodness. (See Chapter 3.)

GLOBAL The view is global in that it says that the consequentialist criterion of evaluation applies not only to beliefs but also to other things including belief-forming dispositions, decision-making procedures, motivational schema, etc. (See Chapter 3 and below.)

VERITIST The view says that the value associated with epistemic deontic terms is instrumenally veritist—i.e., it says that all and only true belief

Right Belief and True Belief. Daniel J. Singer, Oxford University Press. © Oxford University Press 2023.
DOI: 10.1093/oso/9780197660386.003.0008

and the lack of false belief (and accurate credences) have final epistemic value, and it says that other things have derivative epistemic value only insomuch as they conduce to that final value. (See Chapter 4.)

DIACHRONIC The view says that the veritist value associated with epistemic deontic terms should be understood as involving the truth/falsity (accuracy) of collections of beliefs (credences) through time, not just the truth/falsity (accuracy) of the beliefs (credences) when they are adopted. (See Chapter 5.)

The first part of this final chapter will look more closely at the two most novel (and likely most controversial) aspects of the view, the bipartite and global aspects. In Section 7.1, I'll argue that epistemic consequentialists should see epistemic responsibility notions as elements of broader social practices of holding others epistemically responsible. It's the social practices, not our individual uses of the terms, that should be justified in consequentialist terms, I'll argue. This conception of epistemic responsibility both mirrors a prominent approach to ethical responsibility and vindicates the claim repeated in previous chapters that truth-loving epistemic consequentialism is compatible with many first-order conceptions of justification and rationality. Section 7.2 will defend the global aspect of the view. I'll argue that because truth-loving consequentialists should be centrally concerned with good epistemic outcomes, not right belief, they should think many things other than beliefs can be epistemically right and wrong, including things like what reasoning methods agents should use, what experiments they should perform, how scientific lab groups should be set up, which faculty should be hired, how grant money should be distributed, what political institutions we should have, and even what epistemic agents eat and drink.

Sections 7.1 and 7.2 together bring out a way of thinking of truth-loving epistemic consequentialism not just as a theory of right belief, as I have cast it in previous chapters, but also as a general approach to thinking about epistemology, one that is centrally motivated by the idea that there's a unique ultimate epistemic aim of getting the most accurate picture of the world we can. When construed this way, truth-loving epistemic consequentialism acts as a framework for thinking about research and inquiry far beyond the traditional bounds of epistemology. Section 7.3 will give the contours of this broader truth-centric conception of epistemology and show how it can be used in a programmatic way to think about many kinds of inquiry and research. Section 7.4 will compare the global truth-loving consequentialist approach to epistemology to naturalized epistemology, a nearby alternative high-level conception of epistemology. As I'll show, the global truth-loving consequentialist picture of epistemology doesn't conflict with naturalized epistemology as much as it might initially seem.

In this chapter, I'll step back from the first-order normative epistemic theorizing characterized in Chapter 1 and used in Chapters 2 through 6. I'll take a bigger-picture approach by exploring the structural aspects of truth-loving epistemic consequentialism and the broader conception of epistemology it inspires. I hope to convince you that in addition to being a complete and correct first-order theory of normative epistemology that can both capture our truth-loving intuitions and avoid objections, truth-loving epistemic consequentialism can also serve as a broad, programmatic, and fecund framework for epistemic theorizing in general.

7.1 On Epistemic Deontic and Responsibility Terms

Drawing a distinction between epistemic deontic notions and epistemic responsibility notions is one of the most novel elements of the view presented in this book. In Chapter 3, I argued that the epistemic consequentialist should distinguish these two kinds of notions to avoid trade-off objections. In Chapter 4, I argued that the view avoids generalized swamping problem worries by being about epistemic deontic notions, rather than responsibility notions. In Chapter 5, we saw that what seems to be one of the major differences between truth-loving epistemic consequentialists and epistemic utility theorists is that the consequentialist is best seen as giving a view of deontic notions in objective consequentialist terms, whereas the epistemic utility theorist is best seen as using a subjective consequentialist framework to defend a view of epistemic responsibility. And in Chapter 6, I argued that the deontic/responsibility distinction allows the truth-loving epistemic consequentialist to account for many of the intuitions motivating proponents of moral encroachment while still making sense of the epistemic demands on agents. So this distinction does a lot of work making the view feasible. Most of this book has been dedicated to fleshing out and defending an account of epistemic rightness. In this section, I'll sketch how I think epistemic consequentialists should think about epistemic responsibility.

When the distinction between epistemic deontic notions and epistemic responsibility notions was introduced in Chapter 3, I said that we should think of epistemic deontic terms as primarily serving to evaluate beliefs and that we should think of responsibility terms as primarily serving to evaluate agents who have the beliefs. As I noted, the distinction mirrors a distinction typically made by objective consequentialists in ethics between moral deontic notions (e.g., 'right action') and moral responsibility notions (e.g., 'praiseworthy action' and 'blameworthy action'). Among ethical consequentialists, there are two broad approaches to thinking about moral responsibility terms. According to 'instrumentalists' about moral responsibility,[1] our moral responsibility practices are to be explained or justified in consequentialist terms. On the simplest versions of these views, an agent is blameworthy iff holding them blameworthy conduces to the best consequences. The second broad approach flips the direction of the connection between moral responsibility notions and consequentialist accounts of rightness. According to what I'll call 'constraining views,' what we can be morally responsible for constrains the possible consequentialist views of rightness. A simple kind of view like this might hold, for example, that consequentialist conceptions of rightness can only appeal to *foreseeable* consequences because agents can only be responsible for producing that kind of consequence.

Below, I'll consider both of these approaches to understanding moral responsibility notions and ask of each whether it can serve as a good model for making sense of epistemic responsibility. I'll argue that the instrumentalist approach looks more promising and fits truth-loving epistemic consequentialism better than the alternative. There isn't enough space here to work out all of the details of a complete theory of epistemic responsibility. Instead, I'll aim to give a general overview of how the truth-loving epistemic consequentialist should think about these notions on a high level. As we'll see, many different first-order theories of epistemic responsibility are compatible with the truth-loving consequentialist view.

7.1.1 On Constraining Views of Epistemic Responsibility

Let's start by thinking about constraining views. According to constraining views of moral responsibility, consequentialist accounts of rightness should be constrained by what agents can be responsible for. As Mason (2019,

[1] I'm borrowing this terminology from Jefferson (2019) and Vargas (2022). Some authors call these views 'consequentialist' conceptions of responsibility, but using that locution here would obviously be confusing.

p. 221) puts it, constraining views are committed to THE RESPONSIBILITY CONSTRAINT:

> THE RESPONSIBILITY CONSTRAINT A normative theory must give an account of right action such that an agent could reasonably be deemed responsible for acting rightly or wrongly.

Different ways of fleshing this out will have different implications for what kinds of consequentialist views THE RESPONSIBILITY CONSTRAINT rules out. A common thought here is that agents can only be responsible for producing consequences that they can foresee, so THE RESPONSIBILITY CONSTRAINT is sometimes taken to restrict consequentialist views of rightness to only those that take into account foreseeable consequences.[2] Other ways of making consequentialist views more subjective are also inspired by THE RESPONSIBILITY CONSTRAINT. For example, Jackson's (1991) constraining view says that consequentialists should hold that rightness is determined by the expected consequences calculated using the agent's credence and what they ought to desire. We could also imagine views that use THE RESPONSIBILITY CONSTRAINT to limit what actions consequentialist views take to be available to the agent, rather than limiting the range of consequences in play or the subjectivity of the view.[3]

Theorists who go in for constraining views in ethics are typically motivated by the thought that an action can't be right or wrong for an agent unless it is, in an important sense, *the agent's* action, as opposed to someone else's action or something that just happens. (The background thought is that an action being the agent's is a prerequisite for the agent being responsible for it.) For example, proponents of constraining views might appeal to cases where agents are coerced to do something to argue that rightness and responsibility are linked (e.g., that what the agent did wasn't the wrong thing, in part because they couldn't have been responsible for it). Alternatively, they might appeal to the apparent absurdity of thinking an agent is required to do something that in fact conduces to the best consequences if the action also justifiably appears wrong to the agent (e.g., assassinating a toddler who, unbeknownst to the agent, will turn out to be an evil

[2] Mason (2019, p. 221) attributes this kind of view to Bentham (1780), Mill (1863), and Smart (1973), among others.

[3] At some points, Mason (2019, 2020) hints at a relatively simple way of fleshing out a view like this, and Portmore (2011) gives a sophisticated way of working it out.

dictator). The idea here is that the agent couldn't possibly be praiseworthy for doing this nor could they be blameworthy for not doing it (because it's assassination of an apparently normal toddler), and because of that, proponents of constraining views say that it also couldn't be a right action.

Mason (2019, p. 221; 2020, p. 171) argues that what usually motivates authors who go in for THE RESPONSIBILITY CONSTRAINT is a worry that unconstrained ethical consequentialism makes agents responsible for too much, including things that aren't the agent's actions and things beyond the agent's control. For example, Williams gives a case of an agent being forced at gunpoint to kill one person or else let 20 be killed (1973, pp. 98–99). As Mason argues, in cases like this, Williams thinks consequentialists must say that the agent would be responsible for the deaths of the 20 should they not kill the one, even though the killing of the 20 is not an exercise of the agent's agency. Mason (2020, p. 171) argues that consequentialist views with "more subjective accounts of rightness are, implicitly or explicitly, appeals to the need to connect rightness and wrongness with an account of what the agent could be responsible for; what is up to her."

It might seem natural to make a similar move when it comes to epistemic responsibility. As I mentioned in Chapter 1, Alston (1988) argued against what he called the "deontological conception" of justified belief, the conception of justification that aims to understand the notion in terms of "obligation, permission, requirement, blame, and the like." His worry was that we could only be justified in this sense if we could exercise control over what we believe. But in typical cases of belief, we don't exercise our agency at all in what we believe. When I look out the window and see rain, I simply form a belief that it's raining, and in that moment, I couldn't have formed the opposite belief even if I put my entire will behind it. Alston's worry was explicitly about justification, but it might even be more compelling if it were formulated as a worry about epistemic rightness: It seems natural to ask how a belief (credence) could be right/wrong for an agent if the agent doesn't (or couldn't) exercise any agency in its formation, maintenance, or destruction. In this way, Alston's worry is analogous to the worries about ethical consequentialism Mason characterizes as being about consequentialism's propensity to label actions as right or wrong even if they aren't things that are up to the agent.

This Alston-style thought might motivate us to go in for a constraining view of epistemic responsibility by holding something like THE EPISTEMIC RESPONSIBILITY CONSTRAINT:

> THE EPISTEMIC RESPONSIBILITY CONSTRAINT A normative epistemic theory must give an account of right belief (credence) such that an agent could reasonably be deemed epistemically responsible for believing (having credences) rightly or wrongly.

Following the ethical consequentialists mentioned above, it might be natural to apply this to epistemic consequentialist views by limiting the range of consequences in play, making the consequentialist views more subjective, or using an independent theory of epistemic responsibility to limit which beliefs (credences) are open to consequentialist evaluation.

But despite the close resemblance of THE EPISTEMIC RESPONSIBILITY CONSTRAINT to the idea behind constraining views of ethical responsibility, I think that going in for the epistemic constraint is less compelling than the analogous move is for ethical consequentialists. For starters, when it comes to epistemic normativity, epistemologists are generally more open to rejecting the idea that a belief being right requires that the agent be able to exercise their agency over it than ethicists are to rejecting the analogous claim about actions. Feldman (2000), Hieronymi (2008), and Chuard and Southwood (2009) all argue against the claim that for a belief to be epistemically evaluable, it must be under the agent's voluntary control. Feldman (2000), for example, holds that epistemic obligations are what he calls 'role oughts.' These are 'ought's that apply to us in virtue of some role we occupy, regardless of our ability to fulfill them. On Feldman's picture, whether we ought to believe something and whether it's up to us to believe often come apart.

Moreover, insomuch as we take traditional work on justification to be in part about what we should believe, we should see proponents of externalism (e.g., Nozick 1981; Dretske 1981; and the many versions of reliabilism inspired by Goldman 1979) as pushing against the idea that what an agent ought to believe is constrained by what's up to the agent. Externalists hold that whether a belief is justified is dependent (at least in part) on things outside of the believer's ken (such as whether the process that produced the belief is reliable or whether the belief is appropriately causally connected to its content). But if that's right and if justification (they way those theorists were conceiving of it) is about what we should believe, then we must conclude that what we should believe is similarly dependent on things that aren't up to us. The popularity of views like this highlight that it's commonplace among epistemologists to reject the link between right belief and control, even if ethicists don't reject the analogous connection between right action and control. We should worry, therefore, that constraining views of epistemic responsibility are less well motivated than constraining views of ethical responsibility.[4]

There's a second reason to be skeptical of THE EPISTEMIC RESPONSIBILITY CONSTRAINT being a good way for epistemic consequentialists to think about the connection between epistemic deontic and responsibility notions. In many cases, the constraints of these constraining views would eliminate some of the biggest benefits of going in for epistemic consequentialism. Consider, for example, epistemic consequentialist views that limit the consequences in play to foreseeable ones or are made more subjective following Jackson's (1991) ethical consequentialist view. Extreme versions of these views would essentially identify right belief with *what agents take to* conduce to true belief, not what actually does conduce to true belief. Views like that wouldn't be able to predict that right belief is almost always true belief, since we regularly take things to be truth-conducive that are false. This happens anytime we have misleading evidence. Views like this must also give up on a major part of the motivation for truth-loving epistemic consequentialism, namely the idea that epistemic norms are centrally about getting at the truth. According to views like this, epistemic norms would be about getting at *what appears* to be true, rather than what really is true.

More generally, we should worry that epistemic consequentialist views that limit what beliefs might be right/wrong by what beliefs might be justified or rational will end up collapsing that very distinction. As I mentioned at the beginning of this section, distinguishing right/wrong belief (credence) from justified/unjustified and rational/irrational belief (credence) is a key move in defending epistemic consequentialism from many of the most pressing objections against the view. Constraining views of epistemic responsibility, by mirroring constraining views of ethical responsibility, at least partially close this gap, and in doing so, they risk not being able to employ the responses to the objections given in previous chapters.

Finally, I take it that the central idea motivating the kind of epistemic consequentialist view developed here is that what we ought to believe is determined by what gets us at the truth. The goal of the last few chapters

[4] Of course, there are many other responses to Alston's problem, like the compatibilist-inspired response from Steup (2008, 2011). But, the point here is not about whether Alston is right. Rather, the point here is that Alston's intuition about agential control being a prerequisite for epistemic normative terms to apply to a belief is less plausible and less widely accepted than the analogous claims in ethics.

has been to see how far we can get in terms of developing a theory of right belief that stays as close to that original motivation as possible. Were we to adopt a constraining view of epistemic responsibility, we would be giving up on that motivation in an important way. Proponents of constraining views think that when we theorize about what to believe, epistemic responsibility comes first. On these views, what we can be responsible for constrains what we should believe before truth gets into the picture. Truth is no longer the primary driver for epistemic rightness. So going in for a constraining view would involve giving up a pretty significant aspect of that original motivation.

Altogether, what we see is that constraining views of epistemic responsibility aren't as intuitively well motivated as their ethical analogues, that they risk losing out on many of the central benefits of the epistemic consequentialist view I've developed here by collapsing a key distinction, and that they run counter to the original motivating intuition that what we should believe is determined by what gets us at the truth. I don't see these worries as constituting a knock-down argument against constraining views (even taken together). It might be possible to develop a constraining view that is itself well motivated, is able to mesh well with the central motivation for the kind of epistemic consequentialist view considered here, and is able to maintain a meaningful enough divide between right belief and responsible belief to capture the benefits of having that distinction. But walking that tightrope will be hard, and without a clear motivation for pursuing it, it's not clear that it's worth working it out (walking it out?). As I'll argue next, the instrumentalist approach avoids these worries and has some other appealing features, so the instrumentalist approach turns out to be more attractive overall.

7.1.2 On Instrumentalist Views of Epistemic Responsibility

According to instrumentalist views of moral responsibility, our use of moral responsibility terms (or the practices that they're part of) are to be explained or justified in terms of whether they best conduce to some goal. Typically, views like this are advanced by ethical consequentialists, who hope to extend consequentialist theorizing about moral rightness to moral responsibility, but one need not be a consequentialist to go in for an instrumentalist view (see Vargas 2022 on this point). Sidgwick (1907) and Smart

(1963) both give simple direct instrumentalist views of moral responsibility: According to these authors, we should think of praising and blaming as just another kind of activity humans engage in. As such, individual acts of praising or blaming are to be evaluated according to the standard consequentialist criterion of rightness. As Sidgwick (1907) puts it, whether an action should be praised is a question of whether "it is expedient to praise it, with a view to its future production." There are also more sophisticated contemporary instrumentalist views that don't aim to give a particular account of when someone is responsible; they instead give a justification of moral responsibility practices as a whole in terms of whether having those practices conduces to good outcomes (see, for example, Vargas 2013; McGeer 2015; and Jefferson 2019). On these views, whether someone is praiseworthy or blameworthy for an action is determined by norms internal to the social practice of praising and blaming. Those internal norms might say, for example, that an agent is blameworthy if they acted with bad intentions, regardless of the outcomes caused or foreseen. On the more sophisticated intrumentalist conceptions of responsibility notions, it's the social practice as a whole that gets justified in instrumentalist terms.

It's easy to see how we could develop instrumentalist views of epistemic responsibility using instrumentalist views of moral responsibility as a model.[5] The simplest forms of this kind of view would say that we should treat someone's belief as justified (rational) iff doing so conduces to the best epistemic outcome. This simple view is not the same as the simple consequentialist view that says a belief *is* justified (rational) iff having it conduces to the best epistemic outcome. The latter consequentialist view of justification was dispensed with in Chapter 3 (since it is straightforwardly subject to trade-off objections). Analogous to how Sidgwick (1907) and Smart (1963) conceive of the relationship between moral rightness and moral justification, the simplest instrumentalist views of epistemic responsibility would be about the outcomes associated with a particular kind of action, namely *holding a belief to be* justified (rational).

Why might someone accept this simple instrumentalist view? One thing that makes the view attractive is that it is a kind of umbrella view that naturally generalizes many popular conceptions of justification. Reliabilists and evidentialists, for example, both agree that encouraging people to have

[5] Driver (2018) points out this possibility and some of its benefits but doesn't delve very far into developing any particular account.

justified beliefs (by using reliable belief-forming processes or believing what their evidence supports) will generally result in them having more epistemically good beliefs.[6] This is exactly what the simple direct instrumentalist takes to be at the core of when we should treat a belief as justified—i.e., when doing so results in the best epistemic outcomes. Moreover, the simple instrumentalist about justification might be able to make sense of the disagreement between reliabilists and evidentialists (and others) as a disagreement over the standards that best conduce to the epistemic good when we hold people to them. In instrumentalist terms, evidentialists think what best conduces to the epistemic good is treating beliefs as unjustified when they aren't supported by the believer's evidence. Reliabilists, on the other hand, think that treating beliefs as unjustified when they aren't produced by reliable belief-forming processes best conduces to the good. On top of that neat way of understanding the disagreement, if discussants in the conversation could agree on a theory of epistemic value, the simple instrumentalist view also suggests a way to end the debates about justification—empirical research into what standards in fact best conduce to maximizing epistemic goodness.

Of course, for a simple instrumentalist view to work well with truth-loving epistemic consequentialism, the view must also be committed to a veritist theory of value. One might worry that this would make the view run afoul of trade-off objections (see Chapter 3 and Berker 2013a,b) or generalized swamping problem objections (see Chapter 4 and Sylvan 2018). But, mirroring the development of instrumentalist views in ethics, instrumentalists about epistemic responsibility can avoid these issues by going in for an instrumentalist justification of *the practice* of holding beliefs to be justified (rational). The idea here is that when we treat each other's beliefs as justified (rational) or not, we're participating in a system of practices, attitudes, and judgments that collectively conduce to the epistemic good. The practice of holding each other epistemically responsible (as a whole) is what's justified by the epistemic goods it produces, on this more sophisticated view. Importantly, this kind of instrumentalist can remain agnostic about exactly what is involved in a belief being justified (rational) (i.e., whether coherence with evidence matters, whether using

[6] Of course, evidentialists and reliabilists might disagree about what epistemic goodness amounts to. Evidentialists typically think that a belief is epistemically good when it is supported by the holder's evidence, following Feldman (2000), whereas reliabilists more commonly go in for a veritistic conception of epistemic goodness.

reliable belief-forming processes matters, etc.). They'll say that what makes a belief justified (rational) is determined by norms internal to the practice, and it's the practice as a whole that's justified by conducing to the good.[7] (Note the symmetry of the account here with Vargas 2013, p. 2.) By going in for practice-level justifications of our practices of holding epistemically responsible, we avoid the possible worries mentioned above about simpler instrumentalist views.

A benefit of both the simple and more sophisticated instrumentalist views is that on these views, unlike on constraining views of responsibility, rightness is conceptually detached from responsibility. That is, whereas constraining views take responsibility to constrain possible views of rightness, on instrumentalist views, rightness and responsibility are given independent analyses. This means that instrumentalist conceptions of epistemic responsibility avoid the problem that constraining views have about it being hard for them to account for the idea that epistemic norms are centrally about getting at the truth. Constraining views take responsibility to limit the extent to which the norms are about truth. Instrumentalist views, by detaching responsibility from rightness, can treat epistemic norms as solely truth-governed, in exactly the way the truth-loving epistemic consequentialist wants to. So instrumentalist views have that advantage over constraining views.

There's a related second benefit of instrumentalist views. As I argued above, constraining views, by trying to constrain our conception of rightness by what we can be responsible for, risk collapsing the distinction between epistemic rightness and epistemic responsibility. Instrumentalist conceptions of epistemic responsibility don't have this problem, since there is space on instrumentalist views for a real theoretical separation between rightness and responsibility. This is clearest on practice-level instrumentalist views, since it's open to defenders of those views to go in for conceptions of epistemic responsibility that are wildly different from the truth-loving consequentialist conception of rightness, including traditional evidentialist conceptions of justification. But even on simple direct instrumentalist views, epistemic responsibility can come apart dramatically

[7] On the ethical side, McGeer (2015) puts pressure on whether the justification of the practice can be fully independent of the practice-internal norms. Similarly, the practice-internal norms of epistemic justification and rationality might turn out to be more connected to the justification of the practice as a whole than I insinuate here. I don't see that as threatening the general picture, though (again, analogous to how McGeer 2015 thinks it plays out on the ethical side).

from epistemic rightness, since the beliefs that best conduce to the good and the ways of holding responsible that best conduce to the good need not be alike. It seems natural to think, for example, that treating a belief as unjustified is unlikely to best conduce to the epistemic good in cases where the goodness-related effects of the right belief are too causally or temporally distant from the holder of the belief. Cases like that suggest that even defenders of simple instrumentalist views will see epistemic responsibility as more closely tied to an agent's capacities than epistemic rightness. And because advocates of instrumentalist views countenance this difference between rightness and responsibility, they can take advantage of the many theoretical benefits of having that distinction, rather than risking losing out on them like defenders of constraining views.

The key to instrumentalist views is seeing praising and blaming (holding un/justified or ir/rational) as an action or practice that agents are engaged in. The idea is to try to understand what it is *to be* responsible in terms of when we should *hold someone* responsible. This naturally leads to an objection to instrumentalist views that they confuse those two things. It seems natural to think, for example, that there could be cases where someone is morally blameworthy for an action but it isn't appropriate for anyone to blame them.

On the moral side, this objection motivates going in for a practice-level instrumentalist view, rather than one of the simpler views. On the practice-level views, whether an agent is responsible is determined by the norms internal to the practice, not by whether we should hold them responsible (see Vargas 2013, p. 103), so these views aren't subject to this objection. Defenders of the simpler moral instrumentalist views sometimes try to minimize the impact of this objection by showing how their view can make sense of a lot of the apparently problematic cases, but since these authors are often committed to an explicitly revisionist account of responsibility, they're often unmoved by this kind of objection (see Jefferson 2019, sec. III.1). Similarly, on the epistemic side, we should see this kind of objection as motivating a practice-level instrumentalist account of epistemic responsibility, and defenders of simpler views can take cues from the discussion of instrumentalists in ethics about how to develop their view as a more revisionary account. The issues that are brought up by this objection for epistemic instrumentalists mirror the issues already discussed in the literature on moral instrumentalist views (see Arneson 2003; Vargas 2013; and Miller 2014), so we should think instrumentalist accounts of epistemic responsibility are at least as plausible as instrumentalist accounts of moral responsibility in this respect.

But there is one place where instrumentalist views of epistemic responsibility might appear to be on worse footing than instrumentalist views of moral responsibility. As I said above, the central idea behind moral instrumentalist views is trying to understand what it is *to be* responsible in terms of when we should *hold someone* responsible. If you're an ethical consequentialist and you buy this move, then it makes sense to start thinking about responsibility in terms of the consequences of holding someone responsible. Why's that? It's because holding someone responsible is an *action* and ethical consequentialists try to understand right *action* in terms of consequences. The worry is that the analogous move might not make as much sense for the epistemic consequentialist. To see that, suppose that the epistemic consequentialist follows the moral instrumentalist in thinking that we should try to understand what it is to be epistemically responsible in terms of when we should hold someone epistemically responsible. What follows for the epistemic consequentialist? The central instrumentalist idea is to understand responsibility in terms of when we should perform a certain kind of *action*. But epistemic consequentialism is, on a first pass, a view of right belief, not right action. So the worry is that the epistemic consequentialist, unlike the ethical consequentialist, doesn't get any purchase on responsibility by going in for the instrumentalist's central idea.

There are two responses the epistemic instrumentalist should give to this worry. First, recall that in several places in this book, I gave reasons to think that the best versions of epistemic consequentialism are global, in that they take the consequentialist criterion of evaluation to apply to things other than beliefs and credences, including dispositions, decision-making procedures, motivational schema, etc. Following on that, it seems natural to think the epistemic consequentialist criterion of rightness could be used to epistemically evaluate actions. The next section of this chapter will argue for this conception of epistemic consequentialism, so I'll hold further discussion of that idea until then. But notice that if the view is a global consequentialist one, the epistemic instrumentalist can simply follow their ethical conspecifics in giving their account of responsibility in terms of epistemically right action.

The second response is more tailored. The central idea behind instrumentalist views is trying to understand what it is *to be* responsible in terms of when we should *hold someone* responsible. The traditional interpretation of this idea says that holding responsible is a kind of action. A natural move for the epistemic consequentialist who wants to go in for an instrumentalist theory is to insist that holding responsible is not an action but rather the having of a belief. By doing this, their theory of right belief would apply directly, in the same way ethical consequentialist theories are meant to apply to the action-conception of holding responsible. In adopting this view, proponents of the instrumentalist conception of epistemic responsibility might end up more closely aligning themselves with proponents of reactive attitudes accounts of moral responsibility, who typically press the objection mentioned above that moral instrumentalists conflate *when we should act as though* someone is responsible with them actually being responsible (see Wallace 1994 and Shoemaker 2015). As Jefferson (2019, p. 6) points out, instrumentalists and proponents of reactive attitudes accounts actually share the view that responsibility is to be understood in terms of holding responsible. Where they differ is in how they construe that holding. If epistemic instrumentalists use the move proposed here, they would join proponents of reactive attitudes accounts in thinking that holding responsible is a kind of attitude rather than a kind of action (although they will likely disagree with proponents of reactive attitudes accounts about what kind of attitude is in play). So using this move not only would allow them to avoid the worry about how epistemic consequentialism gets a grip on holding responsible, but also might gain them allies in pursuing this general picture of responsibility.

Before concluding this discussion, I want to highlight one final benefit for epistemic consequentialists of going in for an instrumentalist conception of epistemic responsibility. As we saw above, there are many ways of fleshing out the instrumentalist conception of epistemic responsibility. But on all of them, the use of epistemic responsibility notions in our thoughts, words, and actions is treated as a kind of human activity, one to be evaluated in the same ways as other normal human activities, like shopping, working, relaxing, telling jokes, playing games, making promises, making plans, and enjoying artwork. For most human activities, we think that many different kinds of factors, including moral, practical, epistemic, legal, and aesthetic factors, can bear on how they're evaluated. We typically think that the particularities of individuals' situations, individuals' beliefs and desires, and individuals' strengths and limitations can also bear on that. So insomuch as they see holding epistemically responsible as another human activity, proponents of instrumentalist conceptions of epistemic responsibility should be friendly to the idea that non-epistemic factors might bear on whether a belief is justified or rational.

One thing this means is that epistemic instrumentalist views are particularly well suited to account for the intuitions that motivate proponents of pragmatic and moral encroachment (discussed in the last chapter). This is clearest on practice-level instrumentalist views, since those views leave open what the practice-internal norms say about what bears on the justification of individual beliefs, and so they leave open the possibility that the practice-internal norms say that moral and pragmatic factors bear on the justification and rationality of beliefs.[8] But practice-level instrumentalists can think that moral and pragmatic factors bear on the justification of the practices too. This kind of view would hold that there's more to the justification of our epistemic responsibility practices than the production of epistemic goodness; the production of other kinds of value might also matter. Similarly, proponents of simpler instrumentalist views can say that if an individual act of holding responsible is ultimately justifiable, it can't be that the moral, practical, etc. factors that bear on it ultimately undermine its justifiability. This kind of move allows instrumentalist consequentialists to get quite far in accounting for the intuitions that motivate pragmatic and moral encroachers.

Moreover, if instrumentalists buy into the idea that non-epistemic factors can bear on when we hold each other epistemically responsible (at either the individual-act level, practice-internal level, or overall practice-justification level), they can give a novel story about why there would be persistent disagreement about the nature of epistemic justification and rationality. Even if the epistemic factors that bear on the justifiability of a practice or an individual instance of holding responsible are fixed, the web of other things that bear on which human activities are best is complex and often deeply dependent on the particular situations, strengths, limitations, beliefs, and desires of the individuals involved. This gives the proponent of this kind of view the resources to account for why foundationalists, coherentists, reliabilists, etc. would perpetually jab at each other. The idea is that we should expect that in different cases, different practices

[8] This move also allows practice-level instrumentalists to account for a sense in which moral and pragmatic factors might also *be* epistemic factors, in the way some proponents of moral pragmatic encroachment claim. By acting internally to our practices of holding epistemically responsible, these moral and pragmatic factors can bear on justified and rational belief in the same kinds of ways paradigmatic epistemic factors do.

of holding epistemically responsible will be ultimately justifiable because of the differences in the non-epistemic factors in play in those cases.[9] This is another benefit of going in for an instrumentalist conception of epistemic responsibility that sees our practices of holding responsible as just one of many human practices in which we're all constantly engaged.

It would be impossible to fully flesh out a theory of epistemic responsibility in this chapter (that would surely take another book-length work). Instead, my goal was only to show that there's a way to think about epistemic responsibility notions that both is independently plausible and fits well with the truth-loving epistemic consequentialist picture of right belief. I hope to have convinced you that going in for an instrumentalist conception of epistemic responsibility is a promising route for the truth-loving epistemic consequentialist. I argued above that constraining views, the most natural alternative, face several challenges. Neither view is without its limitations, but instrumentalist accounts avoid the challenges of the constraining views, fit the truth-loving motivations better, allow for the kind of conceptual separation needed between deontic and responsibility notions, and offer the possibility of making sense of many different conceptions of epistemic justification and rationality under a single umbrella theory. For these reasons, truth-loving epistemic consequentialists should go in for an instrumentalist conception of epistemic responsibility.

7.2 Going Global

As Mueller (2017) says, the "boring textbook definition" says that epistemic normativity is about what to believe, whereas practical normativity is about what to do. I've already hinted at some ways in which I think that "definition" is false. In Chapter 3, I argued that epistemic consequentialists should treat their view not just as a view about what to believe but also as a view about what dispositions, decision-making procedures, and motivational schema agents ought to have and use. Here I'll flesh out further the conception of epistemic normativity that fits most naturally with this way of thinking, the *global* consequentialist conception of epistemic normativity. I'll ask whether the view is well motivated and coherent, and I'll argue

[9] This might push proponents of this kind of view to a kind of pluralism about rationality and justification like the kind discussed by Kopec (2018), but pluralism isn't demanded by this view. A complex kind of relativism would likely also work.

that it is, despite being at odds with the "boring textbook definition." In the next section, I'll ask about the implications of this view for future work on epistemic normativity, and I'll argue that they're broad, programmatic, and fecund. But first, I'll start by clarifying exactly what the view is.

7.2.1 What Global Epistemic Consequentialism Is

According to the traditional story, epistemic and practical normativity are distinguished by what they apply to. Epistemic normativity is supposed to be the same thing as the normativity of belief. On this picture, claims about what we ought to believe or have reason to believe can only possibly be epistemic 'ought's and reasons. The flip is true as well: On this picture, if there's a claim about what we ought to do or have reasons to do (where the 'doing' is not having a belief), then it can't be a true epistemic 'ought' or reason claim.[10]

The truth-loving epistemic consequentialist agrees with the traditional theorist that epistemic normativity tells us what we ought to believe, but the truth-loving epistemic consequentialist should deny that the evaluation of belief is the unique and exclusive domain of epistemic normativity. In Chapter 3, I argued that epistemic consequentialists should think that their method of evaluating belief can be fruitfully extended to evaluating agents' dispositions, decision-making procedures, motivational schema, and the like. I'll argue here that it makes sense for consequentialists to extend epistemic evaluation further to include how agents reason, how agents collect evidence, what experiments agents perform, how agents collect and process data and information, what mundane actions agents do (like what they eat), how scientific labs are set up, how schools are funded, and even how society is structured more generally. Following similar views in ethics, I'll call this 'global epistemic consequentialism' (cf. Pettit and Smith 2000).

On the global truth-loving epistemic consequentialist view, the epistemically right way for agents to reason is, among those available, the way that best conduces to true belief and the lack of false belief (accurate credence). The epistemically right way for agents to collect evidence is, among those available, the way that best conduces to true belief and the

[10] Feldman (2000), for example, thinks that all of epistemic normativity can be captured by a single norm requiring agents to have only the attitudes supported by their evidence. For more examples of folks who seem to take this view of epistemic normativity to be standard and maybe even definitional, see Berker (2017), Raz (2009), Sylvan (2016), Turri (2009).

lack of false belief (accurate credence). The epistemically right way to set up public schools is, among those available, the way that best conduces to true belief and the lack of false belief (accurate credence). And, in case the general idea isn't clear, for any object of evaluation, the global truth-loving epistemic consequentialist holds that the epistemically right object of evaluation is, among those available, the one that best conduces to true belief and the lack of false belief (accurate credence).

7.2.2 Why Global Rather Than Local Consequentialism

Some of the benefits of global epistemic consequentialism were mentioned in previous chapters. As I argued in Chapter 3, by approving or disapproving of certain dispositions, decision-making procedures, motivational schema, and so on consequentialists are able to make sense of the ways in which agents in trade-off cases are doing something wrong (like not using generally truth-conducive belief-forming dispositions) even though their belief is right. This helps undermine some of the worrisome intuitions about how consequentialists handle trade-offs. In Chapter 4, I argued that the global aspect of the view, which separates the evaluation of dispositions, belief-forming processes, and so on from the evaluation of belief, is one feature of the view that allows it to avoid the generalized swamping problem objection from Sylvan (2018).

It shouldn't be surprising to anyone familiar with the literature on ethical consequentialism that going global helps the epistemic consequentialist. As Greaves (2020) discusses, most contemporary ethical consequentialists are sympathetic to the global version of their view (see Greaves 2020, p. 425 for a long list that includes Driver 2001, Hare 1981, Parfit 1984, Railton 1984, Smart 1973). Greaves argues that, for ethical consequentialist views, going global (1) reduces the plausibility that the view gets the wrong results in some cases, (2) helps the view avoid self-underminingness objections, and (3) helps the view avoid an objection about it being silent about much of morality (like about what motives and character traits agents ought to have). I argued in previous chapters that global epistemic consequentialism has features analogous to the first two of these. I'll recap those briefly before arguing that it also has the third.

The first benefit Greaves discusses of going in for global ethical consequentialism is that being a global consequentialist gives the consequentialist more resources to make sense of apparently difficult cases. We saw this in Chapter 3, where the focus was trade-off cases. There, I argued that global consequentialists could at least minimize the impact of some trade-off objections by holding that the belief-forming processes of those who accept trade-offs is generally epistemically problematic, even if the trade-off belief itself isn't wrong. This allows the consequentialist to at least partially explain our intuition that there is something amiss in accepting problematic trade-offs. Although the focus was on trade-offs in that chapter, the point generalizes to many other purported counterexamples to ethical and epistemic consequentialism. By going in for a global view, there are more resources available to the consequentialist to explain why the view might appear to make incorrect predictions. When the objector says that the consequentialist gets the wrong result about some particular object of evaluation, the global consequentialist can often point to a nearby object of evaluation that does have the objector's desired evaluative valence. This is the generalized version of what Greaves (2020) takes to be benefit (1) of the global ethical consequentialist view.

The second feature of global ethical consequentialism that Greaves (2020, sec. 4) highlights is that it can avoid an objection that the view is self-undermining. Because global consequentialism evaluates many different things, the worry is that it might give inconsistent verdicts. In Chapter 3, we discussed an example of this involving what the view says about trade-off cases. There, the view held that the agent in the trade-off cases ought to believe in God while also having and trying to foster a disposition that would have them not believe in God. Greaves considers an ethical example in which the view predicts that a mother ought to benefit a stranger's child in a particular case but also that the mother ought to love her own child when that love will lead to her benefiting her own child over the stranger's.

In Chapter 3, I argued that if there is an inconsistency in cases like these, it isn't a practical kind of inconsistency, one that would make the theory impossible for an agent to adopt and follow. To argue for that, I gave a recipe for doing what global sophisticated epistemic consequentialism says to do. I followed Railton (1984) in saying that for limited agents like us, the view enjoins us to adopt a standing commitment to the truth goal. Having a standing commitment to the truth goal means that agents aim to live a life that best conduces to achieving the goal. Agents with this kind of commitment do not make their day-to-day decisions by explicitly aiming at the goal. They instead foster in themselves the dispositions, decision-making procedures, character traits, and so on that will help them best reach the goal. Fostering and having these traits means that these agents will sometimes fail to do the right thing. But the idea is that, for limited agents like us, we'll do better overall if we foster these ways of living than if we explicitly aim to do what is best in each individual case.

Greaves (2020, sec. 4) gives a different kind of response to the inconsistency objection. As she sees it, there are several different formulations of the objection, and she thinks that for each formulation of the objection, the problem being pointed to either is not really a problem or is a generic problem about norms, not one that's specifically about global consequentialism (or consequentialism at all). One formulation of the objection, for example, says that there's a contradiction because the mother in the situation above is supposed to both do some action A (benefit the stranger's child) while also doing some action B (loving her own child) that will lead her to not do A. But as Greaves (2020, p. 433) points out, it's not a contradiction to think that we ought to do A, we ought to do B, and doing B would lead to us not doing A (e.g., it can be the case that we ought to do some frustrating activity now at work that would lead us to be snippy toward a stranger on the bus ride home, even though we ought not be snippy toward the stranger). Other interpretations of the objection involve subtleties about how to understand in what sense it is or isn't *possible* for the mother to both love her child and benefit the stranger. Greaves (2020, sec. 4.3) shows that these versions of the objection also rely on independently implausible assumptions. For brevity, I won't recount them further here, but do note that there's no reason to think that the replies Greaves gives to each ethical version of the objection wouldn't work equally well against the epistemic versions of the objection, since nothing about the objections or replies depends on anything particularly ethical or 'actiony' about the considerations in play. So the second benefit Greaves points to for global ethical consequentialism translates to global epistemic consequentialism as well.[11]

The last benefit of global ethical consequentialism that Greaves points out is its ability to respond to what she calls 'the silence objection' to act consequentialism. The silence objection accuses local (non-global) act consequentialism of being too narrow. The claim is that it's part of the goal

[11] See also Driver (2014, p. 175) and de Lazari-Radek and Singer (2014, pp. 315–316) for other responses to ethical inconsistency worries that could be translated to global epistemic consequentialism.

of ethics to understand what motives people should have, what kinds of character traits we should have, and so on, but act consequentialism is silent on those issues; it's only a theory of right action. Global ethical consequentialism responds to this objection by extending the criterion of rightness to motives, character traits, and so on.

I hope it's clear that we *could* level an analogous 'silence' objection to local versions of epistemic consequentialism that only give verdicts about what constitutes right belief (credence). The purported worry might be that such a view is silent about epistemically right and wrong kinds of reasoning, ways of reflecting on and combining evidence, ways of doing thought experiments and physical experiments, ways of doing research, and so on. But one might worry that silence objections make more sense when leveled against views of ethics than they do when leveled against views of epistemology. Traditionally, ethics has been taken to be about not only what we should do but also what character traits we should have, what kinds of people we should be, and so on. The traditional conception of epistemology, on the other hand, holds that epistemology, properly construed, is only about knowledge and beliefs, not practical issues like how to set up experiments. Feldman (2000), for example, holds that epistemic norms apply only to synchronic belief states and that any norm that applies to what we should do or think through time must be moral or practical. On that traditional picture of epistemology, such a 'silence' objection wouldn't be very compelling.

In contrast to the traditional view, I think we should see global epistemic consequentialism's ability to account for epistemic evaluations of things other than synchronic belief states as a benefit. I'll offer many reasons to think that's true, starting with what I take to be the least controversial: It seems that we often do want to give epistemic evaluations of non-beliefs (non-credences). It's natural to think, for example, that there could be epistemically right and wrong ways of reasoning. It's natural, for example, to think that wishful thinking is epistemically problematic while regular scientific induction is epistemically permissible. Reasoning isn't a belief, though. Reasoning is a process agents go through to create, maintain, and destroy beliefs (or credences). So, if we can epistemically evaluate reasoning, then epistemic evaluations must extend beyond right and wrong belief (credence).

Hall and Johnson (1998) argue that there is an epistemic duty to seek out new evidence. Those authors might take that argument further than some readers will find intuitive, but I hope the reader will join me in thinking that *in some cases*, it makes sense to think agents epistemically ought to collect more evidence. Consider, for example, a scientist who is about to form a belief about whether some vaccine is effective, an issue she previously suspended belief about. She currently has *just enough* evidence to justifiably believe, but she could easily get ten times as much evidence simply by opening a file on her computer. It seems natural to think she has an epistemic reason to open the file (perhaps along with a practical reason). To make sense of that, we have to think epistemic norms apply to things other than belief.

In addition, there already exists a large literature outside of the narrow traditional bounds of epistemology, where authors seem to think (and write) as though epistemic norms bear on things other than what beliefs we should have. Many seminal works in the philosophy of inquiry and methodology of science take epistemic considerations to bear on questions about inquiry and the structure of science (e.g., Scheffler 1963; Kitcher 1993). Friedman (2020) takes this head-on and argues that we should think norms of inquiry are epistemic norms. It is also a standard assumption in the literature on the social structure of science that scientific communities can be epistemically evaluated (Grim et al. 2013, Kitcher 1990, Strevens 2003, Thoma 2015, Weisberg and Muldoon 2009, Zollman 2007), and Kornblith (forthcoming) argues for a conception of epistemic justification that applies to the kind of epistemic communities discussed in this literature.

Closer to traditional epistemology, Hookway (2003) argues that virtue epistemologists ought to motivate their view by appeal to the idea that epistemic norms apply to activities and virtues. A lot of work in social epistemology also assumes that epistemic norms bear on non-beliefs. Goldman (2011, p. 222) makes this explicit and holds that epistemic norms apply to what we assert, whether and how to search for evidence, and choices of institutions. Many discussions in social epistemology also accept that epistemic norms apply to non-beliefs but leave this implicit. Discussions of epistemic injustice, for example, typically assume that epistemic norms can bear on how we treat each other in epistemic communities, like how much credit we give people and whether we exclude certain classes of people from epistemic resources (see, e.g., Fricker 2007; Dotson 2014; and Kidd et al. 2017). Goldman (1999) and Greco (2020) give systematic treatments of issues in social epistemology that treat epistemic norms as bearing on things like how communities are structured, how we should regulate the quality of the information we have (at both the social and individual levels), and how information should move in social systems. So, despite the traditional epistemologist's claim that epistemic norms are limited in their application to beliefs at times, it's actually quite common to think that the norms apply a lot more broadly.[12]

Sara Aronowitz and I (Singer and Aronowitz 2022) argue that even traditional evidentialists like Feldman (2000) should think there can be epistemic reasons to do things like use certain reasoning patterns over others, consider certain hypotheses, use certain statistical tests, do certain thought experiments, take time to listen to the testimony of others, organize scientific labs in certain ways, distribute grant money in certain ways, hire certain post-docs, and even eat sandwiches or drink energy drinks. A significant part of that argument works by appeal to a weak transmission principle, one that essentially enjoins us to do something when we know that doing it would bring about us believing more of what our evidence supports. I expect that traditional evidentialists would reject that transmission principle, but the plausibility of that argument is at least another reason to think epistemic evaluation applies to more than just synchronic belief states.

What these examples should make is think us that there actually is a compelling analogue of the ethical silence objection to non-global forms of epistemic consequentialism. Local epistemic consequentialism can only make sense of epistemic evaluations of belief, not the myriad other ways we use epistemic evaluation. Global epistemic consequentialism neatly responds to that objection by extending the criterion of evaluation to all possible evaluands.

This means that the three benefits of global ethical consequentialism that Greaves (2020) discusses all have analogues for global epistemic consequentialism, and so we should see those as benefits of global consequentialist views in general, not just consequentialist views in one sub-domain of normativity or the other. That said, while I find these reasons for accepting global consequentialism over its local alternatives compelling, I think there's a more compelling motivation for global

[12] I'm very thankful to folks in the "Board Certified Epistemologists" Facebook group for suggesting many of these examples. Among things suggested was also Ballantyne (2019), which gives a recent treatment of what he calls 'regulative epistemology,' the goal of which is to systematically give us practical guidance to reach epistemic ideals. This strikes me as a clear example of the kind of project in epistemology I have in mind, one in which epistemic norms are taken to apply far beyond beliefs. I imagine critics will say that Ballantyne is speaking loosely when he treats these as epistemic norms. I've relegated it to this footnote for that reason.

epistemic consequentialism that also mirrors an argument for global ethical consequentialism. I'll turn to that argument now.

In *Reasons and Persons*, Parfit (1984, p. 24) says that the central claim of ethical consequentialism is that "there is one ultimate moral aim: that outcomes be as good as possible." The standard consequentialist analysis of right action falls out of this central claim, but importantly, what the consequentialist centrally cares about is outcomes, not actions. Because of that, the consequentialist shouldn't place any special stock in a theory of right *action* rather than right *anything*. As Pettit and Smith (2000) spell out, if a consequentialist theory were to prioritize a particular kind of evaluand (be it action or anything else) over the others, it would risk losing out on the value produced by things that aren't of that kind. Local act consequentialists, for example, will miss out on the goodness produced by non-actions, such as having good motives and character traits. So, as Parfit (1984, p. 25) says, because what consequentialists centrally care about is outcomes, we should expect them to give a theory that "covers anything that could make outcomes better or worse."

This way of thinking applies equally well to the epistemic consequentialist picture as it does to the ethical consequentialist one. In Chapter 2, I motivated truth-loving epistemic consequentialism by appeal to the prevalence of work in epistemology that begins by quoting William James's command "Believe truth! Shun error!" (1979, p. 24) or a discussion of how belief "aims at the truth." We noted that in *The Meditations*, one of the classic sources for motivating questions in epistemology, Descartes took his goal to be "to arrive at the truth" and "avoid ever going wrong" (1985, p. 41). And we saw that Alston (1985, p. 83) took 'the epistemic point of view' to be "defined by the aim of maximizing truth and minimizing falsity in a large body of beliefs." It's this outcome-oriented conception of epistemology that motivated truth-loving epistemic consequentialism in the first place. At base, the truth-loving epistemic consequentialist is someone who is centrally motivated by the idea that there is one ultimate epistemic aim, that our doxastic attitudes be as accurate as possible. But if that is the central guiding idea of truth-loving epistemic consequentialism, then just like global ethical consequentialists, epistemic consequentialists should put no special stock in evaluating belief (or credence) over any other possible evaluand. The truth-loving epistemic consequentialist should care about anything that influences how accurate our picture of the world is, which includes our beliefs, our dispositions, our motives, our actions, our institutions, and everything else. Were the epistemic consequentialist to give priority to any one of those, they'd risk missing out on the value that might be produced by the others (again, by analogy to ethical consequentialism à la Pettit and Smith 2000). What this means, I claim, is that if we're going to be truly *truth-loving* epistemic consequentialists, we should be global truth-loving epistemic consequentialists. And again here, we see that the best versions of epistemic consequentialism mirror their ethical counterparts, including by being global consequentialist views.

7.2.3 The Broader Global Truth-Loving Epistemic Consequentialist Picture

In Chapter 1, I introduced the term 'epistemically right belief.' It was meant to pick out what we epistemically ought to believe. I suggested that we embark on a kind of inquiry about right belief that I termed 'normative epistemology.' Normative epistemology was meant to mirror normative ethics in aiming to give a complete and correct account of what we ought to believe, analogous to how normative ethics aims to give a complete and correct account of what we should do.

In previous chapters, I argued that the truth-loving epistemic consequentialist can give a theory of right belief that springs from the idea that what is ultimately of value in beliefs and credences is their accuracy. There, I primarily defended truth-loving epistemic consequentalism as a theory of normative epistemology. In the previous subsection, I argued that we should see truth-loving epistemic consequentialism as going far beyond a theory of right belief. The truth-loving epistemic consequentialist is best seen as someone who is centrally motivated by the idea that there is one ultimate epistemic aim, that our doxastic attitudes be as accurate as possible. This truth-loving epistemic consequentialist isn't exclusively concerned with what beliefs or credences we should have. The truth-loving epistemic consequentialist is equally concerned with anything that affects whether we have true beliefs (and accurate credences), so I argued that they should extend epistemic rightness evaluations to those things as well.

But recall what Mueller (2017) said was the "boring textbook definition" of epistemic and practical normativity—i.e., that epistemic normativity is about what to believe and practical normativity is about what to do. According to global epistemic consequentialism, in addition to belief, epistemic norms are about what dispositions to have, what reasoning processes to use, what experiments to do, and even what mundane actions to perform. So the global epistemic consequentialist denies that epistemic normativity is the normativity of belief. Here I'll ask how much we should care about giving up on the "boring textbook definition" and whether there's an alternative definition to be had.

The first thing to notice is that, like global epistemic consequentialists, global ethical consequentialists also deny the "boring textbook definition." As Parfit (1984, p. 25) puts it, global ethical consequentialism "covers anything that could make outcomes better or worse." Presumably that includes what attitudes agents have. So, if there's a problem here, it's a problem for both global epistemic consequentialists and global ethical consequentialists. But luckily, I don't think there's a problem here.

Instead of going in for the traditional way of distinguishing epistemic and practical normativity by what kind of thing they govern (belief and action, respectively), global consequentialists should hold that different kinds of normativity are individuated by the kinds of value that are central to them. Epistemic norms, on this view, are the norms that enjoin us to conduce to the epistemic good. Moral norms are the ones that enjoin us to conduce to the moral good. And generally, global consequentialists should hold that we can individuate different kinds of norms by the kind of value they promote. Let's call this the 'value-driven' way of distinguishing kinds of normativity.

The focus of this book is, of course, epistemic normativity. As such, I haven't given a reason to go in for a value-driven conception of ethical normativity per se, except insofar as one is moved by theoretical symmetry. But note that we don't need to be global consequentialists (or even consequentialists) about all kinds of normativity to accept a value-driven way of thinking about epistemic normativity. It's possible, for example, to think (a) that practical normativity just is the normativity that applies to actions while still thinking (b) that epistemic normativity is defined by the promotion of epistemic goodness. Doing this leaves one with a disjointed way of carving up the normative landscape, but perhaps the proponent of such a view would have a reason for doing so.

One might argue that a reason for wanting to stick with the traditional view over the value-driven way of distinguishing kinds of normativity is that it better preserves the intuition in cases like Pascal's Wager that epistemic reasons and only epistemic reasons apply to belief (discussed in Chapter 1). There are several responses the proponent of the value-driven view can give to this.

First, if we use a veritist conception of epistemic value, the value-driven way of distinguishing kinds of normativity can make sense of there being a tight connection between epistemic normativity and doxastic attitudes. The tight connection is not, as the traditional view claims, that epistemic normativity is the only kind of normativity that bears on doxastic attitudes. Rather, it's that epistemic normativity is the only kind of normativity that works in service of good doxastic attitudes, since epistemic goodness, on this view, just is good doxastic attitudes (i.e., *accurate* doxastic attitudes). Similarly, the defender of the value-driven view should highlight that, on their view, whenever we're considering how to promote epistemic goodness, we're considering how to promote good doxastic attitudes. Again, that's because on the veritist theory of value, anytime epistemic value is affected, it's affected by way of affecting a doxastic attitude. So on the veritist view, it shouldn't be surprising that epistemic normativity bears a tight connection to doxastic attitudes, even if epistemic normativity is not a kind of normativity that has exclusive domain over doxastic attitudes.

Those considerations help explain one aspect of our intuitive judgments about Pascal. In particular, they help explain why we think that epistemic reasons are the kind of reason that Pascal should be using in place of the practical reasons he does use. Ideally, the view would also explain why we think that Pascal's practical reasons don't apply to belief, as he takes them to. But, insomuch as the primary goal here is to defend an account of epistemic norms, not practical norms, it's unclear that my account must explain that particular intuition. As I pointed out above, the traditional conception of practical reasons (as not applying to belief) is compatible with a value-driven conception of epistemic normativity. (This was the "disjointed way of carving up kinds of normativity" discussed above.)

That said, there are two more considerations that might help proponents of the value-driven veritist conception of epistemic normativity explain this second intuition about Pascal. First, notice that it's natural to think that, for agents like us, having true beliefs usually is what best conduces to us maximizing practical value. (Kornblith 1993, for example, gives a theory of epistemic normativity that has a stronger version of this idea at its core.) If that's right, then it could help explain why it seems like Pascal should be using epistemic reasons, rather than practical ones, to govern his beliefs. The idea is that if Pascal cares about practical value, then it's epistemic reasons (the ones that help him get true beliefs), rather than practical reasons, that will help him achieve his practical aims.

The second idea involves taking cues from defenders of pragmatic and moral encroachment, many of whom hold that pragmatic and moral factors affect whether a belief is justified but only do so indirectly. The indirect way that pragmatic and moral factors bear on justification can help explain why these factors have been overlooked by traditional theorists of justification. For example, many defenders of pragmatic and moral encroachment go in for threshold-raising views that say that pragmatic and moral factors affect the threshold of evidence needed for a belief to be justified (e.g., Fantl and McGrath 2002, Pace 2011). On these views, whether a belief is justified is, in one sense, only a question of whether the belief is sufficiently supported by the holder's evidence, but what counts as sufficient support is determined in part by pragmatic and moral factors. (For overviews, see Kim 2017 and Bolinger 2020a.) On these views, pragmatic and moral factors play a subtle, indirect role in justified belief. Defenders of value-driven views of kinds of normativity can borrow this idea as a model for understanding how practical reasons might bear on right belief but in a non-obvious way. The story would say that the traditional theorist is right to hold that these factors don't bear *directly* on right belief, but it would also hold that defenders of the traditional story have overlooked subtle and non-obvious ways that practical normativity indirectly bears on right belief, just as traditional theorists of justification overlooked the indirect ways that pragmatic and moral factors bear on justification, according to proponents of pragmatic and moral encroachment.

Altogether, we see that there are a few ways for value-driven conceptions of normativity to fend off the claim that intuitions in cases like Pascal's Wager support the traditional way of cleaving epistemic and practical normativity. Settling exactly how to individuate different kinds of normativity is a task that would require yet another book, so I won't continue it here. But before closing this brief discussion, I'd like to highlight one additional benefit of going in for the value-driven approach.

The additional benefit of going in for the value-driven way of distinguishing kinds of normativity is that the value-driven approach seems like it's better suited than the alternative to be fully general in distinguishing different kinds of normativity. Here is what I mean: According to the traditional view, we distinguish epistemic from practical normativity by the kind of thing that they're norms for (belief and action, respectively). The problem is that this way of distinguishing kinds of normativity doesn't work in general. Even if this way of cleaving epistemic from practical normativity perfectly draws that distinction, we won't be able to use this method to distinguish other kinds of normativity from each other, like moral, legal, and aesthetic normativity along with social norms like norms of etiquette (since all of these also bear on action). The value-driven approach has a systematic way of distinguishing these kinds of normativity. On the value-driven approach, practical normativity is the kind of normativity that works in service of practical value. Moral normativity is the kind of normativity that works in service of moral value (presumably a kind of practical value). Aesthetic normativity is the kind of normativity that works in service of aesthetic value. Et cetera. So the value-driven approach appears to be more useful at a theoretical level in distinguishing kinds of normativity. That's another reason to go in for the picture of kinds of normativity that fits most naturally with the global epistemic consequentialist picture.

Overall, I hope to have convinced you in this section that the best way to flesh out the truth-loving epistemic consequentialist view is as a global consequentialist view. The global truth-loving epistemic consequentialist gives a schema for the epistemic evaluation of beliefs, but they also give one for evaluating everything else, including reasoning patterns, patterns of considering hypotheses, uses of statistical tests, uses of thought and physical experiments, ways of incorporating the testimony of others, ways of organizing scientific labs, ways of distributing grant money, ways of hiring postdocs, ways of setting up institutions like public schools, and ways of doing mundane tasks like eating and drinking. On this way of conceiving of it, global truth-loving epistemic consequentialism is a theory of epistemically right belief. But it is also a theory of epistemically right *anything*. As I argued above, this view comes with certain benefits (like being supported by the epistemic consequentialist's motivating intuition and being able to make sense of the broad and varying ways we use epistemic evaluation) while avoiding apparent objections (like that it's committed to inconsistent verdicts). Going in for this view requires a revision in how we think of the nature of epistemic normativity. We should think of epistemic normativity as individuated by the kind of value that it's in service of, namely having true beliefs (accurate credences) and not having false beliefs (inaccurate credences). But thinking of epistemic normativity this way is supported by the original motivation for the view, so its proponents should be happy to accept that revision to the traditional metanormative picture.

7.3 The Global Truth-Loving Framework for Inquiry

Many aspects of our lives and the institutions we have are devoted to getting at the truth about something: The field of biology aims to get at the truth about living creatures. English literature departments aim to get at the truth about English literature. Car engineering teams aim to get at the truth about ideal car production. Cancer research aims to get at the truth about how to end cancer. Tons of legal institutions (juries, investigative offices, inspection divisions, etc.) are about getting at the truth about things of legal importance. My friend's research into different college majors aims to get at the truth about which majors are best for her. My planning for next weekend aims to get at the truth about whether there will be a tasty lunch available on my bird-watching route. And when you read the newspaper over your breakfast, you aim to get at the truth about the topics in the paper. Global truth-loving epistemic consequentialism is a complete theory, not only of what we should believe, but also of the ways we (and our institutions) should pursue the truth and how we should set up our lives (and those institutions) to pursue the truth. In that way, global truth-loving epistemic consequentialism acts as a foundation for theorizing about getting at the truth in all of the ways we do it. In this last section, I'll try to convince you that global truth-loving epistemic consequentialism motivates a general truth-loving approach to epistemology, inquiry, and research, one that can be used to think about many important projects both inside and outside of philosophy. The hope is that the reader will see how fecund the truth-loving approach is, not just in philosophy and our personal lives but also in science, law, business, engineering, and many other areas.

Let's look at a few examples, starting with simple ones. Consider small group deliberations, like the deliberation of a faculty about what its degree requirements should be or the deliberation of a school board about whether it should require masks in school. In the social science, social psychology, social epistemology, and business management literature, there are many discussions of how groups should be structured and what kinds of deliberation patterns they should adopt. In the *Harvard Business Review*, for example, Sunstein and Hastie (2014) give six pieces of advice about how to structure group discussion to foster more information sharing. The advice includes things like having a "red team," a subgroup of the larger group that tries to play devil's advocate. Ideas in this vein are supported by work in social psychology suggesting that people tend not to highlight the information they uniquely have in group discussions but instead focus on the information that's shared in the group (see, e.g., Stasser and Titus 1985, 1987). How should we evaluate proposals like this?

Global truth-loving epistemic consequentialism gives a natural way to evaluate the proposals: We should evaluate them with respect to how well they will help groups reach the truth in their deliberations. In "Don't Forget Forgetting: The Social Epistemic Importance of How We Forget" (2019), my co-authors and I give an example of how the global truth-loving picture can be used to evaluate aspects of groups like this. We compare the veritistic effects of ways of structuring group conversations with the veritistic effects of individuals' memory limitations. Using agent-based computer models of small group discussions, we argue that there's good reason to think that how agents manage their limited memory can have a greater veritistic effect on the group overall than how the group structures its discussion. What this means is that if we want to make groups epistemically better off, we might do better to focus on how individuals manage their memory than to focus on how the group discussion is structured.

In "The Epistemic Role of Diversity in Juries" (2021), my co-authors and I consider a slightly more complex case in legal philosophy. We ask about different ways the diversity of a jury might impact how well the jury does at getting at the truth. As we outline there, diversity can play four quite different roles in affecting the accuracy of the verdicts. Importantly, these roles sometimes conflict in their general impact on the likelihood of a jury getting the right answer. Global truth-loving epistemic consequentialism provides a framework for evaluating the overall performance of juries with differing levels of diversity. It's the overall conduciveness of the jury to getting accurate verdicts that ultimately makes one level of diversity or another epistemically right, the theory holds.

In a similar way, global truth-loving epistemic consequentialism can serve as a framework for thinking about many other discussions in philosophy and nearby social sciences. In political philosophy, for example, there has recently been a push toward assessing the merits of political institutions on epistemic grounds. The main thrust of this goes under the heading "epistemic democracy" (e.g., Anderson 2006; Landemore 2012; Grim et al.

2020), where the central concern is how well political institutions do with respect to epistemic ends. There is a related but distinct literature on the epistemic value of diversity. In a highly influential paper, Hong and Page (2004) argue that groups of intellectually diverse people can be expected to perform better than groups of experts in solving particular kinds of problems. Several authors have followed on that line (e.g., Singer 2019, Thoma 2015, Weisberg and Muldoon 2009, Zollman 2010). There is also a literature on the social structure of science that uses agent-based computer models to evaluate scientific institutions by how well they reach the truth (e.g., Betz 2012, Borg et al. 2017, Grim et al. 2013, Zollman 2007). In all of these literatures, there are questions about how groups should deliberate or how institutions should process information, and different structures are evaluated with respect to how well they reach the truth. Global truth-loving epistemic consequentialism provides a theoretical and conceptual foundation for all of these projects by offering a framework for thinking about how to epistemically evaluate these political institutions, small groups, and scientific groups and institutions.

Those examples are all straightforward applications of global truth-loving epistemic consequentialism. In fact, many of the authors in those literatures simply assume that the group reaching the truth is the goal and compare different evaluands (group structures, political institutions, groups of varying diversity) with respect to how they affect the group reaching the truth, which is exactly what the global truth-loving epistemic consequentialist would say they should do. Global truth-loving epistemic consequentialism enables more sophisticated understandings and measures of this kind of research too, though. Consider the work on the social structure of science by Mayo-Wilson et al. (2011) that shows that what is conducive to true belief for individual scientists can clash with what is conducive to *groups* of scientists getting true beliefs.[13] Here, the global consequentialist framework can help us make sense of what might otherwise be a rather puzzling situation. In these cases, there is one thing that is epistemically right for the agent to do or believe: that which, among the available options for that agent's actions or beliefs, best conduces to accurate doxastic states. Then there is something else that is epistemically right for the group to do or believe: that which,

[13] These authors demur on whether their result is really about true belief or optimal action. They argue on pp. 662–663 that their results can be interpreted as being about belief, but they don't take up their own suggestion. Either way, global truth-loving epistemic consequentialism gives a natural way to think about these cases, since the view applies to both action and belief.

among the available options for the group's actions or beliefs, best conduces to accurate doxastic states. Since the options for actions and beliefs that are available to the group can differ from what is available to the agent, it's no surprise that those things can come apart. As the global consequentialist sees it, these cases are the social analogues of the cases considered above and in Chapter 3 where what the right belief is for an individual to have in a particular situation might be different from the belief the agent would have using the dispositions they epistemically ought to use.

Global truth-loving epistemic consequentialism can also help us think about research and the structure of research institutions more generally. A large part of the work in any scientific discipline is establishing, evaluating, and improving the methodology used to perform the research. We can see this clearly when we notice that in almost every field, graduate students are required to take methods courses, and even in classes that aren't methods courses, typically a lot of time is spent explaining and considering the methods and techniques used. Grant applications for major scientific granting agencies typically require extended discussions of the methods to be used, and researchers often make their name by pioneering or perfecting some technique. The entire field of statistics is concerned with methods for gleaning truth from data, and much of the research in data science, artificial intelligence, and machine learning has a similar aim. Global truth-loving epistemic consequentialism gives us a framework for evaluating and guiding research into scientific methods, both at the level of its application (like in particular lab groups and methods classes) and also at the theoretical level (as is done in statistics research). According to the view, in any context, the epistemically right method to use is the one that best conduces to accurate doxastic states. This fits intuitively with what many scientists think about how they choose methods, but the value of the framework goes beyond vindicating those intuitions. Global truth-loving epistemic consequentialism explains both why it makes sense for research to be done at the theoretical level about statistical methods and data science, and why it makes sense for so much of scientific practice to be about methodology.

On the global truth-loving epistemic consequentialist picture, most academic research on scientific methodology, statistics, and data science should be seen as working out the contours of *epistemically ideal* inquiry. Suppose there's a statistician, for example, who is working on a particular statistical method and wants to argue that in some particular class of cases, their particular inference technique is a better predictor of the truth than some alternative method. If the statistician is right, the global truth-loving epistemic consequentialist can account for why we should use the statistician's technique in that class of cases. That's because, according to the global truth-loving epistemic consequentialist, when we're doing a statistical inference, the epistemically right method to use is the one that best conduces to accurate doxastic states. So the global truth-loving epistemic consequentialist will endorse the statistician's technique, at least in some sense.

The "at least in some sense" modifier is important at the end of that last paragraph. That's because real human scientists are limited in their knowledge and ability to use statistical techniques correctly and in the right situations. Often, real researchers are unsure of how to analyze their data, they're limited in their methodological expertise and ability, they're error-prone, and the cutting-edge methodological and statistical research is inaccessible to them. So even though a methodological/statistical method might best conduce to true beliefs in theory, it might not best conduce to true beliefs for real researchers 'on the ground.' What the global truth-loving epistemic consequentialist should hold is that the epistemically right method to use in any situation is the one that in fact best conduces to accurate doxastic states, including in that calculation the limitations and abilities of the agent involved and the complexities of the research situation. This way of thinking about things means that the global truth-loving epistemic consequentialist has an elegant explanation of both the place of high-level theoretical research about methods (like the kind done by statisticians and data scientists) and the place of the lower-level discussions and disagreements about methods we see in methods classes and discussion sections of scientific papers. The global truth-loving epistemic consequentialist sees statisticians and data scientists as advancing our understanding of ideal methods of inquiry, whereas the discussions of methods that happen in methods classes are about what methods are epistemically right for real non-ideal researchers to use in real non-ideal situations.

What these examples show is that the global truth-loving epistemic consequentialist picture of inquiry is a broad and fecund framework. It applies to many aspects of our lives and our institutions, including the structure of scientific and political institutions, the construction of juries and other deliberative groups, and the nature of statistical and scientific methodology. I hope it's clear that the same approach can be used to give similar analyses of all kinds of questions about inquiry and research, ranging from high-level things like how granting agencies should be organized to low-level things like how my neighbors should decide what kinds of plants are best for their backyards. Global truth-loving epistemic consequentialism gives us a highly general and generative way of thinking about all areas of human and institutional inquiry, not just particular questions about what agents should believe in particular situations.

7.4 Global Truth-Loving Consequentialism and Naturalized Epistemology

In the previous chapters, I primarily discussed truth-loving epistemic consequentialism as a theory of normative epistemology, one that says that right belief is to be understood in terms of getting true beliefs and avoiding false beliefs. I tried to argue that the theory of right belief can be developed in ways that avoid the most pressing objections while still capturing the motivating intuitions. Two of the most significant aspects of the view that helped it avoid the objections were the bipartite and global aspects. In this chapter, the discussion brought out that by being bipartite and global, the view has implications for questions about epistemology and metanormativity that extend far beyond questions about what we should believe. What we saw is that global truth-loving epistemic consequentialism can serve as a general approach to epistemology, one that can guide us in thinking about the nature of epistemology and many of the different kinds of questions it might encompass. In this last section, I'll briefly discuss how global truth-loving epistemic consequentialism compares to what some might see as a competitor approach for thinking about epistemology at that general level, naturalized epistemology.

Naturalized epistemology was most famously characterized by Quine (1969, p. 82), who claimed that "epistemology, or something like it, simply falls into place as a chapter of psychology and hence of natural science." There is much debate over exactly what constitutes naturalized epistemology in the wake of Quine, but I'll follow Rysiew (2020) in thinking that most contemporary forms of naturalized epistemology can be characterized by rejecting some collection of the following four tenets of traditional epistemology: (a) that epistemology is to be done a priori without significant empirical work; (b) that epistemology is autonomous from science in that science can't answer any distinctively epistemic questions; (c) that epistemology is essentially normative in that it tells us what beliefs are right, rational, or justified; and (d) that giving an answer to skepticism is a central project of epistemology. Rysiew (2020) catalogues the ways in which different naturalized epistemologists reject different collections of these claims. I won't recount that here, except as needed to compare naturalized epistemology to global truth-loving consequentialism.

As I see it, global truth-loving epistemic consequentialism isn't really a competitor to most forms of naturalized epistemology. The view is actually quite friendly to many of naturalized epistemology's ideas and agnostic about most others. Global truth-loving epistemic consequentialists agree with those naturalized epistemologists who reject (a) and (b). As I've argued in several places in the book, global truth-loving epistemic consequentialists think that what is epistemically right is determined by what in fact conduces to us having accurate doxastic states, and what does that is an empirical matter, to be determined by science. In several places, I've appealed to empirical claims in defending the view. In Chapters 2 and 3, for example, I aimed to show that truth-loving consequentialism predicts that right belief typically lines up with true belief. To do that, I appealed to several claims about how real human beliefs interact. Those were empirical claims, and should they turn out to be false, the defense of the view would need to change. But, as I said there, they seem likely to be true, and their truth (not their 'non-empiricalness') is what is needed to defend the view. This is just one example of how global truth-loving epistemic consequentialists agree with naturalized epistemologists that epistemology is neither exclusively a priori nor are its questions autonomous from science. So global truth-loving epistemic consequentialists should be happy to join naturalized epistemologists in rejecting (a) and (b).

Unlike some parts of traditional epistemology, global truth-loving epistemic consequentialism isn't centrally concerned with responding to skepticism. Even though I've cast global truth-loving epistemic consequentialism as a general approach to epistemology, the view need not pretend to answer *all* questions about epistemology. Global truth-loving epistemic consequentialists see questions about what we should believe as central to epistemology; that leaves room for other questions to be equally central. So global truth-loving epistemic consequentialists can remain agnostic about Rysiew's aspect (d)—i.e., whether responding to skepticism should be a central topic in epistemology.

You might think that there's a more interesting contrast between global truth-loving epistemic consequentialism and naturalized epistemology in comparing the views' takes on (c), that epistemology is distinctly normative. Quine is typically construed as claiming that epistemology should completely get out of the business of making normative claims. Of course, epistemic consequentialists must disagree with that. But Kim's (1988) critique of Quine's naturalized epistemology argued that, if they're actually doing epistemology, naturalized epistemologists must make normative claims too, and contemporary naturalized epistemologists tend to agree with Kim. Instead of trying to get out of the business of making normative claims, contemporary naturalized epistemologists typically aim to give a naturalistically acceptable account of that normativity. The two most prominent approaches are (1) the semantic approach of Goldman (1986), which says that epistemic normative terms get their normative force in virtue of their meaning, and (2) the pragmatic approach of Kornblith (1993, 2002), which aims to ground epistemic normativity in the practical value of having true beliefs (or a cognitive system that gives rise to them).

The debate between Kornblith and Goldman is best understood as a debate in 'metaepistemology,' the subfield of epistemology that's more analogous to metaethics than normative ethics. The debate is about how to understand epistemic normativity at a theoretical level; it's about the concept or source of epistemic normativity. It's not about what is epistemically right or wrong, justified or unjustified, etc. in particular situations. As a theory primarily of the latter, global truth-loving epistemic consequentialism need not take a stand on the source of epistemic normativity—i.e., whether that's to be explained in terms of the concepts involved, in terms of the role true belief plays for us, or in any other terms. (Compare how hedonist utilitarians can remain agnostic about the source of moral normativity.) So when it comes to normativity in epistemology (Rysiew's aspect (c)), global truth-loving epistemic consequentialists agree with contemporary naturalized epistemologists that epistemology is normative, and epistemic consequentialists need not take a stand on the main debate that animates naturalized epistemologists in this area, namely how to give a naturalistically acceptable explanation of the source of that normativity.

A more extreme kind of naturalized epistemology is endorsed by Bishop and Trout (2004), who offer an approach to epistemology that is deeply applied and prescriptive. At the heart of Bishop and Trout's proposal is what they term 'strategic reliabilism,' which roughly holds that reasoning better is synonymous with reasoning in a more truth-conducive way. What makes the proposal 'strategic' is that it takes seriously the strengths and limitations of real human reasoners, and so it endorses things like doing cost-benefit analyses to determine how much truth will be gathered at what cost with different methods. On the view they endorse, the main work of epistemologists should be to use scientific research to help us reason better in this way. Bishop and Trout contrast their prescriptive approach to epistemology with what they label 'standard analytic epistemology' (SAE). SAE, the way they conceive of it, is characterized by a highly conservative methodology that is overly obsessed with giving characterizations of what well-off Western philosophers take knowledge and justified belief to be. In their more spirited moments, Bishop and Trout seem to endorse something close to Quinian replacement naturalism, the view that SAE should be replaced by empirical research. "The main problem with SAE is methodological," Bishop and Trout (2004, p. 22) say, and "its goals and methods are beyond repair." The authors go on to argue that epistemologists should be mirroring work in psychology and related fields that helps real people reason better, by helping us to do things like use statistical prediction rules and cognitive tricks to make more accurate predictions.

There is a lot for global truth-loving epistemic consequentialists to like about Bishop and Trout's project. Global truth-loving epistemic consequentialists should endorse the applied and prescriptive aspects of the project, since like Bishop and Trout, global truth-loving epistemic consequentialists see reasoning better as a matter of reasoning in more truth-conducive ways, and like Bishop and Trout, global truth-loving epistemic consequentialists should reject the idea that epistemology is only about understanding knowledge and justified belief. But global truth-loving epistemic consequentialists need not take Bishop and Trout's extreme revolutionary stance about traditional epistemology.

What the previous chapters of this book show is that truth-loving epistemic consequentialism can give a satisfying account of right belief while avoiding the kinds of objections that traditional epistemologists have thrown at it. In that sense, those chapters defend the truth-centric approach to epistemology using the methodology of standard analytic epistemology that Bishop and Trout reject. Global truth-loving epistemic consequentialism vindicates the central tenet of Bishop and Trout's view that right reasoning is to be understood in terms of truth-conducive reasoning, and the theory we end up with is one that endorses the highly empirical approach to that topic that Bishop and Trout employ. Global truth-loving epistemic consequentialism even takes Bishop and Trout's truth-loving idea to another level by allowing us to see the purview of epistemology as not limited to the beliefs and reasoning patterns of individuals. Global truth-loving epistemic consequentialists endorse a Bishop-and-Trout-style prescriptivism about how groups should deliberate, how to set up experiments, how to distribute grant money, how to set up public schools, etc. So, insomuch as the work of the previous chapters has been successful, it shows that we can have a conception of epistemology that, in Bishop and Trout's (2004, p. 7) words, is "normatively reason guiding," is "genuinely capable of benefiting the world," and brings the "potential benefits of epistemology to ordinary people's lives" without throwing out the methods of standard analytic epistemology. And more generally, what we see is that truth-loving epistemic consequentialism offers an approach to thinking about first-order normative epistemic questions that's friendly to a broadly naturalized approach, but unlike some naturalized epistemologists, it doesn't outright reject standard methods in epistemology nor does it exclude other questions (like questions about skepticism) from playing a role.

7.5 Conclusion

This book started out by outlining a kind of inquiry that I dubbed 'normative epistemology,' the aim of which is to give a complete and correct theory of what we should believe. The rest of the book argued for a simple epistemic consequentialist theory of what we should believe that can both capture the intuition that what we should believe is determined by what gets us at the truth while also avoiding well-known objections to epistemic consequentialist views. In the previous chapters, I focused primarily on showing how truth-loving epistemic consequentialism can avoid objections while discussing it chiefly as a view about right belief. In this chapter, I showed how the view can serve as a framework for a broader approach to epistemology, one that's centrally concerned with the ultimate epistemic goal of making our doxastic attitudes as accurate as possible. The view we end up with has several defining features, each of which mirrors a defining feature of prominent act consequentialist views in ethics. The view is a *sophisticated consequentialist* view that says that an object of epistemic evaluation is right iff it best conduces to epistemic goodness and doesn't say that agents ought to aim for epistemic goodness in their everyday thoughts and decisions. This enables the view to capture the intuition that epistemic normativity works in service of epistemic goodness by enjoining agents to adopt a standing commitment to the truth goal. The view is *diachronically veritistic* in that it takes epistemic goodness to consist in having accurate doxastic states through time. This enables the view to capture the central intuition that epistemic normativity is principally about getting at the truth. The view is *bipartite* in that it distinguishes two classes of epistemic normative notions, those that primarily serve to evaluate objects (like beliefs and credences) and those that serve to evaluate agents with respect to those objects. This allows the view to distinguish between what conduces to the good and in what ways agents are or are not responsible for that. Finally, the view is a *global consequentialist* view that evaluates all kinds of objects, not just beliefs. This enables the view to extend to all evaluands that affect whether we believe the truth, including reasoning patterns, experimental setups, grant funding institutions, and the like. What we should believe is that it's this global truth-loving epistemic consequentialist view that best explains the connection between right belief and true belief.

References

Ahlstrom-Vij, K. and Dunn, J. (2014). A Defence of Epistemic Consequentialism. *Philosophical Quarterly*, 64(257):541–551.

Alston, W. (1988). The Deontological Conception of Epistemic Justification. *Philosophical Perspectives*, 2:257–299.

Alston, W. (2005). *Beyond Justification: Dimensions of Epistemic Evaluation*. Cornell University Press.

Alston, W. P. (1985). Concepts of Epistemic Justification. *The Monist*, 68(1):57–89.

Anderson, E. (2006). The Epistemology of Democracy. *Episteme*, 3(1–2):8–22.

Andow, J. (2017). Do Non-Philosophers Think Epistemic Consequentialism Is Counterintuitive? *Synthese*, 194:2631–2643.

Appiah, K. A. (1990). Racisms. In Goldberg, D., editor, *Anatomy of Racism*, pp. 3–17. University of Minnesota Press.

Arneson, R. (2003). The Smart Theory of Moral Responsibility and Desert. In Olsaretti, S., editor, *Desert and Justice*, pp. 233–258. Clarendon Press.

Ashenfelter, O., Ashmore, D., and Lalonde, R. (1995). Bordeaux Wine Vintage Quality and the Weather. *Chance*, 8(4):7–14.

Audi, R. (2010). *Epistemology: A Contemporary Introduction to the Theory of Knowledge*. Routledge.

Bales, R. E. (1971). Act-Utilitarianism: Account of Right-Making Characteristics or Decision-Making Procedure? *American Philosophical Quarterly*, 8(3):257–265.

Ballantyne, N. (2019). *Knowing Our Limits*. Oxford University Press.

Basu, R. (2021a). Radical Moral Encroachment: The Moral Stakes of Racist Beliefs. *Philosophical Issues*, 29(1):9–23.

Basu, R. (2019b). The Wrongs of Racist Beliefs. *Philosophical Studies*, 176(9):2497–2515.

Basu, R. (2021a). The Specter of Normative Conflict: Does Fairness Require Inaccuracy? In Beeghly, E. and Madva, A., editors, *An Introduction to Implicit Bias: Knowledge, Justice, and the Social Mind*, pp. 191–210. Routledge.

Basu, R. (2021b). A Tale of Two Doctrines: Moral Encroachment and Doxastic Wronging. In Lackey, J., editor, *Applied Epistemology*, pp. 99–118. Oxford University Press.

Basu, R. and Schroeder, M. (2019). Doxastic Wronging. In Kim, B. and McGrath, M., editors, *Pragmatic Encroachment in Epistemology*, pp. 181–205. Routledge.

Bentham, J. (1780). *An Introduction to the Principles of Morals and Legislation*. Dover Publications.

Berker, S. (2013a). Epistemic Teleology and the Separateness of Propositions. *Philosophical Review*, 122(3):337–393.

Berker, S. (2013b). The Rejection of Epistemic Consequentialism. *Philosophical Issues*, 23(1):363–387.

Berker, S. (2017). A Combinatorial Argument against Practical Reasons for Belief. Unpublished manuscript.

Betz, G. (2012). *Debate Dynamics: How Controversy Improves Our Beliefs*. Synthese Library, volume 357. Springer Science & Business Media.

Bishop, M. A. and Trout, J. D. (2004). *Epistemology and the Psychology of Human Judgment*. Oxford University Press.

Boghossian, P. A. (2003). The Normativity of Content. *Philosophical Issues*, 13(1):31–45.

Bolinger, R. J. (2020a). The Rational Impermissibility of Accepting (Some) Racial Generalizations. *Synthese*, 197(6):2415–2431.

Bolinger, R. J. (2020b). Varieties of Moral Encroachment. *Philosophical Perspectives*, 34(1):5–26.

BonJour, L. (1985). *The Structure of Empirical Knowledge*. Harvard University Press.

Booth, A. R. and Peels, R. (2010). Why Responsible Belief is Blameless Belief. *Journal of Philosophy*, 107(5):257–265.

Borg, A., Frey, D., Šešelja, D., and Straßer, C. (2017). An Argumentative Agent-Based Model of scientific inquiry. In *International Conference on Industrial, Engineering and Other Applications of Applied Intelligent Systems*, pp. 507–510. Springer.

Brink, D. (1993). The Separateness of Persons, Distributive Norms, and Moral Theory. In Frey, R. G. and Morris, C., editors, *Value, Welfare, and Morality*, pp. 252–289. Cambridge University Press.

Brown, C. (2011). Consequentialize This. *Ethics*, 121(4):749–771.

Byrne, T. (2016). Might Anything Be Plain Good? *Philosophical Studies*, 173(12):3335–3346.

Caie, M. (2013). Rational Probabilistic Incoherence. *Philosophical Review*, 122(4):527–575.

Capes, J. A. (2012). Blameworthiness Without Wrongdoing. *Pacific Philosophical Quarterly*, 93(3):417–437.

Carr, J. R. (2017). Epistemic Utility Theory and the Aim of Belief. *Philosophy and Phenomenological Research*, 95(3):511–534.

Chappell, R. Y. (2005). Inquiry and Deliberation. *Philosophy, et Cetera* (blog). http://www.philosophyetc.net/2005/08/inquiry-and-deliberation.html.

Chignell, A. (2018). The Ethics of Belief. In Zalta, E. N., editor, *The Stanford Encyclopedia of Philosophy*. Spring 2018 edition.

Christensen, D. (2010). Higher-Order Evidence. *Philosophy and Phenomenological Research*, 81(1):185–215.

Christensen, D. (2013). Epistemic Modesty Defended. In Christensen, D. and Lackey, J., editors, *The Epistemology of Disagreement: New Essays*, pp. 76–97. Oxford University Press.

Chuard, P. and Southwood, N. (2009). Epistemic Norms Without Voluntary Control. *Noûs*, 43(4):599–632.

Clifford, W.K. 1877 [1999], "The ethics of belief", in T. Madigan, (ed.), *The Ethics of Belief and Other Essays*, pp. 70–96. Amherst, MA: Prometheus.

Code, L. (1987). *Epistemic Responsibility*. University Press of New England.

Comesaña, J. and Klein, P. (2019). Skepticism. In Zalta, E. N., editor, *The Stanford Encyclopedia of Philosophy*. Winter 2019 edition.

Dancy, J. (1985). *An Introduction to Contemporary Epistemology*. Basil Blackwell.

Dancy, J. (2009). Moral Particularism. In Zalta, E. N., editor, *Stanford Encyclopedia of Philosophy*, Spring 2009 edition.

Daniels, N. (1979). Wide Reflective Equilibrium and Theory Acceptance in Ethics. *Journal of Philosophy*, 76(5):256–282.
David, M. (2001). Truth as the Epistemic Goal. In Steup, M., editor, *Knowledge, Truth, and Duty*, pp. 151–169. Oxford University Press.
Davidson, D. (1986). A Coherence Theory of Truth and Knowledge. In *Truth and Interpretation: Perspectives on the Philosophy of Donald Davidson*, pp. 307–319. Basil Blackwell.
Dawes, R. M. (1971). A Case Study of Graduate Admissions: Application of Three Principles of Human Decision Making. *American Psychologist*, 26(2):180.
de Lazari-Radek, K. and Singer, P. (2014). *The Point of View of the Universe: Sidgwick and Contemporary Ethics*. Oxford University Press.
Descartes, R., Cottingham, J., Stoothoff, R., and Murdoch, D. (1985). *The Philosophical Writings of Descartes*. Cambridge University Press.
DeVaul, R. A., Jervey, F., Chappell, J. A., Caver, P., Short, B., and O'Keefe, S. (1987). Medical School Performance of Initially Rejected Students. *JAMA*, 257(1):47–51.
Dotson, K. (2014). Conceptualizing Epistemic Oppression. *Social Epistemology*, 28(2):115–138.
Dreier, J. (2011). In Defense of Consequentializing. In Timmons, M., editor, *Oxford Studies in Normative Ethics, Volume 1*. Oxford University Press.
Dretske, F. I. (1981). *Knowledge and the Flow of Information*. MIT Press.
Driver, J. (2001). *Uneasy Virtue*. Cambridge University Press.
Driver, J. (2005). Consequentialism and Feminist Ethics. *Hypatia*, 20(4):183–199.
Driver, J. (2006). *Ethics: The Fundamentals*. Basil Blackwell.
Driver, J. (2011). *Consequentialism*. Routledge.
Driver, J. (2014). Global Utilitarianism. In Eggleston, B. and Miller, D. E., editors, *The Cambridge Companion to Utilitarianism*, pp. 166–176. Cambridge University Press.
Driver, J. (2018). The "Consequentialism" in "Epistemic Consequentialism." In Ahlstrom-Vij, K. and Dunn, J., editors, *Epistemic Consequentialism*, pp. 113–122. Oxford University Press.
Egan, A. (2011). Comments on Gendler's "The Epistemic Costs of Implicit Bias."*Philosophical Studies*, 156(1):65–79.
Elga, A. (2007). Reflection and Disagreement. *Noûs*, 41(3):478–502.
Fantl, J. and McGrath, M. (2002). Evidence, Pragmatics, and Justification. *Philosophical Review*, 111(1):67–94.
Fantl, J. and McGrath, M. (2009). *Knowledge in an Uncertain World*. Oxford University Press
Feldman, R. (2000). The Ethics of Belief. *Philosophy and Phenomenological Research*, 60(3):667–695.
Feldman, R. (2003). *Epistemology*. Prentice Hall.
Feldman, R. (2006). Reasonable Religious Disagreements. In Antony, L., editor, *Philosophers Without Gods: Meditations on Atheism and the Secular Life*, pp. 194–214. Oxford University Press.
Feldman, R. and Conee, E. (1985). Evidentialism. *Philosophical Studies*, 48(1):15–34.
Fieser, J. (2020). Ethics. In *Internet Encyclopedia of Philosophy*. https://iep.utm.edu/ethics/.
Firth, R. (1998). Part III: The 1978 Schneck Lectures. In *In Defense of Radical Empiricism: Essays and Lectures by Roderick Firth*, pp. 317–370. J. Troyer, editor. Rowman & Littlefield.

Fischer, J. M. and Ravizza, M. (1998). *Responsibility and Control: A Theory of Moral Responsibility*. Cambridge University Press.
Fisher, R. (1925). *Statistical Methods for Research Workers, First Edition*. Oliver and Boyd.
Fitzpatrick, S. (2022). Simplicity in the Philosophy of Science. In *Internet Encyclopedia of Philosophy*.
Foot, P. (1967). The Problem of Abortion and the Doctrine of Double Effect. *Oxford Review*, 5:5–15.
Freeman, S., Eddy, S. L., McDonough, M., Smith, M. K., Okoroafor, N., Jordt, H., and Wenderoth, M. P. (2014). Active Learning Increases Student Performance in Science, Engineering, and Mathematics. *Proceedings of the National Academy of Sciences*, 111(23):8410–8415.
Fricker, M. (2007). *Epistemic Injustice: Power and the Ethics of Knowing*. Oxford University Press.
Friedman, J. (2020). The Epistemic and the Zetetic. *Philosophical Review*, 129(4): 501–536.
Fritz, J. (2017). Pragmatic Encroachment and Moral Encroachment. *Pacific Philosophical Quarterly*, 98(S1):643–661.
Fumerton, R. A. (1995). *Metaepistemology and Skepticism*. Rowman & Littlefield.
Garcia, J. L. A. (1996). The Heart of Racism. *Journal of Social Philosophy*, 27(1):5–46.
Gardiner, G. (2020). Relevance and Risk: How the Relevant Alternatives Framework Models the Epistemology of Risk. Synthese 199(1–2):481–511.
Geach, P. T. (1956). Good and Evil. *Analysis*, 17(2):33–42.
Gendler, T. S. (2011). On the Epistemic Costs of Implicit Bias. *Philosophical Studies*, 156(1):33–63.
Gibbard, A. (2005). Truth and Correct Belief. *Philosophical Issues*, 15(1):338–350.
Gibbard, A. (2007). Rational Credence and the Value of Truth. In *Oxford Studies in Oxford Studies in Epistemology*, volume 2, pp. 143–164. Oxford University Press.
Ginet, C. (2001). Deciding to Believe. In Steup, M., editor, *Knowledge, Truth and Duty*, pp. 63–76. Oxford University Press.
Glasgow, J. (2009). Racism as Disrespect. *Ethics*, 120(1):64–93.
Goldberg, S. (2017). Should Have Known. *Synthese*, 194(8):2863–2894.
Goldberg, S. C. (2018). *To the Best of Our Knowledge: Social Expectations and Epistemic Normativity*. Oxford University Press.
Goldman, A. (1999). *Knowledge in a Social World*. Oxford University Press.
Goldman, A. (2001). The Unity of the Epistemic Virtues. In Fairweather, A. and Zagzebski, L., editors, *In Virtue Epistemology: Essays on Epistemic Virtue and Responsibility*, pp. 30–48. Oxford University Press.
Goldman, A. I. (1979). What Is Justified Belief? In Pappas, G. S., editor, *Justification and Knowledge*, pp. 1–23.
Goldman, A. I. (1986). *Epistemology and Cognition*. Harvard University Press.
Goldman, A. I. (2011). A Guide to Social Epistemology. In Goldman, A. I. and Whitcomb, D., editors, *Social Epistemology: Essential Readings*, pp. 11–37. Oxford University Press.
Goldman, A. I. (2015). Reliabilism, Veritism, and Epistemic Consequentialism. *Episteme*, 12(2):131–143.
Goodman, N. (1983). *Fact, Fiction, and Forecast*. Harvard University Press.
Greaves, H. (2013). Epistemic Decision Theory. *Mind*, 122(488):915–952.

Greaves, H. (2020). Global Consequentialism. In Portmore, D. W., editor, *The Oxford Handbook of Consequentialism*, pp. 423–440. Oxford University Press.
Greaves, H. and Wallace, D. (2006). Justifying Conditionalization: Conditionalization Maximizes Expected Epistemic Utility. *Mind*, 115(459):607–632.
Greco, J. (2020). *The Transmission of Knowledge*. Cambridge University Press.
Grim, P., Bramson, A., Singer, D. J., Berger, W. J., Jung, J., and Page, S. E. (2020). Representation in Models of Epistemic Democracy. *Episteme*, 17(4):498–518.
Grim, P., Singer, D. J., Bramson, A., Holman, B., Jung, J., and Berger, W. J. (2021). The Epistemic Role of Diversity in Juries: An Agent-Based Model. Unpublished manuscript.
Grim, P., Singer, D. J., Fisher, S., Bramson, A., Berger, W. J., Reade, C., Flocken, C., and Sales, A. (2013). Scientific Networks on Data Landscapes: Question Difficulty, Epistemic Success, and Convergence. *Episteme*, 10(4):441–464.
Grimm, S. (2009). Epistemic Normativity. In Haddock, A., Millar, A., and Pritchard, D., editors, *Epistemic Value*, pp. 243–264. Oxford University Press.
Hájek, A. (2008). Arguments for—or Against—Probabilism? *British Journal for the Philosophy of Science*, 59(4): 793–819.
Hájek, A. (2012). Interpretations of Probability. In Zalta, E. N., editor, *The Stanford Encyclopedia of Philosophy*. Winter 2012 edition.
Hájek, A. (2018). Pascal's Wager. In Zalta, E. N., editor, *The Stanford Encyclopedia of Philosophy*. Summer 2018 edition.
Hall, R. J. and Johnson, C. R. (1998). The Epistemic Duty to Seek More Evidence. *American Philosophical Quarterly*, 35(2):129–139.
Hare, R. M. (1981). *Moral Thinking: Its Levels, Method, and Point*. Oxford University Press.
Hieronymi, P. (2006). Controlling Attitudes. *Pacific Philosophical Quarterly*, 87(1):45–74.
Hieronymi, P. (2008). Responsibility for Believing. *Synthese*, 161(3):357–373.
Hong, L. and Page, S. E. (2004). Groups of Diverse Problem Solvers Can Outperform Groups of High-Ability Problem Solvers. *Proceedings of the National Academy of Sciences of the United States of America*, 101(46):16385–16389.
Hooker, B. (2015). Rule Consequentialism. In Zalta, E. N., editor, *The Stanford Encyclopedia of Philosophy*. Winter 2015 edition.
Hookway, C. (2003). How to Be a Virtue Epistemologist. In Zagzebski, L. and DePaul, M., editors, *Intellectual Virtue: Perspectives From Ethics and Epistemology*, pp. 183–202. Oxford University Press.
Horowitz, S. (2016). Accuracy and Educated Guesses. In Gendler, T. S. and Hawthorne, J., editors, *Oxford Studies in Epistemology, Volume 6*, pp. 85–113. Oxford University Press.
Horwich, P. (2006). The Value of Truth. *Noûs*, 40(2):347–360.
Hurley, P. (2020). Consequentlalizing. In Portmore, D. W., editor, *The Oxford Handbook of Consequentialism*, pp. 25–45. Oxford University Press.
Ichikawa, J. J. and Steup, M. (2018). The Analysis of Knowledge. In Zalta, E. N., editor, *The Stanford Encyclopedia of Philosophy*. Summer 2018 edition.
Jackson, E. and Fritz, J. (2021). Belief, Credence, and Moral Encroachment. *Synthese* 199(1–2):1387–1408.
Jackson, F. (1991). Decision-Theoretic Consequentialism and the Nearest and Dearest Objection. *Ethics*, 101(3):461–482.

James, W. (1979). The Will to Believe. In *The Will to Believe and Other Essays in Popular Philosophy*, pp. 13–33. F. Burkhardt, F. Bowers, and I. Skrupskelis, editors. Harvard University Press.

Jefferson, A. (2019). Instrumentalism About Moral Responsibility Revisited. *Philosophical Quarterly*, 69(276):555–573.

Jenkins, C. S. (2007). Entitlement and Rationality. *Synthese*, 157(1):25–45.

Johnson, R. and Cureton, A. (2019). Kant's Moral Philosophy. In Zalta, E. N., editor, *The Stanford Encyclopedia of Philosophy*. Spring 2019 edition.

Joyce, J. M. (1998). A Nonpragmatic Vindication of Probabilism. *Philosophy of Science*, 65(4): 575–603.

Joyce, J. M. (2009). Accuracy and Coherence: Prospects for an Alethic Epistemology of Partial Belief. In Huber, F. and Schmidt-Petri, C., editors, *Degrees of Belief*, Synthese Library, volume 342, pp. 263–297. Springer.

Joyce, J. M. (2013). Why Evidentialists Need Not Worry About the Accuracy Argument for Probabilism. Unpublished manuscript.

Kagan, S. (1998). *Normative Ethics*. Westview Press.

Kelly, T. (2010). Peer Disagreement and Higher Order Evidence. In Goldman, A. I. and Whitcomb, D., editors, *Social Epistemology: Essential Readings*, pp. 183–220. Oxford University Press.

Kidd, I. J., Medina, J., and Pohlhaus, G., editors. (2017). *The Routledge Handbook of Epistemic Injustice*. Routledge.

Kim, B. (2017). Pragmatic Encroachment in Epistemology. *Philosophy Compass*, 12(5):e12415.

Kim, J. (1988). What Is "Naturalized Epistemology?" *Philosophical Perspectives*, 2:381–405.

Kitcher, P. (1990). The Division of Cognitive Labor. *Journal of Philosophy*, 87(1):5–22.

Kitcher, P. (1993). *The Advancment of Science*. Oxford University Press.

Kopec, M. (2018). A Pluralistic Account of Epistemic Rationality. *Synthese* 94(3):357–376.

Kornblith, H. (1993). Epistemic Normativity. *Synthese*, 94(3):357–376.

Kornblith, H. (2002). *Knowledge and Its Place in Nature*. Oxford University Press.

Kornblith, H. (forthcoming). Two Kinds of Epistemic Evaluation. In Reed, B. and Flowerree, A. K., editors, *Towards an Expansive Epistemology: Norms, Action, and the Social Sphere*. Routledge.

Kvanvig, J. (2000). Review: Zagzebski on Justification. *Philosophy and Phenomenological Research*, 60(1):191–196.

Landemore, H. (2012). *Democratic Reason: Politics, Collective Intelligence, and the Rule of the Many*. Princeton University Press.

Lasonen-Aarnio, M. (2014). Higher-Order Evidence and the Limits of Defeat. *Philosophy and Phenomenological Research*, 88(2):314–345.

Leitgeb, H. and Pettigrew, R. (2010a). An Objective Justification of Bayesianism I: Measuring Inaccuracy. *Philosophy of Science*, 77(2):201–235.

Leitgeb, H. and Pettigrew, R. (2010b). An Objective Justification of Bayesianism II: The Consequences of Minimizing Inaccuracy. *Philosophy of Science*, 77(2): 236–272.

Lemos, N. (2007). *An Introduction to the Theory of Knowledge*. Cambridge University Press.

Lewis, D. (1971). Immodest Inductive Methods. *Philosophy of Science*, 38(1):54–63.

Lewis, D. (1980). A Subjectivist's Guide to Objective Chance. In Carnap, R. and Jeffrey, R. C., editors, *Studies in Inductive Logic and Probability*, volume 2, pp. 83–132. University of California Press.

Littlejohn, C. (2012). *Justification and the Truth-Connection*. Cambridge University Press.

Littlejohn, C. (2018). The Right in the Good: A Defense of Teleological Non-Consequentialism in Epistemology. In Dunn, K. A. J., editor, *Epistemic Consequentialism*, pp. 23–47. Oxford University Press.

Lord, E. (2015). Acting for the Right Reasons, Abilities, and Obligation. In Shafer-Landau, R., editor, *Oxford Studies in Metaethics, Volume 10*, pp. 26–52. Oxford University Press.

Lynch, M. (2004). *True to Life: Why Truth Matters*. MIT Press.

Lynn, M. (2007). Race Differences in Restaurant Tipping: A Literature Review and Discussion of Practical Implications. *Journal of Foodservice Business Research*, 9(4):99–113.

Marušic, B. and White, S. (2018). How Can Beliefs Wrong? A Strawsonian Epistemology. *Philosophical Topics*, 46(1):97–114.

Mason, E. (2019). Consequentialism and Moral Responsibility. In Seidel, C., editor, *Consequentialism: New Directions, New Problems?*, pp. 219–236. Oxford University Press.

Mason, E. (2020). Consequentialism, Blame, and Moral Responsibility. In Portmore, D. W., editor, *The Oxford Handbook of Consequentialism*, pp. 162–178. Oxford University Press.

Mayo-Wilson, C., Zollman, K. J. S., and Danks, D. (2011). The Independence Thesis: When Individual and Social Epistemology Diverge. *Philosophy of Science*, 78(4):653–677.

McGeer, V. (2015). Building a Better Theory of Responsibility. *Philosophical Studies*, 172(10):2635–2649.

Meehl, P. E. (1954). *Clinical Versus Statistical Prediction: A Theoretical Analysis and a Review of the Evidence*. University of Minnesota Press.

Meehl, P. E. (1986). Causes and Effects of My Disturbing Little Book. *Journal of Personality Assessment*, 50(3):370–375.

Mill, J. S. (1863). *Utilitarianism*. Parker, Son & Bourn.

Miller, D. E. (2014). Reactive Attitudes and the Hare–Williams Debate: Towards a New Consequentialist Moral Psychology. *Philosophical Quarterly*, 64(254): 39–59.

Miracchi, L. (2015). Competence to Know. *Philosophical Studies*, 172(1):29–56.

Moore, G. E. (1939). Proof of an External World. *Proceedings of the British Academy*, 25:273–300.

Moss, S. (2018). Moral Encroachment. *Proceedings of the Aristotelian Society*, 118(2):177–205.

Mueller, A. (2017). How Does Epistemic Rationality Constrain Practical Rationality? *Analytic Philosophy*, 58(2):139–155.

Munton, J. (2019). Beyond Accuracy: Epistemic Flaws with Statistical Generalizations. *Philosophical Issues*, 29(1):228–240.

Nagel, J. (2014). *Knowledge: A Very Short Introduction*. Oxford University Press.

Neyman, J. and Pearson, E. S. (1933). On the Problem of the Most Efficient Tests of Statistical Hypotheses. *Philosophical Transactions of the Royal Society A*, 231: 289–337.

Nolfi, K. (2018). Why Only Evidential Considerations Can Justify Belief. In McHugh, C., Way, J., and Whiting, D., editors, *Metaepistemology*, pp. 179–199. Oxford University Press.

Nolfi, K. (2019). Epistemic Norms, All Things Considered. *Synthese*, 198(7):6717–6737.

Norcross, A. (1997). Consequentialism and Commitment. *Pacific Philosophical Quarterly*, 78(4):380–403.

Nozick, R. (1981). *Philosophical Explanations*. Harvard University Press.

Oddie, G. (1997). Conditionalization, Cogency, and Cognitive Value. *British Journal for the Philosophy of Science*, 48(4):533–541.

Pace, M. (2011). The Epistemic Value of Moral Considerations: Justification, Moral Encroachment, and James' "Will to Believe." *Noûs*, 45(2):239–268.

Parfit, D. (1984). *Reasons and Persons*. Oxford University Press.

Pascal, B. (1941). *Pensées. W. F. Trotter, editor.* Modern Library.

Peels, R. (2017). Responsible Belief and Epistemic Justification. *Synthese*, 194(8):2895–2915.

Pettigrew, R. (2016). *Accuracy and the Laws of Credence*. Oxford University Press.

Pettigrew, R. (2019). Epistemic Utility Arguments for Probabilism. In Zalta, E. N., editor, *The Stanford Encyclopedia of Philosophy*. Winter 2019 edition.

Pettit, P. and Smith, M. (2000). Global Consequentialism. In Hooker, B., Mason, E., and Miller, D., editors, *Morality, Rules and Consequences: A Critical Reader*, pp. 121–133. Edinburgh University Press.

Philips, M. (1984). Racist Acts and Racist Humor. *Canadian Journal of Philosophy*, 14(March):75–96.

Plato (1969). *Plato in Twelve Volumes*. Translated by Paul Shorey. Harvard University Press.

Portmore, D. W. (2009). Consequentializing. *Philosophy Compass*, 4(2):329–347.

Portmore, D. W. (2011). *Commonsense Consequentialism: Wherein Morality Meets Rationality*. Oxford University Press.

Pritchard, D. (2018). *What Is This Thing Called Knowledge*. Routledge.

Pritchard, D., Turri, J., and Carter, J. A. (2018). The Value of Knowledge. In Zalta, E. N., editor, *The Stanford Encyclopedia of Philosophy*. Spring 2018 edition.

Putnam, H. (1975). The Meaning of "Meaning." *Minnesota Studies in the Philosophy of Science*, 7:131–193.

Quine, W. (1969). Epistemology Naturalized. In *Ontological Relativity and Other Essays*, 69–90. Columbia University Press.

Rachels, S. and Rachels, J. (2015). *The Elements of Moral Philosophy*. McGraw-Hill Education.

Railton, P. (1984). Alienation, Consequentialism, and the Demands of Morality. *Philosophy and Public Affairs*, 13(2):134–171.

Ramsey, F. P. (1926). Truth and Probability. In Braithwaite, R., editor, *The Foundations of Mathematics and Other Logical Essays*. Kegan, Paul, Trench, Trubner & Co.

Rathbone, A. (1997). *Windows 95 for Dummies*. IDG Books.

Rawls, J. (2005). *A Theory of Justice*. Harvard University Press.

Raz, J. (2009). Reasons: Practical and Adaptive. In Sobel, D. and Wall, S., editors, *Reasons for Action*. Cambridge University Press.

Rysiew, P. (2020). Naturalism in Epistemology. In Zalta, E. N., editor, *The Stanford Encyclopedia of Philosophy*. Fall 2020 edition.

Saul, J. (2018). (How) Should We Tell Implicit Bias Stories? *Disputatio*, 10(50):217–244.

Scheffler, I. (1963). *The Anatomy of Inquiry: Philosophical Studies in the Theory of Science*. Routledge.

Schervish, M. (1989). A General Method for Comparing Probability Assessors. *The Annals of Statistics*, 17(4):1856–1879.

Schroeder, M. (2011). Ought, Agents, and Actions. *Philosophical Review*, 120(1):1–41.

Schroeder, M. (2012). Stakes, Withholding, and Pragmatic Encroachment on Knowledge. *Philosophical Studies*, 160(2):265–285.

Schroeder, M. (2015). Knowledge Is Belief for Sufficient (Objective and Subjective) Reason. In Gendler, T., and Hawthorne, J., editors, *Oxford Studies in Epistemology*, Volume 5, pp. 226–252. Oxford University Press.

Schwitzgebel, E. (2019). Belief. In Zalta, E. N., editor, *The Stanford Encyclopedia of Philosophy*. Fall 2019 edition.

Shah, N. (2003). How Truth Governs Belief. *Philosophical Review*, 112(4):447–482.

Shah, N. and Velleman, J. D. (2005). Doxastic Deliberation. *The Philosophical Review*, 114(4):497.

Sharadin, N. (2018). Epistemic Consequentialism: Haters Gonna Hate. In Kyriacou, C. and McKenna, R., editors, *Metaepistemology*. Palgrave Innovations in Philosophy. Palgrave Macmillan.

Shaver, J. P. (1993). What Statistical Significance Testing Is, and What It Is Not. *The Journal of Experimental Education*, 61(4):293–316.

Shelby, T. (2002). Is Racism in the "Heart"? *Journal of Social Philosophy*, 33(3):411–420.

Shoemaker, D. (2015). *Responsibility from the Margins*. Oxford University Press.

Sidgwick, H. (1907). *The Methods of Ethics*. 7th edition. Macmillan.

Singer, D. J. (2012). Doxastic Normativity. PhD thesis, University of Michigan, Ann Arbor.

Singer, D. J. (2018a). How to Be an Epistemic Consequentialist. *Philosophical Quarterly* 68(272):580–602.

Singer, D. J. (2018b). Permissible Epistemic Trade-offs. *Australasian Journal of Philosophy* 97(2):281–293.

Singer, D. J. (2019). Diversity, Not Randomness, Trumps Ability. *Philosophy of Science*, 86(1):178–191.

Singer, D. J. and Aronowitz, S. (2022). What Epistemic Reasons Are For: Against the Belief-Sandwich Distinction. In Plunkett, D. and Dunaway, B., editors, *Meaning, Decision, and Norms: Themes from the Work of Allan Gibbard*. Maize Books, pp. 74–94.

Singer, D. J., Bramson, A., Grim, P., Holman, B., Kovaka, K., Jung, J., and Berger, W. (2019). Don't Forget Forgetting: The Social Epistemic Importance of How We Forget. *Synthese*, 198(6):5373–5394.

Sinnott-Armstrong, W. (2015). Consequentialism. In Zalta, E. N., editor, *The Stanford Encyclopedia of Philosophy*. Winter 2015 edition.

Sklar, L. (1974). *Space, Time, and Spacetime*. University of California Press.

Skyrms, B. (1980). *Causal Necessity: A Pragmatic Investigation of the Necessity of Laws*. Yale University Press.

Smart, J. J. C. (1963). Free Will, Praise and Blame. *Mind*, 70(279):291–306.

Smart, J. J. C. (1973). An Outline of a System of Utilitarian Ethics. In Smart, J. J. C. and Williams, B., editors, *Utilitarianism: For and Against*, pp. 1–74. Cambridge University Press.

Sosa, E. (1991). *Knowledge in Perspective*. Cambridge: Cambridge University Press.

Sosa, E. (2007). *A Virtue Epistemology: Apt Belief and Reflective Knowledge, Volume I*. Oxford University Press.

Souza, D. (1995). *The End of Racism: Principles for a Multiracial Society*. Free Press.

Stanley, J. (2005). *Knowledge and Practical Interests*. Oxford University Press.

Stasser, G. and Titus, W. (1985). Pooling of Unshared Information in Group Decision Making: Biased Information Sampling During Discussion. *Journal of Personality and Social Psychology*, 48(6):1467.

Stasser, G. and Titus, W. (1987). Effects of Information Load and Percentage of Shared Information on the Dissemination of Unshared Information During Group Discussion. *Journal of Personality and Social Psychology*, 53(1):81.

Steglich-Petersen, A. (2006). No Norm Needed: On the Aim of Belief. *Philosophical Quarterly*, 56(225):499–516.

Steup, M. (2008). Doxastic Freedom. *Synthese*, 161(3):375–392.

Steup, M. (2011). Belief, Voluntariness and Intentionality. *Dialectica*, 65(4):537–559.

Stich, S. (1990). *The Fragmentation of Reason*. MIT Press.

Strevens, M. (2003). The Role of the Priority Rule in Science. *Journal of Philosophy*, 100(2):55–79.

Sunstein, C. R. and Hastie, R. (2014). Making Dumb Groups Smarter. *Harvard Business Review*, 92(12):90–98.

Swets, J. A., Dawes, R. M., and Monahan, J. (2000). Psychological Science Can Improve Diagnostic Decisions. *Psychological Science in the Public Interest*, 1(1):1–26.

Sylvan, K. (2016). Epistemic Reasons I: Normativity. *Philosophy Compass*, 11(7):364–376.

Sylvan, K. (2018). Veritism Unswamped. *Mind*, 127(506):381–435.

Sylvan, K. L. (2020). An Epistemic Non-Consequentialism. *The Philosophical Review*, 129(1):1–51.

Talbott, W. (2016). Bayesian Epistemology. In Zalta, E. N., editor, *The Stanford Encyclopedia of Philosophy*. Winter 2016 edition.

Thoma, J. (2015). The Epistemic Division of Labor Revisited. *Philosophy of Science*, 82(3):454–472.

Thomson, J. (1997). The Right and the Good. *Journal of Philosophy*, 94(6):273–298.

Thomson, J. J. (1976). Killing, Letting Die, and the Trolley Problem. *The Monist*, 59(2):204–217.

Thomson, J. J. (2008). *Normativity*. Open Court.

Timmons, M. (2012). *Moral Theory: An Introduction*. Rowman & Littlefield.

Tognazzini, N. and Coates, D. J. (2014). Blame. In Zalta, E. N., editor, *The Stanford Encyclopedia of Philosophy*. Spring 2016 edition.

Turri, J. (2009). The Ontology of Epistemic Reasons. *Noûs*, 43(3):490–512.

Turri, J. (2010). On the Relationship Between Propositional and Doxastic Justification. *Philosophy and Phenomenological Research*, 80(2):312–326.

Turri, J., Alfano, M., and Greco, J. (2019). Virtue Epistemology. In Zalta, E. N., editor, *The Stanford Encyclopedia of Philosophy*. Fall 2019 edition.

Vahid, H. (1998). Deontic vs. Nondeontic Conceptions of Epistemic Justification. *Erkenntnis*, 49(3):285–301.

Vargas, M. (2013). *Building Better Beings: A Theory of Moral Responsibility*. Oxford University Press.

Vargas, M. (2022). Instrumentalist Theories of Moral Responsibility. In Nelkin, D. K. and Pereboom, D., editors, *Oxford Handbook of Responsibility*, pp. 3–26. Oxford University Press.

Wallace, R. J. (1994). *Responsibility and the Moral Sentiments*. Harvard University Press.

Weatherson, B. (2008). Deontology and Descartes's Demon. *Journal of Philosophy*, 105(9):540–569.

Weatherson, B. (m.s.). Do Judgments Screen Evidence? Unpublished manuscript.

Wedding, D. (1983). Clinical and Statistical Prediction in Neuropsychology. *Clinical Neuropsychology*, 5(2):49–55.

Wedgwood, R. (2002). The Aim of Belief. *Philosophical Perspectives*, 16:267–97.

Wedgwood, R. (2016). Objective and Subjective "Ought." In Charlow, N. and Chrisman, M., editors, *Deontic Modality*, pp. 143–168. Oxford University Press.

Weisberg, M. and Muldoon, R. (2009). Epistemic Landscapes and the Division of Cognitive Labor. *Philosophy of Science*, 76(2): 225–252.

Whiting, D. (2010). Should I Believe the Truth? *Dialectica*, 64(2):213–224.

Williams, B. (1973). A Critique of Utilitarianism. In Smart, J. J. C. and Williams, B., editors, *Utilitarianism: For and Against*, pp. 77–150. Cambridge University Press.

Williams, B. A. O. and Atkinson, W. F. (1965). Ethical Consistency. *Aristotelian Society Supplementary Volume*, 39(1):103–138.

Williamson, T. (2000). *Knowledge and Its Limits*. Oxford University Press.

Zagzebski, L. (2000). From Reliabilism to Virtue Epistemology. *The Proceedings of the Twentieth World Congress of Philosophy*, 5:173–179.

Zagzebski, L. T. (1996). *Virtues of the Mind: An Inquiry Into the Nature of Virtue and the Ethical Foundations of Knowledge*. Cambridge University Press.

Zollman, K. J. S. (2007). The Communication Structure of Epistemic Communities. *Philosophy of Science*, 74(5):574–587.

Zollman, K. J. S. (2010). The Epistemic Benefit of Transient Diversity. *Erkenntnis*, 72(1):17–35.

Index

Ahlstrom-Vij, Kristoffer and Dunn, Jeffrey, 54, 69, 72, 89, 167
Alston, William, 37–38, 42, 49, 81, 107, 194
applied ethics, 18–19

backward-lookingness. *See* directionality
Bayesianism, 14, 17, 54, 123–154
See also credence
Berker, 35, 53–55, 75–77, 86–87, 93
birds, 10, 42, 109, 136, 137–138, 140, 219
Bishop, Michael and Trout, J.D., 226–228

Carr, Jennifer, 142–154
changes of worldview, 58–61
complete (theory) 19, 20, 22, 29
computer operating system, 1
correct (theory) 19, 24
correct belief, 25–29
credence, 17, 48, 51, 123–154

degree of belief. *See* credence
deontic terms, epistemic, 73–75, 77–83
deontology, 19–20
directionality, 35, 55, 76, 86–87, 104

epistemic utility theory, 123–154
ethical consequentialism, 19–20, 54, 72–75, 90, 91, 113–121, 192
See also global consequentialism
ethics, 2, 18–23
See also normative ethics, metaethics, applied ethics, ethical consequentialism, deontology, paradox of hedonism
ethics of belief, 13
evidentialism, 13, 14, 32, 39–41, 44–45, 166, 199

first-personal-deliberative cases, 55–56
For Dummies, 1–2
formal epistemology. *See* Bayesianism, credence
forward-lookingness. *See* directionality

global consequentialism, 91, 104–105, 189, 207–214
Goldman, Alvin, 42, 49, 53, 54, 69, 107
Greaves, Hilary, 53–55, 69, 123–154, 207–212
guide, 39, 44, 167

hedonistic utilitarianism, 20, 31
See also ethical consequentialism, paradox of hedonism

independence, 65
indirect consequentialism, 53, 73, 89
indirect doxastic decision, 61–64
intuitions, 20–22, 36, 37, 65

justification, epistemic, 14, 74, 77, 82, 86, 170, 191–205

knowledge, 11, 12–14, 15, 72, 78–79

metaethics, 18, 29, 226
microwave, 12, 41, 74
morally right action, 18, 22–23, 24, 31, 34, 193, 202

normative epistemology, 10–38, 197–199
normative ethics, 2, 18–23

objective consequentialist, 51, 191
objective ought, 25–29, 31–34

paradox of hedonism, 90, 91, 138–139
Pascal's Wager, 23, 63–64, 215–217
pedagogy, 43–44, 56–58, 84
peer disagreement, 14, 15, 38, 68
positive arguments by supposition, 67–68
positive dependence, 66
practical reasons, 23, 216–217
principles, 19, 21, 35, 89, 91, 93, 167
psychology, 46–47, 92, 220, 224, 227

responsibility terms, epistemic, 73–75, 77–83, 191–205
right belief, 23–38
    definition of, 24
rules. *See* principles

separateness of
    persons, 54, 76
    propositions, 54, 67, 76
Shah, Nishi, 25, 39, 55–56
skepticism, 14, 141, 225
statistics, 45–46, 49, 63, 155, 179, 222–223
statistical prediction rules, 47, 227
swamping problem, 102–105

theory of knowledge, 11–12
trade-offs
    Benefits of, 67–69
    Objections, 71–100
    Permissible, 52–70
    Rarity of, 65–66
trademark lawsuit, 1
traditional epistemology, 11–16, 224–225, 227
transparency, 39, 55–56, 96
truth begets truth, 65, 84, 152
truth-loving epistemic consequentialism
    definition of, 48
    features of, 189–190

veritism, 48, 102

Wedgwood, Ralph, 25, 85, 95–96, 114
what we should believe. *See* right belief